WIND, WATER AND STEAM

WIND, WATER AND STEAM

The story of Hertfordshire's mills

HUGH HOWES

Hertfordshire Publications
an imprint of
UNIVERSITY OF HERTFORDSHIRE PRESS

First published in Great Britain in 2016 by
Hertfordshire Publications
an imprint of
University of Hertfordshire Press
College Lane
Hatfield
Hertfordshire
AL10 9AB

© Hugh Howes 2016

The right of Hugh Howes to be identified as the author of this work has been asserted by him in accordance with the Copyright, Designs and Patents Act 1988.

All rights reserved. No part of this book may be reproduced or utilised in any form or by any means, electronic or mechanical, including photocopying, recording or by any information storage and retrieval system, without permission in writing from the publisher.

British Library Cataloguing in Publication Data
A catalogue record for this book is available from the British Library

ISBN 978-1-909291-73-7

Design by Arthouse Publishing Solutions Ltd
Printed in Great Britain by Charlesworth Press, Wakefield

Contents

List of illustrations	vi
Acknowledgements	xi
Abbreviations	xiv
Notes for readers	xiv
Preface	xv
1. Hertfordshire's milling heritage	1
2. Conflicts in the catchments	30
3. Milling in Hertfordshire today	45
4. The eight accessible mills	59
5. Corn milling	81
6. Hertfordshire's windmills	123
7. Paper mills	153
8. Silk mills	169
9. At the margins of milling	179
10. Reflections on the restoration and preservation of Hertfordshire's mills	189
Appendices	
1. 'The country mill in wartime', extract from *The Miller*, 1 April 1918, by 'Excelsior'	207
2. London: Docks and Mark Lane	210
3. The archaeology of Hyde Mill, Ickleford	215
4. 'Mr B. Coles new mill at Luton, Bedfordshire', extract from *The Miller*, 1 May 1893	218
5. 'Mr Toovey's New Roller Flour Mill At King's Langley, Herts', extract from *The Miller*, 4 September 1893	220
6. 'Mr J.G. Knowles and Sons', extract from *The Miller*, 3 April 1911	223
7. 'Successful country mills', extract from *The Miller*, 4 August 1902	225
8. 'A model country mill', extract from *The Miller*, 7 May 1906	228
Glossary	229
Gazetteer	233
Bibliography	245
Index	249

Illustrations

1.1	Advertisement for Chapman Bros, Standon New Mill	2
1.2	Sawbridgeworth Town Mill, *c.*1900	2
1.3	Destruction of Gamnel End windmill, Tring	4
1.4	Kings Langley Mill in 1978	6
1.5	Advertisement for Carter/Turner roller mills, 1883	12
1.6	Roller mill installation at Station Mills, Hitchin	13
1.7	Stanstead Abbots Mill, *c.*1900	14
1.8	Diagram of an Armfield turbine	15
1.9	Turbine at Broxbourne	16
1.10	Cole's horse-drawn wagon	17
1.11	Narrow boats at Sawbridgeworth Town Mill	18
1.12	Castle Mill, Berkhamsted, in 1997	18
1.13	Siding serving Standon New Mill	20
1.14	Bowman's steam lorry	20
1.15	Burton's steam lorries at Sawbridgeworth	23
1.16	Dickinson's motor lorry	23
1.17	Advertisement for an auxiliary steam engine	27
2.1	Hertfordshire's contours and river catchments	31
2.2	River transport at Ware in 1890	32
2.3	View of the Grand Junction Canal at Berkhamsted	35
2.4	Dickinson's canal boats at Apsley Mill	37
2.5	Water-level gauge at Sawbridgeworth Town Mill	41
2.6	Lea barges frozen in	42
3.1	Millstone at the Town Mill, Bishops Stortford	47
3.2	Allinson's complex at Bishops Stortford	48
3.3	The south side of Station Mill, Royston, in 1905	49
3.4	Tring steam mill and windmill in 1893	50
3.5	Station Mills, Hitchin, in 1950	52
3.6	Ickleford Mill, *c.*1910	53
3.7	Ponders End Mill, *c.*1950	54
3.8	The waterwheel being installed at Lemsford Mill	56
4.1	Location of the eight accessible mills in Hertfordshire	60
4.2	Mill Green Mill	61

ILLUSTRATIONS

4.3	Cross section of Mill Green Mill	62
4.4	Kingsbury Mill	64
4.5	Moor Mill in the 1990s	65
4.6	The railway connection to Hyde Mill	68
4.7	The stone floor at Hyde Mill	69
4.8	Diagram of roller mill plant at Hyde Mill	70
4.9	Cromer Mill, *c*.1900	72
4.10	Cromer Mill in 1930	73
4.11	Sketch of a detail of Cromer Mill, 1931	74
4.12	Cromer Mill fantail and ladder	74
4.13	Aerial view of the Apsley paper mills	76
4.14	The Waltham Abbey Powder Mills in 1739	78
5.1	The location of corn mills in the Colne Valley	82
5.2	Watford Mill in 1903	83
5.3	Noake Mill in the 1950s	84
5.4	Piccotts End Mill in 1955	84
5.5	Kings Langley Mill from the canal	85
5.6	Hunton Bridge Mill, *c*.1890	86
5.7	Grove Mill, Watford	87
5.8	Bourne End Mill, *c*.1900	88
5.9	Shafford Mill	90
5.10	The lay-shaft at Sopwell Mill	91
5.11	The power train at Park Mill in 1983	92
5.12	The location of corn mills in the Lea Valley	94
5.13	Batford Mill	95
5.14	Lemsford Mill in 1935 before conversion	96
5.15	Lemsford Mill today	96
5.16	Essendon Mill	98
5.17	The rivers and mills in Hertford	99
5.18	Town Mill, Hertford, in 1954	99
5.19	Rescued millstones at Ware Town Mill	100
5.20	*A Hertfordshire Mill* by Beatrix Potter	101
5.21	Ware Flour Mills today	102
5.22	Broxbourne Mill in 1905	104
5.23	Kimpton Mill before conversion	105
5.24	Welwyn Mill, *c*.1910	106
5.25	Walkern Mill	107
5.26	Watton Mill in 1912	107
5.27	Braughing Mill	109
5.28	Standon New Mill in 1913	110

5.29	Wadesmill in the 1960s, before conversion	110
5.30	Ware Park Mill	112
5.31	Parsonage Mill, Bishops Stortford	113
5.32	South Mill, Bishops Stortford, in 1905	114
5.33	Twyford Mill in 1910	115
5.34	Harlow Mill	116
5.35	Hunsdon Mill, *c.*1890	116
5.36	The location of mills in the Ouse catchment	118
5.37	Oughton Head, or West Mill, Ickleford, in the 1930s	118
5.38	Hyde Mill, Ickleford, *c.*1880	120
5.39	Purwell Mill, Hitchin	121
6.1	The location of Hertfordshire's windmills	124
6.2	Goff's Oak tower mill, *c.*1900	125
6.3	Barkway post mill in 1905	129
6.4	Post and smock mills at Great Hormead, *c.*1928	130
6.5	High Wych post mill in 1870	131
6.6	The smock mill at Little Hadham in 1927	132
6.7	Bushey Heath smock mill in 1904	135
6.8	Smock mill at Graveley	136
6.9	Brent Pelham smock mill today	136
6.10	Smock mill at Snow End, Anstey	138
6.11	Reed tower mill in 1910	140
6.12	Gammel End tower mill, Tring	142
6.13	Arkley tower mill, *c.*1900, before restoration	142
6.14	Goldfield tower mill	143
6.15	Breachwood Green tower mill in ruins	144
6.16	Croxley Green tower mill in 1970	146
6.17	Lannock tower mill, Weston	148
6.18	Colney Heath tower mill	149
6.19	Much Hadham tower mill	150
7.1	Continuous paper-making machine	154
7.2	Croxley Mills in 1865	156
7.3	Locomotive for use at Croxley Mills	157
7.4	Croxley Mills being demolished in 1982	158
7.5	Nash Mills House	158
7.6	Scotsbridge Mill today	162
7.7	Hamper Mill, *c.*1910	163
7.8	The Old Paper Mill, Standon	165
7.9	The waterwheel at the Old Paper Mill, Standon	166
7.10	The preserved pit wheel at the Old Paper Mill, Standon	167

ILLUSTRATIONS

8.1	The location of Hertfordshire's silk mills	170
8.2	Fire at Grove Mill, Hitchin, in 1889	172
8.3	The hydraulic system at Tring Silk Mill	173
8.4	The workforce at Tring Silk Mill, *c*.1880	174
8.5	The waterwheel at Tring Silk Mill	175
8.6	Abbey Mills, St Albans, *c*.1900	176
9.1	Codicote fulling mill in 1967	180
9.2	Fulling stocks at Horns Mill	180
9.3	Horns Mill shortly before demolition	182
9.4	The railway connection to Horns Mill	182
9.5	The cotton mill at St Albans, by an unknown artist	183
9.6	Cecil sawmill, Hatfield, in 1954	183
9.7	Foster's sawmill, Boxmoor	184
9.8	The Pulhamite works at Broxbourne today	184
9.9	Waterpump at The Grove, Watford	186
9.10	Waterpump at Cassiobury Park, Watford	186
9.11	Waterpump at Chaulden House, Boxmoor	186
9.12	Waterpump at Marden Hill House, Tewin	186
9.13	Waterpump at Panshanger	186
9.14	Waterpump at Panshanger	186
9.15	Waterpump at Langleybury, Hunton Bridge	186
9.16	Waterpump at Chorleywood House	186
10.1	Grove Mill, Watford, today	190
10.2	Sele Mill, Hertford, today	192
10.3	Cromer Mill, *c*.1920	194
10.4	Roydon Mill, *c*.1890s	197
10.5	Breachwood Green windmill today	198
10.6	Reed tower mill after conversion, *c*.1978	199
10.7	Codicote fulling mill today	200
10.8	Park Mill before conversion	202
10.9	Park Mill after conversion	202

Appendices

1	Interior of Hitchin Corn Exchange	211
2	Bishops Stortford Corn Exchange	212
3	The mill race and site of the waterwheel at Hyde Mill, Ickleford	215
4	Recovered section of waterwheel	216
5	Reconstruction of waterwheel	216

Plates
1   Mill Green Mill
2   Hurst frame and machinery at Mill Green Mill
3   Moor Mill in 1990
4   The stone floor at Moor Mill before conversion
5   The lay-shaft drive at Redbournbury Mill
6   Redbournbury Mill
7   Diagramatic view of Redbournbury Mill
8   The stone floor at Redbournbury Mill
9   Hyde Mill
10 Upper Mill, Berkhamsted, *c.*1900
11 Cromer Mill
12 The roundhouse at Cromer Mill
13 The meal floor at Cromer Mill
14 The stone floor at Cromer Mill
15 Waterwheel at the Royal Gunpowder Mills, Waltham Abbey
16 Waterwheel at Hunton Bridge Mill
17 Waterwheel at Sopwell Mill in 1990
18 Waterwheel at Redbournbury
19 Hertingfordbury Mill before conversion
20 Hertingfordbury Mill after conversion
21 Hatch controls at Hertingfordbury Mill
22 Wheathampstead Mill
23 Roydon Mill

Hertfordshire's artists
24 *The Water Mill* by William Henry Hunt
25 *Buntingford Windmill* by James Wilcox
26 *Corey's Mill, Stevenage* by Sidney Massie
27 *Welch's Windmill, Gaping Hill* by Samuel Lucas
28 *Rowley's Mill, Ickleford* by Samuel Lucas
29 *Ickleford Mill* by E.M. Seebohm
30 *Sailing Barge at Dicker Mill, Hertford* by Edgar Wigram

Acknowledgements

The main structure of the book is based on historic records and old documents, but the richness of detail has been provided through the kindness of the many individuals who I have had the pleasure to meet in the course of my research. Their enthusiasm, encouragement and kindness have been outstanding and to all of them I am profoundly grateful. Not only have I been welcomed into their private houses, but I have been supplied with much information that has not been in the public domain. The sheer length of the list of the staff at the variety of institutions and organisations whose collections I consulted, and of the private individuals who gave me information, gives an idea of the complexity of the milling that has taken place in Hertfordshire. Many of the illustrations have come from these sources. My thanks go to the many people listed below.

Museums and archives
The Hertfordshire Archive and Local Studies Library: Chris Bennett and his staff.
The staff of the Mills Archive at Reading: Mildred and Ron Cookson, Luke Bonwick, Elizabeth Trout and Nathanael Hodge, and members David Jones, Martin and Susan Watts, Alan and Jenny Crocker, Jenny West and Jeff Hawksley.
Hertfordshire Building Preservation Trust: Dorothy Abel Smith, Robin Webb and Tony Bradshaw.
The Royal Society: Fiona Keates.

Local museums
Mike Stanyon (The Paper Trail), Catherine Newley (St Albans Museum), Yvonne Fackney (Loweswood Museum), Mike Bass, Shelley Savage and Tim Amsden (Tring Museum), Jenny Sherwood (Dacorum Museum), Isobel Cranmer (Redbourn Museum), Beryl Gafney (Ware Museum), Jo Ward (Stevenage Museum), David Hodges (Hitchin Museum), Audrey Adams (Bushey Museum), Terry Ransome (Hitchin British Schools Trust), Victoria Jones (Watford), Sarah Keeling (Hertford), Robin Mann and Roger Yapp (Abbots Langley Local History Society) and Roy Wood (Hemel Hempstead Local History and Museum Society).

WIND, WATER AND STEAM

The milling industry
David Wright and Alan Cave (Ponders End Mill), Robert Dunderdale and Adrian Seeley (Cereform at Royston), Sue Freestone, Matt Lupton and Maureen Edwards (Allinson at Bishops Stortford), Paul Messenger (Heygates at Tring), Peter Titmuss (Wheathampstead), Guy Horlock and David Jupp (French and Jupps, Stanstead Abbotts), Mags Humphrey and Ron Gosling (Christy Turner, Ipswich), Mike Sheppard (North Herts Farmers Grain Ltd), Nigel Bennett (National Association of British and Irish Millers) and Charles Doble (Green and Carter).

The eight accessible mills
Justin James (Redbounbury Mill), Ben Cole (Hyde Mill), Linda Dobbs and Joe Taylor (Mill Green Mill), Jo Gaze (Kingsbury Mill), Laurie Hart (Moore Mill), and Richard Thomas and Les Tucker (Royal Gunpowder Mills), Mike Stanyon (Frogmore Mill) and Robin Webb (Cromer Windmill).

Watermills
Roger Hands (Boxmoor), Gloria Thompson (Hamper), Michael Harveson (Watford), Will Templeton (river Chess), Angela Colman (Sarratt), Paul Barnes (Shafford), Steve Russell (Prae), Mark and Beccy Boxer (Sopwell), Simon Hudson (St Albans), Annette Cotter and Paul Chamberlain (Lemsford), Peter Sinclair and Tony Burgess (Ware), Bernard Barwick (Broxbourne), Oliver Kelly (Whitwell), Nicholas Maddex (Codicote), Tony Rook (river Mimram), Ian Frazer (Welwyn), Virginia Maunder Taylor, William Vigus and Mary Fitzgerald (Hertingfordbury), Clare and James Currey (Walkern), Simon Garratt (Hertford), John Phillpot (Standon), Mike Smith (Puckeridge), Wally Wright (river Stort and Sawbridgeworth), Richard Nixon (re Burton's steam lorries), Derek Rochall (Hallingbury), Bob Freeman (Ickleford), Ruth Jeavons and Andrew Robley (Wheathamstead), and Anthony Boswell (Chorleywood).

Windmills
Richard Sisson (Breachwood Green), Jenny Wrench and Kerry and Gill Jenkins (Goldfield), Theo van de Bilt (High Wych), Jon Sass (Much Hadham), John Lucas and Bridget Howlett (Gaping Hills), Sheila White (Goff's Oak) and Jon Sass (Much Hadham).

Silk mills
Martin Wheeler (Tring).

Pictures
Tom Doig, Susan Watts, Stephen Ruff, Alan Stoyal, Alan Rattue, Darran Mustoe, Peter Eyre, David Huggins, John Brandrick, Roger Yapp, Brian Johnson, Derek Miles, Diana Parrott and Chris Howes.

ACKNOWLEDGEMENTS

Maps
Sarah Wroot

For technical help
Bryan Magee (roller mills), Hugh O'Reilly (Panshanger), Stanley Cauvain (Chorleywood Bread Process), Edwin Trout (Pulhamite) and Malcolm Green (for information on the gunpowder industry).

Abbreviations

CWS	Cooperative Wholesale Society
GNR	Great Northern Railway
HALS	Hertfordshire Archive and Local Studies
HBPT	Hertfordshire Building Preservation Trust
HER	Historic Environment Record
RSA	Royal Small Arms
SPAB	Society for the Protection of Ancient Buildings

Note on access

I must remind readers that the majority of mills are in private hands and there is no right of public entry. At the time of writing Hyde Mill, on the river Lea, can be viewed only by appointment with the owner, Ben Cole.

Note on glossary

Terms included in the glossary are indicated in the text with the use of a dagger (†).

Preface

My researches on Bedfordshire's mills suggested that, with the minor exception and scant evidence of a pug mill for chopping clay for brickmaking, mills were used exclusively for corn. In contrast, Hertfordshire boasts no fewer than nine uses to which water, wind and steam power was put: corn, paper, gunpowder, silk, cotton, fulling, sawmilling, stone crushing and water pumping. Of these different uses, almost all are now redundant, for the various reasons described herein.

What is the unique quality of Hertfordshire's mills? English builders were especially adept at realising the potential of new technologies and making them uniquely appropriate to the landscapes and societies in which they were built, and Hertfordshire is notable for the amazing variety of applications of milling technology. It is also unusual to find several medium-sized milling companies that have survived either independently or as separate entities, under the umbrella of Allied Mills.

Despite the loss of so much of the county's milling heritage, there is a remarkable range of examples demonstrating the rapid evolution of milling technology from the late eighteenth to the twentieth century. Waterwheels, for example, include simple low breast shot wheels with rudimentary paddles and multi-bucketed overshot wheels, while an unusual find has been two examples of millstones driven by a lay-shaft layout.

Milling was once one of the most important of Hertfordshire's industries. Now it is only peripheral. This book attempts to aggregate the evidence of its glory days in an economic history reflecting the dynamic nature of the technological advances, with successful survival being as important as heritage. It is about hard-faced commercialism colliding with equally hard-faced economics, about those who could 'ride the tiger' against those who could not. It conveys something of the 'grittiness' or 'edginess' of a struggle against adverse economic circumstances.

The Hertfordshire Historic Environment Record (HER) is the base which I have used as my starting point. The HER is comprehensive, and has been constantly enhanced with fresh information as it has become available. However, there are many instances in which the details of machinery have been lost and cannot be recovered. In years gone by it was frequently the case that, on the sale of a mill, milling equipment was removed for scrap without any official record being made.

Mills are now regarded as an important part of the national heritage and looked on with affection by the conservation movement. Moreover, a cosy nostalgia in some quarters for all things past has given rise to many a cheerful painting of the countryside in which there are roses round the cottage door and the sun always shines. Such scenes often include a windmill on the hill or a watermill nestling in the valley, with a jolly miller or happy smocked peasant. The packaging of flour for retail often contained such images of rustic windmills, suggesting that the source of the product was this, rather than the massive industrial mills from which it actually came. Milling has had its part to play in the nostalgic quest for a perceived, rather than actual, lost rural idyll. I myself used to live in a mill house in Oxfordshire. The mill building itself was long gone but the wheel pits and grooves for the headstocks were clearly visible and the odd milling artefact remained, including a grinding stone complete with its handle and millstones reused to form doorsteps. I have a vivid memory of listening to the restful sound of the waters of the river Windrush pouring over the mill race into the pool below. It has been a pleasure to have been reminded of these sounds on some of my visits to Hertfordshire's converted watermills.

However, this bucolic idyll is far removed from the reality of a working mill. We need to remember that the words 'dark' and 'satanic' are also associated with them. They were hot, noisy, dusty and dangerous places in which to work and there are frequent references to fatal accidents. William Vigus recalls the working conditions, for example, in Hertingfordbury Mill: 'It was not a nice place to work. The whole building shook. It was so hot and dusty with no ventilation. You were lucky not to lose fingers in the elevators.'

The purpose of this book is, first, to explain why milling in the county is but a shadow of its former self and to explain the events, developments and changes that have brought this about. I have sought to recapture the now largely forgotten social and economic role that mills once fulfilled, whether in the form of paper mills, gunpowder mills, corn mills, fulling mills or silk mills. Second, it presents, as far as is possible, a comprehensive record of the milling industry that was once so dominant in the county.

Hugh Howes
February 2016

1

Hertfordshire's milling heritage

Hertfordshire has an unusually rich and diverse milling heritage. Apart from the long tradition of corn milling, which is not untypical of the home counties, Hertfordshire enjoyed an extensive and wide-ranging reputation for the milling of a whole variety of products. The county shared with its eastern neighbours the capacity to produce great amounts of wheat, and processing this wheat kept the vast majority of the county's mills busy. However, there is also a long history of pioneering paper-making, primarily in the west of the county, as well as a legacy of the manufacture of gunpowder and small arms in the east and of silk mills, fulling mills, leather works and mills for oil seed cake, cotton and artificial stone for rockeries made from claystone. Despite this rich history, little of this heritage remains today. The decline of local corn milling and the concentration of flour production in very large industrial mills, mainly outside the county, are typical of the region as a whole. What makes the situation in Hertfordshire special is that the county's other kinds of milling all but disappeared within a few years, making the contraction of milling far more pronounced than elsewhere.

In Hertfordshire, as in other counties, milling, in the form of watermills, can be traced back to Saxon times. The mills themselves may have been rebuilt several times, but their sites did not change. Local mills served village communities and often enjoyed a monopoly throughout the medieval period. This began to change only at the start of the nineteenth century, when there was an increase in the demand for flour from an expanding population in the growing cities. The next hundred years are often described as 'the golden age of milling' because of an ever-increasing demand for flour. It is this period of rapid evolution with which this book is mainly concerned.

Changes to the milling community in this period were the result of national and international developments, technical changes and increasingly sophisticated marketing opportunities. Any one of these developments would have had a significant impact on milling practices: coming together, they brought a complete revolution to the millers' world. For instance, mill owners began to augment their water and wind power by steam engines. New mills were built that relied wholly on steam and were footloose in terms of where they could be located. Mills sited adjacent to railway stations had great advantages: Sherriffs at Hatfield, Bowmans at Hitchin, Smiths at Station Mill, Royston and Chapmans at New Mill, Standon are examples.

STANDON FLOUR MILLS, HERTS.

Chapman Bros. :— Registered Proprietors of "Nutros."

Telegrams: Chapman Bros., Puckeridge.
Telephone: No. 3, Puckeridge.

Flour Mills, STANDON, HERTS.

Figure 1.1 Chapman Bros proudly advertising their new flour mill in the early years of the twentieth century. Kindly supplied by S. Ruff.

Figure 1.2 Burton's Sawbridgeworth Town Mill in its prime at the start of the twentieth century. Reproduced by kind permission of the Mills Archive.

The success, or otherwise, of the mill owners in meeting these challenges depended on the extent to which individual millers were able to adapt to these evolving economic circumstances. Up-to-date milling equipment and good access to both imported grain and expanding markets were the key to survival. The individual mills in the county bear the evidence of how far millers were willing or able to go to confront the new challenges of technologies, transport and the increasingly sophisticated markets for bread and confectionery products. At one extreme they built new industrial-style mills located next to modern transport links and equipped with the latest in roller milling technologies; at the other, they persevered with obsolete equipment in rural backwaters until declining profitability forced their closure. Between these extremes most millers went some way to adapting to the changing economic environment by modernising their mills and adapting their existing transport links. By these means they were able to extend the working lives of their mills until their sheer lack of capacity rendered them redundant. The following chapters will explore the extent to which the individual mills were adapted to these evolving conditions and how successful they were in meeting these challenges.

Many mill buildings have subsequently found new uses, ensuring that a small but significant part of the county's milling heritage has been preserved. Many watermills have been converted to dwellings or offices. Lemsford Mill, for example, now the offices of Ramblers Worldwide Holidays, offers an intriguing vision of a sustainable use of water power. Here an historic building enjoys a new lease of life as a modern commercial office whose electricity is generated by a new waterwheel which harvests the power of the river Lea. Hertfordshire's HER reveals 110 watermill sites, of which seven are now accessible to the public and 31 have survived in a reasonable state of preservation: of these, 15 have been converted into houses or apartments. A further 64 have been demolished. There are also records of 71 windmills, of which seven have tangible remains; only one, Cromer post mill, is well preserved in its original form and open to the public.

There were several milling dynasties in Hertfordshire ready to take advantage of the new circumstances. They included Meads (who sold out to Heygates) at New Mill (otherwise known as Gamnel Mill), Tring; Bowmans at Hitchin and subsequently at Ickleford; Edwards (subsequently Allinson) at Beech Mill (or Town Mill) at Bishops Stortford; and Cereform at Station Mill at Royston. All continue in production today, specialising in niche-market flour products. There were also the Knowles of Bourne End and Castle Mill, Berkhamsted, the Chapmans of New Mill, Standon (Figure 1.1), the Burtons of Sawbridgeworth (Figure 1.2), the Browns and Frenchs of Ware Flour Mills, the Coles of Hyde Mill, Harpenden, the Garratts of Sele Mill, Hertford and the Pulhams of Broxbourne. Some of their mills, such as the Town Mill in Ware, New Mill in Standon and Sele Mill in Hertford, were closed down only after being taken over by one of the big milling conglomerates after World War II. All were substantial

Figure 1.3 The fate of redundant technology: in May 1911 Mead's Gamnel End windmill at Tring was demolished to make way for an extension to the steam-powered mills. The lower brickwork was carefully replaced by wooden struts and a steel cable and winch pulled them out, ensuring that it fell in the right direction. Courtesy of the Tring Local History Society.

buildings that have enjoyed a new life as apartments. Others, such as Toovey's Mill at Kings Langley, have been demolished, and Sawbridgeworth Town Mill has been lost to fire. Some older rural mills, such as Bourne End Mill near Hemel Hempstead and Hyde Mill near Harpenden, were also successfully updated and continued in production for many years.

The losers were the newly constructed tower windmills† and those watermills that had been re-equipped with the latest millstone technology, which was itself, within a few decades, rendered obsolete by the widespread adoption of the much more efficient roller mills (Figure 1.3). Several of these brick-built windmills, the final flowering of windmill technology, were built towards the end of the 'golden age', at Colney Heath (1854), Great Offley (1855), Goff's Oak, near Cheshunt (1860) Breachwood Green, near King's Walden (1860), Patmore Heath, near Albury (1860/1) and Much Hadham (1892). The Browns flour mill at Ware was newly built in 1851 with five sets of stones, but appears to have fallen out of use by 1880. It was augmented by a new mill when J.W. French and Co took over the site in 1897. These mills all had the disadvantage of using millstones, which, at the time of their construction, were already becoming obsolete, and were also remote from modern transport links. They can hardly have repaid the substantial investment that their construction had incurred. Reliance on wind power was a further disadvantage, as a comment concerning Goff's Oak windmill demonstrates: 'Sometimes, however, owing to lack of wind (or too strong a wind) the Mill would be idle for as long as 10–14 days at a time.'[1]

These changing economic circumstances and new technologies, and the limitations of wind and water power, were summarised nearly 50 years ago by W. Branch Johnson, the noted antiquary who did so much to record Hertfordshire's built heritage immediately after World War II. In his seminal work *Industrial monuments in Hertfordshire*, which traced the history of Hertfordshire's industries, he said:

> The decline in the Hertfordshire milling industry over the last century may be accounted for generally by the advantages enjoyed by port millers in being able to unload grain from overseas direct from ship to silo and, particularly in Hertfordshire, by the steady fall in the water table, which has put more than one old-established mill out of action. Where capital was lacking millers had no means either of modernising their plant or of meeting the cost of transport.
>
> From the middle third of the 19th century water mills, and a few windmills, began to supplement their water or wind power by steam; later mills were built wholly for steam. From the 1880s mills began to adopt roller milling, thus doing away with the old fashioned millstones.[2]

The chief influences on the economic environment for milling from the middle of the nineteenth century can be summarised as the free trade movement, the increasing impact of London and its docks, the revolution in milling technology and the growing importance of access to modern transport, as explored below.

Free trade

During the first half of the nineteenth century corn milling was entirely local. Farmers within the catchment of a wind or watermill would bring their corn to it and would then distribute the flour to local bakers. This situation began to change with the repeal of the Corn Laws in 1846. This legislation, by eliminating tariffs on imported grain, succeeded in providing cheap bread to the growing new industrial centres. It was a triumph for liberal thinking and resulted in a doubling of inter-continental trade. Despite these benefits, however, it had an increasingly adverse effect on the local corn milling industry.

Initially the impact was limited, such was the rapid growth in the demand for food. From 1846 until 1880 the demand for flour seemed to be almost limitless. During this time, however, imported grain began to make inroads into a rapidly

Figure 1.4 Toovey's Mill, Kings Langley, in 1978, with the miller's house on the left. The Grand Union Canal is behind the mill. Photo by M.J. Hemming. Reproduced courtesy of the Kings Langley Local History and Museum Society.

expanding urban market, a trend which set in train the long-term decline in local corn milling. The emphasis gradually shifted to industrial-scale mills, particularly at the ports, where imported corn was milled straight from ocean-going ships at the point of entry, the flour then being sent, by rail, to bakeries in the growing industrial cities. Home-grown corn was protected to some degree by the Crimean War in the 1850s and the American Civil War in the 1860s, both of which restricted the amount of imported wheat, but the economic basis of local flour milling was, nevertheless, changing fundamentally. Lewis Dean of the Toovey family, who operated the mill at Kings Langley (Figure 1.4), explained:

> An increase in population had resulted in a growing demand for flour, which was met by greatly increased imports of wheat. As a result far more was imported than was grown at home, so of course a port was a better place for a mill than in the country. On the other hand, biscuit flour required the characteristics which were absolutely met by English wheat which was then grown, and so these mills should be where the wheat was.[3]

In the late 1870s a series of poor harvests affected both agriculture and milling, and those mills that were purely local declined rapidly thereafter. From then on, with the exception of the war years, the picture of corn milling in Hertfordshire reflected the growing influence of London as a market for flour and the corresponding decline of 'country' mills.

Corn milling was not alone in being affected by the reforms to the tariff system mentioned above. The Cobden–Chevalier Commercial Treaty of 1860 eased tariff barriers with France but, for the silk 'throwing' industry, the provisions of the treaty were devastating. French protective duties were to be reduced to a maximum of 25 per cent over five years with free entry for French products. This placed British silk producers at an impossible disadvantage and most silk mills closed soon afterwards (see Chapter 8). The paper-making industry was doubly disadvantaged, in that the Treaty imposed a tariff not only on the importation of rags but also on the export of finished paper products. The industry relied on the import of substantial quantities of rags from both France and Germany, and the cost of rags in Paris was half that in London. The introduction of esparto grass as a substitute for rags was one initiative that attempted to circumvent these taxes (see Chapter 7).

The influence of London

The proximity of London had a significant and increasing influence on corn milling in Hertfordshire in terms of both supplies of imported corn and rapidly growing metropolitan market opportunities. It is no exaggeration to say that the decline in local milling in Hertfordshire, and indeed in the other home counties, was, in no small measure, due to two developments outside the county: the development of large-scale mills in London's docklands and the rapid growth of the corn exchanges in Mark Lane in the City, near the Tower of London (see Appendix 2).

The imported grain that came into the Surrey Docks offered a new opportunity for those of Hertfordshire's corn millers who were in a position to re-equip their mills and have the grain delivered by water or by rail. The main sources at that time were Canada, the Ukraine and Argentina. Following the initial imports from these countries, docks specialising in the import of grain were constructed, firstly at Wapping and subsequently at the Royal Docks. This was particularly important as it coincided with a period in the late 1870s when local corn became scarce. Millers who turned to this new source were successful, while those who could not, or did not, went out of business. These developments go a long way towards explaining the decline of local milling generally and in Hertfordshire in particular.

An example of the effects of these emerging economic difficulties is Waterford Mill, on the river Beane, which was destroyed by fire in 1870:

> It is a matter of conjecture how long the watermill at Waterford would have survived had it not been for the disastrous fire. The decline of local milling throughout the country was sealed when the Repeal of the Corn Laws in 1846 permitted the import of cheap grain from abroad. This was mostly processed in large purpose built mills at or near the main ports. Milling had now become big business. The small miller soon lost trade to these large new mills using modern power sources to drive steel rollers instead of the old circular grinding stones used for many centuries before. Trade with small mills often survived only due to the loyalty of local farmers.[4]

The revolution in milling technology

A traditional set of millstones consists of a lower bedstone† and an upper runner†. Grain is fed into the hoppers immediately above the stones and thence into the central eye of the stones themselves. The ground flour emerges from the outer edge of the stones and is collected within the wooden casing, before being fed down a chute to the floor below.

Favourable economic conditions in the period up to 1880 had disguised the uncomfortable fact that technology was moving on, and that the traditional millstones were unproductive and difficult to maintain. In 1876 an article in *The Miller*, the trade paper for the milling industry, explained how little technical progress had been made:

> Milling has, in reality, made very little progress since ancient times. It still consists in reducing wheat to flour and bran by the friction of stones, and

afterwards by various modes of sifting. No doubt great improvements have been attained both as to the quality and quantity, but still the old principles have been adhered to. During the last fifty years various efforts have been made to replace millstones by more suitable machines, and many more or less successful experiments have been made. One of these machines – the Roller Mill – has attained of late years a very high degree of perfection, and should certainly engage the attention of millers.[5]

Roller mills made redundant the laborious and time-consuming task of 'stitching' or 'fluting'† that millstones regularly required. This process involved removing the wooden tuns† from the stones, lifting the runner stone, which could weigh three-quarters of a ton, and sharpening the grooves in the face of the stones. Everything then had to be replaced and the stones balanced to ensure that they ran true. Roller mills were a great step forward and produced a finer, and more hygienic, flour at lower cost. The pioneer of roller mills† was Henry G. Simon of Manchester, who, well aware that roller mills had already become widespread in Hungary, Austria and his native Germany, introduced the 'gradual reduction' milling system into Britain. In 1879 he described the technical change with a degree of whimsy:

> You are all aware of the revolution which, slowly in some places, quicker in others, but certainly in almost all civilised countries, is coming over the flour milling industry. The autocratic reign of King Millstone is being questioned. He has already had to make concessions to his subjects, and the spirit of the times may force him before long to grant a constitution with parliamentary government in imitation of the sultan of Turkey.[6]

The new process itself he described in the following terms:

> To carry out the principles and the results and advantages already mentioned, the grinding of the grain by the roller-mill process is divided into three main operations. First, the granulation or separation of the outer husk or bran of the grain from the kernel; secondly, the purification of the broken kernel or semolina obtained by granulation from such portions of the bran as have been mixed with it; and thirdly the gradual reduction of the purified semolina into flour.[7]

Subsequently, in 1882, he explained the disadvantages of traditional milling methods:

> In the old stone mill a serious expense was occasioned by the necessity of redressing the surface of the stones. This is necessary, say every ten to

fifteen days, when at work day and night. The expense for performing this operation is stated to be about £15 per annum per pair of stones.[8]

And the advantages of the new technology:

> The principal advantage of roller-milling is that the bran or husk, and the germ of the grain, are flattened out by the action of rolling, and can consequently easily be sifted out by proper application of dressing machinery. This advantage cannot be over-estimated, seeing the detrimental action which both bran and germ have on the keeping and baking qualities of flour. Where the oily germ is ground up with the semolina, the flour easily gets musty when kept. Such flour is therefore totally unfit for export.

A modern view of the revolution in milling is given by Lewis Dean, who, referring to Toovey's Mill at Kings Langley, describes the new technology:

> The whole essence of this new roller mill process was gradual reduction. The rolls were made of chilled cast iron with a steel spindle at each end. They varied in length from about 2ft to 5 ft., whip becoming excessive if the length were made greater than this, and were about 9ins in diameter. The rolls ran together in pairs like the rollers of a mangle but in some pairs one would run faster than the other. Some had spiral flutes cut into them making one or two revolutions in the length of the roll. These were known as 'break rolls', and their purpose was to break open the kernel of wheat. As one of the pair revolved faster than the other there was a tendency for it to hold the wheat while the other scraped it. The branny particles were then separated by a combination of air currents and sieves from the pure inner part of the grain, which had not been much reduced in size and was in fact semolina. This was then passed through a pair of smooth matt rolls which would probably both be running at the same speed and whose function was to reduce the size of the particles by crushing them a little.[9]

It is impossible to overstate the scale of the revolution in the milling world represented by the advent of roller mills, which has been well documented; Simon himself published papers with both the Institution of Mechanical Engineers and the Institution of Civil Engineers. Being aware of the relative backwardness of his adopted country was one thing, however, but overcoming its inertia was quite another. An obituary of Simon illustrated the problem:

> In the face of very strong opposition, himself not a British-born subject, having to advocate principles of manufacture which were opposed to the lifelong ideas of the master millers of the time, in his struggles to introduce an expensive process according to the prevailing opinion, he had an uphill fight against the prejudices of time-honoured institutions. It will, therefore, be admitted that the contest which he entered upon in the seventies was one beset with immense difficulties, and only to be successfully accomplished by some masterful man. Some of us have scarcely forgotten the obloquy, ridicule and adverse criticisms which were launched against the new-fangled notions enunciated by the pioneers of roller milling. Anything foreign seems to be, to the average Englishman, a thing to be despised and rejected; but the argument which overcomes even these sentiments is to be found to be all powerful when it takes the form of an increased profit promised to those who can swallow their prejudice and adopt the new principles suggested.[10]

Millers were certainly becoming aware of the advantages of the system of roller mills from the mid-1870s. However, traditional customers of the industry of milling machinery were often opposed to the new technology, to some extent because it was perceived as 'foreign'. However accurate Simon's observations may have been, as an immigrant, his comments about the ways of Englishmen can hardly have endeared him to his British audience.

Nevertheless, the science of milling subsequently evolved rapidly in the last quarter of the nineteenth century, aided by advances in engineering technology and spurred on by the demand for white bread. Simon summed up the revolution in milling in a paper to the Institution of Mechanical Engineers in 1889: 'The completeness of the revolution that has taken place is exemplified by the fact that practically, in less than ten years, the machinery and methods of corn milling have been radically altered, at the cost of an immense amount of capital.'[11]

Roller mills, purifiers† and sifters† thus came to replace millstones and traditional sieving equipment. The 'Simon System' was on the market by 1880 and Simon's equipment was installed in the Ware Town Mill, Bowman's Ickleford Mill and Garratt's Sele Mill at Hertford. E.R. & F. Turner of Ipswich were manufacturing rollers from 1882. J. Harrison Carter, a milling expert based in Mark Lane, London, designed a complete roller milling system, the necessary machinery for which was manufactured, too, by E.R. and F. Turner (Figure 1.5). The company was a pioneer in providing the new technology. It was the first to install roller milling systems in the UK and supplied complete flour milling products throughout the industrialised world. Their four-roller mill system was to be installed in a great many mills, including, in Hertfordshire, Meads at Tring, Knowles at Bourne End, Tooveys at Kings Langley and Pearman at Walkern (see Appendices 6, 7 and 8) (Figure 1.6).

Figure 1.5 An advertisement for a Carter/Turner roller mill, which was one of the first for producing white flour. Reproduced from The Miller, 5 March 1883.

Figure 1.6 Roller mills were installed by E.R. & F. Turner of Ipswich at Station Mills, Hitchin, at the beginning of the twentieth century. Reproduced by kind permission of Jas. Bowman and Sons Ltd.

The next 50 years were to be an industrial version of survival of the fittest in terms of the modernisation of mills. Advances in the design and development of milling machinery were accompanied, as noted, by an increasing demand for white bread. The whiter flour required was more easily produced by roller mills than by millstones, which, in turn, were less suited to producing flour in the volumes required by the rapidly expanding market. The innovations were not restricted to the grinding of corn, but extended to sophisticated purifiers and a variety of sifting machinery, such as silk dressing machines, which rendered the traditional sifters with wire brushes obsolete. They also consumed less power and could be operated at the same time as the millstones, something that had not previously been possible. Faced with this revolution in milling, the number of small unmodernised traditional mills dwindled between 1880 and 1914 as they became unviable. Hertfordshire's mills were no exception, with many going out of business.

Figure 1.7 Stanstead Abbotts Mill with its elongated 'luccam' or sack hoist, extending over the mill stream, at the turn of the twentieth century. This enabled grain to be lifted direct from barges on the river Lea to the bin floor. Reproduced by kind permission of the Mills Archive.

Garratts of Hertford and Meads of Tring were the pioneers of the new technology in Hertfordshire. However, installing it was extremely expensive. Some mills, such as Bourne End Mill, Sawbridgeworth Town Mill, and New Mill at Tring, could be converted, or a completely new mill might be built, such as Stanstead Abbotts Mill (Figure 1.7) or Kings Langley. In other cases a roller mill plant might be built alongside the existing millstone installation, as at Hyde Mill (Harpenden) on the river Lea and French's mill at Ware. Several new steam-driven mills, such as the Beech Flour Mill at Bishops Stortford, Station Mill at Royston, Dixon's flour mill at St Albans and Goff's Oak windmill near Cuffley, were built on sites unrelated to water power. There was also a gas-powered mill, Sherriff's Mill, at Hatfield.

The other major technological invention requiring investment was the water turbine†, which significantly improved the power and efficiency of the milling process (Figures 1.8 and 1.9). Joseph J. Armfield, of Ringwood, was the pioneer in its development.[12] However, the advantages of the turbine were soon offset by falling water tables and reduced flows in rivers. They were therefore little more than a stop gap

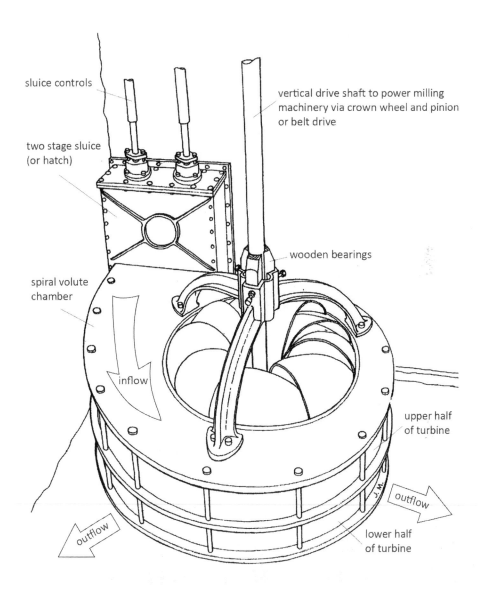

Figure 1.8 A diagram of a 24-hp two-stage water turbine by J.J. Armfield. Kindly supplied by W. Wright. The turbine blades are contained in a spiral 'volute' casing, which is designed to reduce the velocity of flow of the incoming water and to increase its pressure on the turbine blades. For the first stage the inlet sluice is half raised, thereby admitting water to the lower half of the turbine. Fully raising the sluice admits water to the upper half of the turbine, thereby achieving full power.

Figure 1.9 The turbine at Broxbourne survived the destruction of the mill in a complete form. Kindly supplied by D. Housham.

before millers sought to free themselves from these hydraulic constraints altogether by installing steam engines.

Location and transport

Before the advent of quick and easy methods of transport, the local corn mills played a vital role in each village economy, where transport by horse and cart was adequate (Figure 1.10). However, as the nineteenth century progressed, mills that could be accessed only by horse and cart along country lanes were at an immediate disadvantage compared with those with canal wharfage or rail sidings. They had little control over the grain they milled, being limited to those local supplies of grain that farmers brought them. In contrast, those millers with better access could buy the grain of their choice at corn exchanges and sell their flour to London and other urban markets. Only those millers who obtained a supply of imported wheat by using navigations,

Figure 1.10 Early transport: Ben Cole's horse-drawn wagon, which served Hyde Mill on the river Lea. It is now preserved at the Museum of English Rural Life in Reading. Reproduced by kind permission of L. Bonwick.

Figure 1.11 Narrow boats unloading at Sawbridgeworth using a grain elevator by S.S. Stott and Co. of Haslingden in Lancashire (specialising in grain warehousing machines for silos and granaries). It was capable of discharging 180 tons (183 tonnes) of grain per hour. A similar device was used at Ponders End Mill. Kindly supplied by W. Wright from the Ed Goatcher collection.

Figure 1.12 Castle Mill, Berkhamsted, built in 1895, was typical of a number of industrial-style mills dating from that time and equipped with the most up-to-date machinery. Photographed in 1997, after it had been converted to offices. Reproduced by kind permission of Dacorum Museum.

canals, turnpikes or railways were able to continue in business into the twentieth century. If they could also free themselves of often unreliable wind and water power by converting to steam power they stood some chance of prospering.

The navigable waterways offered an immediate advantage to those mills with waterside wharfage. The Lea and Stort Navigations provided ready access to the London docks: initially the imported corn was moved by 100-ton barges either up the Lea Navigation to Broxbourne, Stanstead Abbotts, Ware and Hertford, or up the Stort to Sawbridgeworth and Bishops Stortford (Figure 1.11). The New Mill at Tring took its supplies via the Regent's and Grand Junction Canals to its own mill-side wharf. New canal-side mills were built at Castle Mill (Figure 1.12), Berkhamsted and Kings Langley. However, the problems of water shortages in the navigations, along with floods and ice, meant that the advantage gradually shifted first to the railways and then to the roads. Owen Burton of Thomas Burton Ltd, millers of Sawbridgeworth, explained why water transport was proving unreliable:

> In the old days it would take two days to get a horse-drawn barge, full of grain, from London Docks to Sawbridgeworth along the Lea and Stort Navigation. That was when conditions were favourable. If the water was coming down a river fast against the barges it might take three or four days to make the journey.[13]

Although the Stort Navigation had been substantially improved by the upgrade of the locks, which was completed by 1924, water-borne trade was already in decline. The company found that navigating the Lea and Stort was too leisurely and bought steam lorries to replace the barges.

If millers could free themselves of horse and water transport then they could expand their marketing horizons. Initially this meant access to railheads. The arrival of the railways meant that coal could be purchased more cheaply than before, which made the conversion of mills to steam power a more attractive proposition. Clearly this could help only a minority of millers, however. The railways also offered further advantages to those mills that could make use of them: the Buntingford Line, for example, provided a siding direct into New Mill at Standon (Figure 1.13), while Hyde Mill, near Harpenden, enjoyed a private siding on the Dunstable to Welwyn line. The Great Northern Railway (GNR) was particularly attractive to new purpose-built steam mills – Sherriff's at Hatfield and Bowmans at Hitchin are notable examples.

This was a period when several large steam-driven industrial mills were built adjacent to railway lines. Bowmans at Hitchin and Ickleford, and their third mill at Astwick, just across the Bedfordshire border, were all close to the GNR, newly opened in 1850. Using the railway the company was able to supplement local supplies with imported grain from Canada, America and Australia. They were also able to

Figure 1.13 Railways became a vital artery for successful millers. A view of the siding from the roof of Standon New Mill. Kindly supplied from the S. Ruff collection.

Figure 1.14 Road transport takes over from water and rail: an early Foden steam lorry in 1922. Reproduced by kind permission of Jas. Bowman and Sons Ltd.

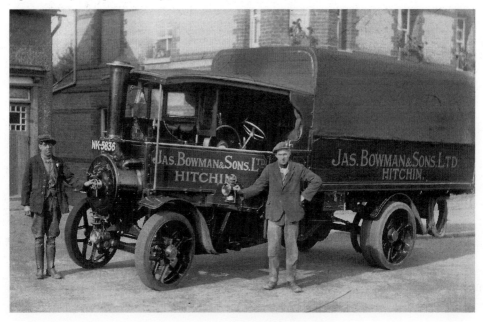

use the railway to access the company's warehouse in Mint Street in the City, which 'transformed the Bowman business because flour could be sent easily and quickly to London and other places between'.[14]

The same applied to Cereoffs at Royston, Sherriffs at Hatfield and Chapmans at Standon. Horns Leather Mill at Hertford was served by a connection to the Hatfield–Hertford branch of the GNR, a subsequent casualty of the Beeching Report. (The surviving Enfield and Stevenage Loop Line was built later: see Figure 9.4.) John Dickinson started to use the London–Birmingham Railway, instead of the Grand Junction Canal, for transporting paper goods from his mills at Apsley:

> Though the mills were all established before the age of railways, Mr. Dickinson, with his usual foresight, chose for his enterprise a locality provided with excellent water-carriage, and though the London and North Western Railway now passes close to three of the mills, and one of the branch lines near the other, water-carriage is still found to be the cheaper and cleaner, so that the greater part of the traffic of all the mills is even now carried on by means of the Grand Junction Canal, on which there are quite a fleet of boats employed in bringing coal and materials to the mills, and in taking away paper and stationery. These boats each carry about twenty five tons at a time, and every evening paper leaves the mills by them and is delivered into London next morning at six at the company's warehouse, Irongate Wharf, Paddington. Furthermore, the whole mill system is closely knitted together by a private telephone service, which also connects them with the London office at 65 Old Bailey, and thus brings them into touch with all the markets of the world.[15]

From the turn of the twentieth century road transport, and particularly the steam lorry (Figure 1.14), proved an enormous advantage to those milling companies who could afford the capital outlay. Commenting on the arrangements of supplying Sele Mill in Hertford, Simon Garratt noted: 'Imported wheat came up the Lee to Ware, where it was transferred to a smaller barge to take it to our wharf in Hertford and from there by horse drawn cart. It sounds very cumbersome and I wonder what the saving was when lorries became available.'[16] The Crystal Palace Motor Show of 1904 included steam wagons by not only the well-known manufacturers – Foden, Thorneycroft, Straker and Coulthard – but several lesser-known ones as well. *The Miller* commented:

> We were impressed with those vehicles which promise to play a great and significant part in the millers' daily trade life … we have given the question of heavy traffic haulage our closest consideration, and we advise its adoption

wherever possible. The motor waggons of today have nothing of that jarring rigidity we associate with earlier types, and have a wonderful resilience which ensures them a long life of usefulness. We call our readers' attention to a few of these – soon to be indispensable – machines, and trust they will be found useful and interesting.[17]

These primitive wagons were to play a critical role in the survival of some millers over others.

The proximity of London markets to the home counties meant that mills, which might normally be of only local significance, could now serve the metropolis. In taking advantage of these new opportunities to improve distribution networks, G.R. Wright was the first to buy a Foden steam lorry, as early as 1907, after which both Mead and Bowmans acquired them. Mead acquired a Foden in 1916 and a Napier in 1918. Bowmans, too, bought a Foden, from surplus World War I stock. This was able to climb the one-in-eight gradient at Offley on the Hitchin–Luton road, which had been too steep for horse-drawn carts, so gaining the company access to a new market in the rapidly expanding town of Luton. Burtons of Sawbridgeworth bought two Garratt steam lorries in the early 1920s specifically to deliver flour to London, where they supplied about 15 bakeries. They also fetched grain from the Surrey Docks, where the lorries could be loaded direct from the ships with Canadian wheat in sacks or barrels. These lorries both offered a quicker delivery than the barges and did not suffer the constraints of low water at critical times. By the 1930s cheaper and less complicated motor lorries were becoming available (Figures 1.15 and 1.16).

The decline of the 'country miller'

All these changes were bad news for the traditional miller. The poor harvests of the late 1870s revealed, all too harshly, the fundamental weaknesses of the domestic milling industry and its inability to function in the newly emerging economic landscape. These weaknesses, as explained above, were in the fields of milling technology and transport. Competition came from larger mills equipped with rollers and that enjoyed improved transport, economies of scale, superior marketing skills and the increasing influence of London, with access to the docks. During this period many local mills, even the recently constructed windmills, lost their markets and gradually fell out of use.

Local wind and watermills thus faced an increasingly adverse economic situation and were often reduced to producing animal feedstuffs. The revenue, although just adequate to cover the marginal costs of running a mill, rarely generated enough for long-term replacement of components or for meeting accident damage. Even such a fine windmill as Lannock was unable to provide a living: 'Farmers and windmillers were having a hard time in England in the 1880s and many were emigrating to America. In 1882 Richard Christie and his family set out to seek their fortunes there

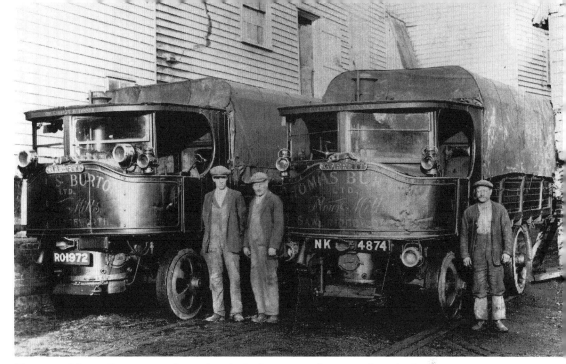

Figure 1.15 Later Garratt steam lorries bought by Burton to collect grain from the Surrey Docks, dating from 1923 (right) and 1925 (left). Kindly supplied by W. Wright from the Ed Goatcher collection.

Figure 1.16 Dickinson's 1922 Commer motor lorry. HALS.

as well.'[18] The final straw usually came when a major repair was needed, as the depleted income stream could not finance such repairs. Windmills were particularly vulnerable here. Major storm damage often meant the end of flour production and the onset of the decay of the mill.

The Miller was very anxious to support 'country millers' during the late nineteenth century and the early years of the twentieth century. It encouraged them to modernise to meet the new challenges. In a series of articles, with upbeat titles such as 'Successful country millers' and 'A model country mill', it featured millers who had re-equipped their mills and held them up as examples for others to follow (see Appendices 4–8).

In the same vein, the articles warned of the dangers of not modernising. An article in 1918 warned of the competition that millers would face in an unregulated post-war world and urged them to modernise or go to the wall. The editor foresaw the threat to 'country millers' when the war-time regulations were removed. This happened in 1921, after which there was, indeed, a further rapid decline. The article indicated that millers would need 'to possess the soundest and most extensive knowledge with practical experience and a well-flowed plant to survive', and that there were all too few millers who would be able to meet the challenge. They faced severe competition and closures were inevitable (see Appendix 1).

Writing in 1971, Lewis Dean seemed to foresee the end of the Kings Langley mill seven years later:

> What is the future for a mill such as this? I think the position today is that any competent accountant looking at the balance sheet and trading account would say that we were not making good use of our assets. There is a lot of money tied up in this concern and not earning as much as it should.

Enterprise rewarded, survival of the few

The companies that rode out these adverse economic circumstances were those that were able to respond by diversifying and moving into a wider range of products and by identifying new markets. While the imported 'hard' grain proved to be superior for bread-making, the softer, locally grown grain was favoured by confectionery bakers for cakes and pastry. In order to cater for both markets the successful millers sought greater control over their supplies and actively engaged in marketing their products. Owen Burton explained: 'Originally the wheat grain came from local fields, but then the Burtons moved into the baker's trade and needed imported strong wheat, three parts imported, one part English (or rather less if a poor crop).'[19]

Inevitably, in the ensuing shake-out of the industry there were many losers, but also some notable successes. Outstanding examples were Burtons of Sawbridgeworth,

Meads of Tring, Bowmans of Ickleford, Tooveys of Kings Langley, Cereform of Royston and Edwards of Bishops Stortford Town Mill in corn milling, J. Maygrove in silk throwing and John Dickinson in paper manufacturing.

The lesson was clear: those mill owners who were prepared to refocus their business, move up the production chain and concentrate on higher-value niche products could succeed in the face of the variety of economic misfortunes that befell the various parts of the milling industry in the later nineteenth and early twentieth centuries. Bowmans, for example, moved into wholesale supply, taking technology further and concentrating on specialist products.

Burton, too, saw the import of grain as an opportunity as much as a threat. The imported grain could be milled to provide a wider range of flour products. The company's post-World War II publicity leaflet stated:

> Here flour of all types is milled. Hard flour for bread and biscuits is made from blends of the world's finest grain harvests from Minnesota, Manitoba, Australasia and Europe.
>
> From the ships which put into London's Surrey Docks grain is brought by barge along the leisurely rivers Lee and Stort to Burton's mill at Sawbridgeworth.[20]

And, emphasising the variety of his products:

> From the local farms, too, comes the fine soft wheat of England, to be milled into that pure white self-raising flour which makes cakes and pastry of such a lovely texture and which is now available from your local grocer.

Burton's success came from his willingness to expand his business by extending their product range, by marketing this range more widely and by moving into the bakery business. Like so many milling companies, Burtons prided themselves on the whiteness of their flour, particularly as no bleaching agent was used:

> Finally comes the milling, that process, part mechanical part human, upon which the final quality and whiteness depends.
>
> Very simply, grain consists of an outer husk of bran and an inner kernel. The final whiteness of the flour depends upon the skill with which the miller can separate the husk from the kernel.
>
> To do this properly calls for great patience and the knowledge of a lifetime. At Burton's, where quality is everything, the grain passes again and again

through the mill, until every trace of husk is gone and only pure white flour remains.[21]

Burtons also diversified into 'provender' (animal foods) for cattle, pigs and poultry. However, the business came to an end in the 1960s, when it was acquired by Garfield Weston.

By the time of World War II some mills were abandoning their own steam engines for electricity, which was becoming widely available through the national grid. Such a decision could be triggered by an apparently isolated event. Owen Burton explained what happened at Sawbridgeworth, where the failure of a single component precipitated the change: 'In 1941, when the Germans invaded Holland, it was vital that the mill be kept going at all costs. Then we had a calamity when a cotter pin broke in the steam engine. We could not afford any delays so we did away with steam power and went electric.'[22]

Wartime reprieve

The outbreak of World War II brought relief for inland mills, as bombing destroyed many of the mills located at the ports. Inland milling companies came under direct government control in terms of what they produced and how much they could charge. Furthermore, because of the threat to imports from the U-boat war in the Atlantic and the agricultural war effort, the mills were using more home-grown wheat.

During the interwar years local millers were aided by the setting up of The Millers Mutual Association, which helped them to enjoy more settled market conditions. Each member was allocated a quota based on a previous volume of trade. If the quota was exceeded an extra premium was required; if there was a shortfall the participating company might be eligible for compensation.

The 'big four' take control of the market

After World War II the big milling companies, Rank/Hovis, Spillers (latterly Dalgety), The Cooperative Wholesale Society (CWS) and Garfield Weston set up new, industrial-scale mills in east London at Millwall and Silvertown. There were some eight to ten such mills within five miles of the docks. At the same time these companies bought up potentially competing local mills, in Hertfordshire and elsewhere, and closed them down, in part to secure distribution networks for their own flour. For example, French's Ware Flour Mills and Sele Mill in Hertford were closed by Spillers and Sawbridgeworth Town Mill was closed by Garfield Weston. This trend further entrenched the focus of milling on London. However, several significant Hertfordshire mill companies retained their independence, including Bowmans at Ickleford, Heygate at Tring, Cereform at Royston and Allinson at Bishops Stortford.

HORIZONTAL FIXED STEAM ENGINES.

These Engines are erected upon an iron foundation plate, made to bolt down upon a bed of brickwork or masonry, thus securing great strength and solidity. The whole arrangement is the simplest that can be adopted, the working parts few, and the liability to get out of repair consequently very slight. The material and workmanship are both of the best description, and the consumption of fuel, in proportion to the amount of power obtained, very small.

The prices, as below, are inclusive of a governor, fly wheel, &c. a Cornish boiler, with safety valve, two guage cocks, glass water guage, blow-off cock, pipes for the steam and water, with their proper connexions; also of an Engineer's time to fix the engine, the masonry or brickwork, with all necessary labourers' assistance being furnished by the purchaser.

PRICE.

3-horse Power	- - - - - -	£90
4 ,,	- - - - - -	112
6 ,,	- - - - - -	150
7 ,,	- - - - - -	170
8 ,,	- - - - - -	190
10 ,,	- - - - - -	230
12 ,,	- - - - - -	270
14 ,,	- - - - - -	310
16 ,,	- - - - - -	350
20 ,,	- - - - - -	430

N.B.—The Engines of 8-horse power and upwards may be had with double expansive slide valves, which are highly conducive to the economy of fuel.

CONDENSING HORIZONTAL ENGINES,
from 10-horse power and upwards.

COMBINED HIGH AND LOW PRESSURE ENGINES,
from 20 to 30 horse-power.

Delivered to London and all Stations on Great Eastern Railway.

Figure 1.17 An advertisement for auxiliary steam power. Reproduced from promotional literature of E.R. & F. Turner, 1868.

Conclusion

From 1860 onwards the whole economic and technical basis of corn milling changed radically. Some millers were able to adapt to the changing circumstances, but many more were not and soon found that their machinery was obsolete or that they lacked modern transport and were redundant.

The traditional milling technology of millstones powered by wind or water was becoming obsolete because of its inability to produce flour in the volumes required for the emerging mass markets. Roller mills, which were being introduced from the 1880s onwards, were much more efficient. The process of modernising mills also included addressing the source of power. Success here meant moving away from the vagaries of wind and water and switching to steam power (Figure 1.17). Waterwheels were being replaced first by water turbines, then by steam engines and finally by electricity, which, at last, freed millers entirely from the problems of achieving a consistent and reliable power source. However, the only mills which could prosper were those which also enjoyed good access by water, rail or, from about 1905 onwards, road.

My intention in this book is to explore these radical evolutions which took place in the nineteenth and twentieth centuries and to show what they meant for the individual milling industries of Hertfordshire. The questions millers faced in the latter half of the nineteenth century were various. Could the existing vernacular mill be adapted or should a new industrial plant be built? Should they retain tried and tested millstones or make a leap into the unknown with rollers? And should they replace the waterwheel with a turbine or augment it with a steam engine? How millers responded, or did not respond, to the new technical developments – turbines, steam engines and roller mills – determined which mills survived and which did not.

This book aims to recapture the problems faced by local millers and the entrepreneurs of the new industrial-style mills. It will explain why so little of the county's milling heritage remains and why mill owners had to move away from wind and water power and use steam power instead. It will look at the milling scene today and those surviving mills where it is possible to learn about milling. Successive chapters will describe corn milling, paper manufacture, silk milling, gunpowder mills, cotton milling, fulling, sawmills, leather production and, finally, the water-driven pumps which supplied Hertfordshire's mansions with potable water and, in the cases of Hatfield House and Tring Park, generated electricity. It concludes with reflections on the issues surrounding the conservation of this important part of Hertfordshire's industrial heritage.

References

1. P.C. Archer, *Historic Cheshunt* (Cheshunt, 1923).
2. W. Branch Johnson, *Industrial monuments in Hertfordshire* (Hertford, 1967).
3. L. Dean, 'The history of King's Langley Mill', *Watford and District Industrial History Society Journal*, 1 (1971), pp. 3–9.

4 M. Pollard, *Mill Cottage and Waterford Mill* (2001).
5 L. Offle, 'On roller mills', *The Miller* (6 March 1876).
6 'Daverio's system', *The Miller* (7 July 1879).
7 H. Simon, 'Roller milling', *The Miller* (7 July 1879) (paper read before the National Association of British and Irish Millers).
8 H. Simon, 'Modern flour milling in England', Institution of Civil Engineers Paper 1874 (16 May 1882).
9 L. Dean, 'The history of King's Langley Mill'.
10 'The late Mr Henry Simon of Manchester', *The Miller* (7 August 1899).
11 G. Jones, *The millers: a story of technological endeavour and industrial success 1870–2001* (Lancaster, 2001) (Reference to a paper by H. Simon to the Institution of Mechanical Engineers, 1889).
12 'Men of mark in milling mechanism, Mr Joseph J. Armfield', *The Miller* (5 August 1901).
13 'The last bag of flour has been ground at Burton's Mill', *Harlow Citizen* (30 January 1970).
14 P. Bowman, 'Bill, thrift and damsel' (unpublished, 1997).
15 *Hemel Hempstead Gazette* (16 April 1904).
16 Telephone interview with Simon Garratt, 13 Febuary 2013.
17 'The Crystal Palace Motor Show', *The Miller* (7 March 1904).
18 C. Moore, *Hertfordshire windmills and windmillers* (Sawbridgeworth, 1999).
19 Interview with Owen Burton, 30 November 1985.
20 'The whitest flour from England's pastures', undated publicity leaflet from Burtons Mill.
21 Since those days, modern nutritional theory has shown that the removal of the bran deprives the flour of its particular qualities which are vital to health. Wholemeal flour is the preferable option: it is the bran that contains the roughage which is thought to be vital in inhibiting cancers of the bowel. A further issue to emerge in recent years is that roller mills, often operating at up to 600 rpm, generate enough heat to kill the enzymes in the grain. Some millers have reduced the speed of the rollers to prevent this happening.
22 *Harlow Citizen* (30 January 1970).

2

Conflicts in the catchments

River water, by its nature, is finite in quantity. It depends on springs, which in turn depend on aquifers. In times of drought the level of water in the aquifer falls and springs dry up. Despite the consequently variable quantities of water, rivers were adequate to power the waterwheels of mills down the years until well into the nineteenth century. The rapid expansion of towns during the Victorian era, however, placed new demands on these limited water resources. These demands were satisfied by taking water either directly from the rivers or from boreholes which, in turn, took water from the aquifers. In either case it meant less water for powering waterwheels. Conflicts therefore developed between existing mill owners and the new water companies and also between millers and boat owners, where both parties were competing for a diminishing quantity of river water.

Water was, in particular, needed in abundance for the paper-making process, but all milling industries were heavily reliant on it and interruptions in the flow could have severe consequences. Summer droughts and prolonged freezing in winter were occupational hazards, during which production could be halted for significant periods. At the beginning of the nineteenth century, as intimated above, supplies were plentiful. By the end of the century, however, the abstraction of groundwater for the supply of potable water to London had started to reduce these supplies. The river valleys contain most of the larger settlements in the county, including, among others, Watford, St Albans, Hatfield and Hertford, as well as, in later years, Welwyn Garden City and Hemel Hempstead New Town, and supplying these growing towns with water has meant that flows in these rivers have been depleted. They would not now have adequate flows to turn the waterwheels that they did a century ago.

The potential for conflicts between millers and users of navigations became more acute as the nineteenth century progressed, particularly in the valleys of the river Colne and on the Grand Junction Canal in the west and in the valleys of the Lea from Hertford downstream and the Stort in the east. Millers, therefore, increasingly sought to free themselves from the limitations of river water by turning to the newly available steam engines as a more reliable source of power to ensure the continuous operation of their mills. There was thus a permanent decline in the use of water power that was underlined by events such as that of 1927, for instance, when the river Ver dried up, bringing corn milling at Shafford Mill to an abrupt and final end.

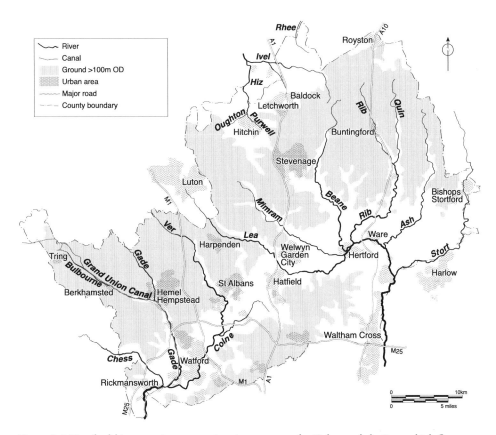

Figure 2.1 Hertfordshire contains two major river systems, the Colne and the Lea, which flow down the dipslope of the Chiltern Hills, providing power for the county's watermills. There are also the headwaters of tributaries of the Great Ouse in the vicinity of Hitchin and Baldock. The Stort and the Lea below Hertford are navigable, while the Gade and the Grand Union Canal form another significant navigation, allowing the distribution of imported grain and an outlet for flour and paper products to the London market.

The rivers Colne and Lea

The distribution of Hertfordshire's watermills relates closely to the two major catchments, the Colne and the Lea. (The only exceptions are sites at Hitchin on the river Hiz, which drains into the Ivel in Bedfordshire, and on the river Rhee, which drains into the Cam in Cambridgeshire.) At their nearest point, at Hatfield, the Colne and the Lea are no more than two miles apart (Figure 2.1). But from there they diverge, flowing to the west and east of London respectively. Both are fed from the chalk-based Chiltern aquifer. These Chiltern chalk streams, which are ecologically valuable in their upper reaches as natural trout streams, both flow down the dipslope of the Chilterns escarpment and consequently have a gradient which ensures an adequate fall for the mills on their courses.

The river Colne rises near Hatfield. Its tributaries, the Gade, Bulbourne and Ver, all have more distant and higher headwaters. It flows through Watford and Rickmansworth before leaving the county on its southward journey through Uxbridge to Staines, where it joins the river Thames. One of its tributaries, the Gade, allowed the most important industrial concentration in Hertfordshire, the paper industry, to become established.

The river Lea is some 42 miles long. Its source is at Leagrave, just north of Luton, at an elevation of some 380' above sea level. It flows for 16 miles through a gap in the Chilterns at Luton Hoo and receives a major flow from the waste-water treatment plant at West Hyde, not far from where it enters Hertfordshire. This means that, since the construction of the plant, it has a fairly consistent flow regardless of climatic conditions. It flows generally eastwards through Harpenden and Wheathampstead, between Welwyn and Hatfield and on to Hertford, which is at a height of 133' above sea level. Thus far it is not navigable, and has much of the character of a Chiltern chalk stream. It powered watermills at Hyde, still very much in its original form, Pickford, Batford, Wheathampstead, Lemsford, Bush Hall and Mill Green, as well as the Cecil sawmill, Essendon and Horns Mill on the western outskirts of Hertford.

The Lea receives three tributaries at Hertford: the Mimram, Beane and Rib. Like the rest of its tributaries in Hertfordshire, these are all on its north side. Below

Figure 2.2 This scene of the river Lea at Ware in 1890 shows how important a navigation it was. On the right is Henry Ward's Page & Co grain dryer for the malthouse, which was burnt down in 1939. Reproduced by kind permission of the Mills Archive.

Hertford it changes in character to a full navigation for 26 miles through Ware and Stanstead Abbotts, before leaving the county at Waltham Abbey to flow south through London's east end to join the tidal Thames at Canning Town. Hertford, at the head of the navigation, became a significant inland port serving an extensive hinterland. A continuous flow of goods such as malt, flour, vegetables and fodder went down the river to London, while sailing barges, narrower than Thames barges, could navigate to Hertford. The river Lea and navigation was, therefore, a vital artery for flour milling in the latter part of the nineteenth century. A.A. Brown, miller at Ware Flour Mills in Amwell End, wrote in 1867: 'The Lee is very useful to me; it acts as a check on the rail and enables me to get foreign wheat from the Thames by barge.'[1]

There were flour mills all along the river and its tributary, the Stort, notably at Hertford, Ware (Figure 2.2), Stanstead Abbotts, Broxbourne, Bishops Stortford and Sawbridgeworth.

Water supplies

Maintaining adequate head flows to drive waterwheels was a constant problem for millers, who had to defend flows against other users of water, actual or potential. In Hertfordshire the conflict was particularly acute. In the Chilterns area public water supplies are more than usually dependent on groundwater† sources, there being only chalk streams and few surface water reservoirs. Water companies, including the New River Company, that sought to supply the capital with potable supplies of water posed a significant threat to the interests of mill owners in the two major river systems of the county, as abstraction reduced the quantities emerging from the headwater springs of the rivers and, hence, the volume of water in the rivers for powering waterwheels and turbines.

From 1880 onwards there was a gradual decline in water power, estimated at 30 per cent in 1904, which adversely affected the operation of mills.[2] Periods of low water became more frequent and of longer duration, as well as getting more serious on each occasion. To add to these problems, the Grand Junction Canal Company and the Lea and Stort Navigations were a further potential source of depletion of mills' headwaters. The passage of barges through the locks could diminish the headwaters to the mills by some 70 million gallons each time a barge passed through. The intensifying battle between these conflicting interests was fought out against a background of a limited understanding of the hydrology of the basin of the lower Thames, a subject into which John Dickinson, the pioneer of continuous paper-making (see Chapter 7), had only recently begun to inquire.

In a pioneering paper in 1850, when knowledge of the interrelationship between geology and hydrology was in its infancy, Dickinson sought to explain that abstracting the amount of groundwater needed to supply London through boreholes would have a detrimental impact on the flow of water in the rivers on the surface. His work was based on practical experiments in the area of Hemel Hempstead. He concluded:

The River Colne would, in consequence of the water pumped up being taken away as proposed, be subjected to a diminution of the supply in all the lower part of its course equivalent to the draught of water from the Wells, but the upper part of the Valley would chiefly suffer by the annihilation of springs and drying up of Wells and ponds and also of a great part of the River for it is indeed from the preceding observations that such must be the result of draining a pervious stratum to a depth of 100 feet beneath the natural outlet.

I am of the opinion that the water obtainable by this mode would be very far short of the supply of the New River but the injurious consequences stated above may be foreseen with as much certainty as the result of any drainage of land by opening channels to a lower outlet.[3]

Sir John Evans (1823–1908), John Dickinson's nephew and son-in-law and also heir to the Dickinson paper empire, was a man of scholarship who produced learned papers on the hydrology of the Chilterns and on the consequences for the chalk streams and rivers of abstracting water from boreholes in terms of their diminished capacity to power the waterwheels of the paper mills in the Gade valley. In a polemical article in 1893 he highlighted the growing conflict between London and its hinterland over the matter of water supply: using phrases more graphic than academic, he referred to 'the insatiable desire of our overgrown neighbour to claim, as of right, the natural water supply of this and other counties that surround her', and argued that 'the covetous eyes of scheming engineers have been cast upon our springs and streams, and the waters of Hertfordshire regarded as legitimate prey'. Particularly interesting is his summary of the respective threats to the two catchments:

On the western side of the county, when companies legitimately constituted for the purposes of local water supply have attempted to extend their Parliamentary powers so as to allow them to supply water in bulk to London, the united efforts of the mill-owners and land-owners within the valley of the Colne have just been able to restrict their powers to the districts which the companies might be said to have a natural right to serve.

On the eastern side of the county, in the valley of the Lea, the attacks of the New River Company upon the water resources of Hertfordshire have been more successful, because less strenuously opposed, and the latent powers which they claim to possess are … of the most alarming nature. Had our County Council been in existence some forty or fifty years ago perhaps the circumstances would have been materially different.[4]

Clearly Evans saw the need to supply London with water as an ongoing threat to the quantity of water in the Chiltern rivers, particularly given the precedent of water being taken by the New River Company in the east of the county.

Dickinson was astutely perceptive. In 1876 the Colne Valley Water Company obtained permission to sink a borehole at Bushey, with the consequences he had foretold. The issue that he identified more than 160 years ago remains the principal hydrological problem in the Colne valley today. The European Water Framework Directive sets standards for improving the chemical and biological quality of river water. Low flows in the Chiltern chalk streams caused by groundwater abstraction are, however, the main constraint and a significant impediment to achieving these standards. Whether abstraction can be reduced in the future clearly remains a major issue for these catchments. The low flow alleviation scheme on the river Ver, for example, has to some degree improved its water level in recent years, to the benefit of Redbournbury Mill.

Figure 2.3 Lock on the Canal, Birkhamsted (sic), *1842. A view of the newly opened Grand Junction Canal at Berkhamsted, by James Wilcox. Reproduced by kind permission of Hertford Museum.*

Navigation

Dickinson and Evans were foremost among the advocates seeking to protect the millers' rights, having been the first to realise the connection between surface and ground waters in a permeable chalk catchment: it was impossible to abstract groundwater without affecting the volume of water in the rivers. Their drawn-out battles with the canal and water companies forced the pace of hydrology scholarship. Abstraction for supplying London with potable water, however, was not the only threat to mills' water supplies in the Gade valley. The Grand Junction Canal Company (Figure 2.3) had a vested interest in maintaining adequate levels of water for the locks and in particular in supplying water to the Tring summit of the canal, a few miles upstream at Cow Roast. To do this they had sunk boreholes, which added to the likelihood of the volume of water in the rivers being depleted. Despite this, commercial waterways were vital to the success of Hertfordshire industries. The paper-making and gunpowder enterprise, as well as the more successful corn mills, all depended on access by water to the London markets; in particular, the Grand Junction Canal was fundamental to the success of the paper-making industry in the Gade valley. Lacking this advantage, all other paper-makers suffered a steady decline. John Dickinson, however, used the canal to full advantage to bring coal from the north, transfer pulp between the mills and take away the finished paper to the south (Figure 2.4).

Lewis Dean of Kings Langley Mill reflected on the Toovey company's dependency on the canal in the 1920s:

> In those days I suppose that 60% or 70% of our raw material came in by canal. The lighters used to go alongside ships in the London Docks and the sacked up wheat would be loaded into them to be taken to Brentford where it would be stored in the Grand Union Canal Company's warehouse which acted as a kind of buffer reservoir. We had two canal boats of a variety you no longer see today. They were 'wide' boats, holding about 45 tons each which is roughly the same as a narrow boat together with its butty†, and used to ply to and fro between Brentford and the mill, regularly and fully employed. They were built by Bushell Bros of Tring and launched sideways into the canal. The last one was built in 1916 and cost £222–10–0.[5]

Significantly before this, however, a dispute had broken out at Kings Langley in 1845 over the taking by Toovey's Mill of so much water out of the canal that many narrow boats had been left stranded and 120 others delayed through lack of water:

> 14 to 15 pairs of boats were aground for many hours between Locks 69 and 69A as Mr Toovey persisted in drawing down water … the Company [The Grand Junction Canal Company] was powerless. Even if unnecessary

Figure 2.4 Dickinson's narrow boats in the loading bay at Apsley Mill. In the background is a wide beam boat which could navigate the Thames but could not go beyond Berkhamsted on the canal. Reproduced by kind permission of the Paper Trail.

working of the mill were proved as a maximum fine for the offence was only £5 … On 12th February Mr Toovey had again worked the water level down and held up 120 boats. He refused indemnity and said that he would not stop his mill again even for £50. He had agreed, however … to sell the mill to the Company for £15,000.

Similarly, the Lea and Stort Navigations were intrinsic to the success of the gunpowder works in Waltham Abbey and to corn mills on the Lea and Stort. These navigations allowed barges from the Thames to reach the heads of navigation at Hertford and Bishops Stortford. The Town Mill at Sawbridgeworth, for example, imported wheat from many parts of the world via the Surrey Docks and up the Lea and Stort Navigations.

Every year the Trustees of the River Lee travelled down the river for which they were responsible. In a barge towed by horses it took a very long day to reach London. Inspections of the navigation were extravagant occasions, but on top of possessing remarkable digestions, the conservators were apparently tireless, as this account of a river inspection revealed:

June 29, 1836

'My bro' Robert and myself rose a little before 4 o'clock, took a cup of tea, and set off together in the gig for Ware. Drove to the bridge where the barges belonging to the Trustees of the River Lee soon arrived at 6 o'clock.

The day was propitious but very hot when we were stationary in the locks, some of which we had to inspect, also the tumbling bay at Carthagena Lock. Breakfasted in the Barge off Broxbourne about half past 9. Most of the party lunched heartily about 2 o'clock. I contented myself with some strawberries, and some time afterwards a glass of porter. We were 12 hours on our passage. Debarked at Limehouse by Richardson's Timber Wharf, and proceeded in three omnibuses, being rather more than forty of us, to Lovegrove's Hotel at Blackwall (the West India docks) where we were joined by several more gentlemen. After brushing, washing etc. we sat down about sixty to an excellent dinner, Rowland Alston Esq in the chair.

There were liberal supplies of turtle soup with lime punch, flounders, soals [sic], small perch, boiled turbot and salmon and lastly white bait, to which luxury all did ample justice, they being nicely done, they being brought up hot and eaten with lemon only. After this several haunches of venison made their appearance. Lots of champagne was drunk; I contented myself with little more than one glass, and took sherry as champagne does not suit me. Retired about half past 9, Mr Robert Hanbury driving us to Brick Lane in his phaeton.[6]

Significant improvements were made at this time to the navigation in terms of canalising the river and rebuilding the locks. In 1868 the Lee Conservancy Board was set up, taking over the functions of the Trustees of the River Lee with responsibility for maintaining and improving the navigation. In 1911 it took over the Stort Navigation as well and began improvement works there.

Conflicting interests

The conflicts of interests that arose over the limited supply of water in the rivers and canals became more frequent as the supply of water came under increasing strain. To a long history of conflicts between adjacent millers was added conflicts between the millers and the organisations responsible for navigation and between the millers and the bargemen using the navigations.

In the first case, a miller could, wittingly or unwittingly, cause trouble for the mills downstream or upstream either by releasing water unexpectedly and flooding the next mill downstream or by holding back water above the mill thereby impairing the efficiency of the waterwheel of the next mill upstream. This is known as 'backwatering'† and is graphically illustrated by a notice for the sale of the paper mill in 1855 at Standon, which was half a mile below the New Mill. The rights of the paper mill's new owner were constrained in the interests of the corn mill upstream:

> The owner of the Standon Corn Mill has a right to enter upon this Paper Mill whenever it is converted into, or used as a Corn or Flour Mill, and to hold the same, and to open the Flood Gates and let off the water to prevent it being used; and also to lower the Tumbling Bay whenever it shall exceed its present height, and to enter onto the adjoining Lands to clean out the River and cut the weeds between the Tumbling Bay and the Corn Mill; and the Purchaser will be bound to repair the Tumbling Bay and the two Standard Posts, and not to allow the same to exceed the present standard height: and to keep open the Water Course leading from the Tumbling Bay into the River.[7]

The fine balance of interests in terms of water levels also left little scope for tolerance at Frogmore Mill, on the river Gade, at the start of the nineteenth century. The miller complained to the mill owner that the papermaster at Apsley Mills (the next mill downstream) had closed his sluices and thus raised the level of the water between the mills by some 12–18 inches in order to gain more power from his waterwheel. In consequence, the two new wheels at Frogmore had become partially immersed and this 'backwatering' had led to a loss of power.[8]

In the Gade valley the canal and river run parallel and are often combined. This meant that the mills and canal were competing for the same water. John Dickinson, who owned and ran the paper mills in and around Apsley, was involved between 1815 and 1849 as plaintiff in several law suits with the Grand Junction Company in an attempt to defend his milling rights. The first case concerned a poorly constructed length of canal, which constantly lost water, adjacent to the Frogmore Mill. The canal company diverted water from the river to the canal, thereby depriving Apsley and Nash Mills of their headwaters. Eventually, after Dickinson had brought a series of actions, the canal was diverted nearer the mill, with an additional lock to avoid the need for deep ones, which required a disproportionate amount of water:

> Action after action for the damage that ensued had to be brought by Mr Dickinson against his powerful neighbour, until an intimation from the Court made the Company perceive that an end must be made to their illegal abstraction of water. They then agreed that the course of the canal should be changed, and that the bed of the river and the canal should, near the two

mills, be, so far as possible, one and the same. Mr Dickinson, with his usual energy, undertook the contract for carrying out the work, which involved the construction of at least three new locks.[9]

The second dispute, in 1849, related to the canal company's previously mentioned borehole at Cow Roast, at the summit of the canal, which lowered the water table and reduced the amount of water available to the paper mills. The scientific evidence of Dickinson and Evans proved decisive, and the Court of Chancery granted a perpetual injunction against the canal. The company:

> had to defend its water-rights from an attack on the part of the Grand Junction Canal Company, who had sunk a well, 'The Cowroast,' a few miles south of Tring, and were beginning to pump water from it for the supply of their canal. An injunction from the Court of Chancery to restrain them from so doing was applied for, and after a series of experiments which conclusively proved that the water pumped from the well would otherwise have gone to supply the river by springs, a perpetual injunction against the company was granted.

The interests of millers and bargemen were equally at variance. A lockful of water used for the passage of a barge meant much less water to turn an adjacent waterwheel. On the other side of the county bargemen on the Stort were obliged to pay each miller 6d for the privilege of using a lockful of water. The conservators of the navigation sought to bring some order to the situation and to defuse potential disputes; eventually, agreement was reached with the millers that a 12-inch head of water for the mills would be maintained all the way through the Stort Navigation (Figure 2.5). If it fell below this level, then barges could not proceed. Clearly, in this matter, the millers had the upper hand over the bargemen. An iron plaque on the wall at Twyford Lock on the Stort provides evidence of the agreement for the Stort Navigation between the Lee Conservation Board and the owner of the mill in 1910: 'The twelve inches marked on this plate creates a working head for this mill'. The multiplicity of channels on the Lea below Hertford, coupled with long mill streams almost independent of the navigation, went some way to resolve these conflicts. As a result, traffic on the Lea tended to be more reliable than on the Stort, where this conflict of interests persisted. Relations between the two parties did not improve; Owen Burton, for instance, decided to stop employing his contractor's barges because 'they were expensive and bloody-minded'. Eventually he tried using narrow boats instead during 1954/5, but these were not safe on the tideway: '… they could not go alongside the big ships in London to load. The grain had to be loaded into a lighter, taken through the Limehouse Cut, and then transferred to the narrow boats, thus making [them] rather uneconomic.'[10]

Figure 2.5 The water-level gauge at Sawbridgeworth Town Mill had its top mark set to the normal working level determined by the weirs. A 12-inch range was to allow the mill to work and to keep the loaded barges afloat and not at risk of being marooned by grounding. Infringement would not necessarily create a stoppage but might incur a fine by the Conservancy Board. Kindly supplied by W. Wright from the Ed Goatcher collection, c.1870–90.

Any bloody-mindedness may perhaps be explained by the working conditions that prevailed in the late 1920s, as shown by an interview with a Sawbridgeworth man in 1985:

> Fred's next job was unloading barges at Burton's Flour Mill. They were loaded with 60 tons of grain, in 18 stone bags (seedcake weighed 21 stone). The two crewmen (driver and horseman) lifted the bags onto his shoulders. Then it was up a ladder and along a plank to the bank and into the mill to stack them two deep. For this the wage was a penny a bag. The crew men went for lunch at The Fox in Station Road, where they also stabled their horse. They would arrive back drunk and then were not very good at placing the bags. These bargees were very hardened characters.[11]

Life in a mill, too, was hard. John Mathews worked in Wheathampstead Mill for seven years in the immediate post-war period:

> There were several jobs: mixing corn meal, crushing oats and polishing corn for pigeons, dressing seed, selecting the best grains of seed and hoisting sacks to the top of the mill.… John had to have three hip replacements during his old age, wearing them out carrying such heavy loads during his work.[12]

Pollution

The River Pollution Commission, set up in 1868, issued its report in 1874, resulting in the Rivers Pollution Act, a permissive piece of legislation that gave local authorities

Figure 2.6 A hazard of riverine navigation: barges could be frozen in for days or weeks at a time. A late nineteenth-century image of the river Stort in winter. Reproduced by kind permission of W. Wright.

the power to take action where appropriate and where funds allowed, and which highlighted a further source of conflict between mill owners and water companies. The latter, understandably, favoured the drilling of boreholes to tap groundwater for public water supply instead of using river water, which was becoming increasingly polluted. However, this resulted in the depletion of the aquifer, with the consequences spelled out by Sir John Evans.

Untreated sewage was a major element in the pollution but, in Hertfordshire, the paper industry, too, had to shoulder its share of blame. The paper mills discharged the water used for washing rags, the water used in the paper-making process itself, residues of china clay and, finally, chlorine, which was used for whitening the paper. The problem was so bad that it led to the closing down of the paper mills on the river Chess. Enforcing higher standards of water quality was a significant factor in the relocation of the paper industry in the Gade valley. One canal user recalled 'the sickly sweet foaming water of paper mill washings'.[13]

While the quality of river water has improved out of all recognition since those times, the disposal of dredgings poses a fresh problem, in that they often constitute 'toxic waste'. In the case of Hyde Mill, near Harpenden, a proposal by the Environment Agency in the 1980s to dredge the mill pond as part of a comprehensive flood relief scheme had to be abandoned because of the cost of disposal of the dredgings, which were polluted with heavy metal from Luton's industries.

Conclusion

While water was fundamental to the development of milling in Hertfordshire, the problems of relying on it exclusively for the powering of watermills became all too clear during the last years of the nineteenth century and the beginning of the twentieth. Water supplies are quite limited in the Chilterns, and ultimately the claims of the water companies had to be acknowledged. Consequently mill owners in turn had to recognise that they could not rely on water power to the extent to which they had been accustomed. They therefore sought to free themselves from reliance on water power altogether by installing steam engines. The final step was to remove the need for generating power on-site altogether by switching to electricity as it became available from the 1930s onwards.

The navigation of rivers and canals for supplying grain was always subject to the vagaries of drought, flood and frost. The winter of 1963 was the culmination of many enforced stoppages, when freezing conditions for six weeks meant virtually the end of commercial water transport (Figure 2.6). And the conflicts between millers and bargemen were often the final straw which persuaded millers to switch to road transport and to liberate themselves from all the problems associated with water. Foremost among these millers were the independent companies which are still in business today and which form the subject of the next chapter.

References

1. A. Burgess, 'Amwell End Mill and House', unpublished private study, 2014.
2. B. Cole, 'Proof of Evidence to Parliamentary Committee concerning the Barnet and District Gas and Water Bill', 1904.
3. J. Dickinson, 'Supply of water from the chalk stratum in the neighbourhood of London', paper given to the Royal Society, Ref AP/33/10 (1850).
4. J. Evans, 'Hertfordshire and its water supply', *Hertfordshire Illustrated Review* (1893).
5. Dean, 'The history of Kings Langley Mill'.
6. G. Curtis, *A chronicle of small beer* (Chichester, 1970).
7. Sale notice relating to the Standon Estate, 1842.
8. Hertfordshire County Record Office, Ref 80623.
9. J. Lewis Evans, *The firm of John Dickinson and Co Ltd* (London, 1896).
10. Interview with Owen Burton, 12 December 1985.
11. Interview with Fred Revell of Sawbridgeworth, 11 November 1985.
12. John Mathews at Wheathamstead Mill.
13. A.H. Faulkner, *The Grand Junction Canal* (Rickmansworth, 1993).

3

Milling in Hertfordshire today

Around the beginning of the twentieth century *The Miller*, the monthly trade journal of the milling industry, took an editorial line of supporting the enterprise of those businessmen who built the new generation of industrial-style mills and conducted a campaign to press home the need for country millers to modernise or lose out, as noted in Chapter 1. Articles described Hyde Mill near Harpenden, Bourne End and Castle Mills, and Kings Langley, Tring and Walkern Mills, all of which had carried out thorough-going programmes of modernisation (see appendices 4–8 for these articles). In an article about Tring New Mill *The Miller* said:

> There is plenty of room for improvement in our mills, and it ought not to be a matter of difficulty or expense to be put and kept in the front line. We know that the country miller is 'waking up,' as we have several times had the satisfaction of testifying to during late months, and we repeat that this gives us pleasure. The milling trade of England must grow, and that extensively, and we are always ready and willing to be the means of showing others what their fellows are doing.[1]

Of the vernacular corn mills, only a few were re-equipped before World War I and remained in business until after World War II. Of the others, some were demolished, others converted to homes, offices or pubs/restaurants, and a very few have remained as they were when they ceased working. The two outstanding exceptions still working and producing flour are Redbournbury and Mill Green Mills. The decline in vernacular mills was accompanied by the building of up-to-date purpose-built industrial mills in the period before World War I. They survived in business until after World War II, but have also had mixed fortunes. Although some remain in production, the majority have either been converted into apartments or offices or been demolished. Today's survivors are among those who invested heavily in the new technology. Such was the superiority of roller mills that some mills, despite having recently re-equipped with iron hurst frames† and new millstones – notably at New Mill, Tring – had the machinery ripped out after a short working life and roller mills installed.

Commercial flour milling today

There are several medium-sized commercial mills in the counties to the north of Hertfordshire, but none in the counties to the south. Hertfordshire's surviving commercial mills are on the periphery of the country's major grain-producing areas and, furthermore, the county is in an advantageous position for flour milling, with its proximity both to these wheat-growing areas and to Tilbury, which is now the main point of entry for imported Canadian grain. It is also well located to serve the increasingly sophisticated niche markets of north London.

The county's major flour producers today are Allinson at Bishops Stortford, Cereform Ltd at Royston, Bowmans at Ickleford, Heygates Ltd at Tring, and, just outside the county, George Wright and Son of Ponders End, Enfield. As the only working mill left on the whole of the river Lea, Wrights Mill is included here to give a flavour of milling in the Lea valley. It is also the only remaining operational mill within the M25. These companies have all prospered by providing niche products outside the main volume bread market.[2]

The mills mentioned above were all late nineteenth-century industrial-style mills equipped with the latest roller mill technology. The sites at Ickleford and Ponders End are sited in traditional watermill locations, but those at Tring, Bishops Stortford and Royston are situated for ease of transport: the proximity of the Grand Junction Canal in the first case, the Stort Navigation in the second case and the GNR in the last. They were all steam-powered, but converted to electric power as it became widely available on the National Grid and as the economy picked up after World War II.

The concentration of flour milling under four big conglomerate companies that took place in the 1960s led to greater integration with the baking industry. Spillers and Ranks started to acquire plant bakeries, whereas Garfield Weston extended his bakery business by moving into milling and acquired mills for that purpose. This is reflected in Hertfordshire today. Garfield Weston (1898–1978), a Canadian businessman and philanthropist, founded Associated British Foods in 1935. It has several business arms, of which Allied Bakeries and Ingredients are two, and is one of the largest suppliers of bread to the nation, marketing loaves under the Kingsmill and Allinson labels. Weston acquired the Town Mill at Bishops Stortford in 1963 and the Station Mill at Royston in 2001. The latter is operated by Cereform, a company owned by AB Mauri, which, in turn, is part of the 'Ingredients' division of Associated British Foods. Cereform is the only company in the UK to produce full-fat soya flour. The other working mills in Hertfordshire have remained staunchly independent. Heygates and Bowmans both have substantial mills outside the county; in contrast, Wrights is concentrated on the one site at Ponders End.

In the last fifty years the number of mills has continued to decline. Sele Mill and Ware Town Mill were prominent casualties within the county, and one of the 'big four', Spillers, went out of business in the 1990s. Another major change over the

Figure 3.1 A glimpse of the past: a French burr stone surviving at the Town Mill, Bishops Stortford.

last half-century has been the increasing use of UK-sourced wheat: while in 1961 only 30 per cent of flour was produced from UK wheat, the figure is now 85 per cent. The surviving milling companies owe their success to their ability to respond to the emerging markets for specialist flours. An increasingly sophisticated market in London and the home counties requires a wide variety of milling products and many companies, particularly in Hertfordshire, have moved away from supplying flour in bulk to the baking companies and now concentrate on supplying niche flours for such goods as artisanal and ethnic breads supplied in pre-pack form for home baking.

Following major rebuilding and expansion in the 1980s, all these mills are of sufficient capacity still to be viable against competition from the very much larger mills in the Thames estuary, and form the foundation of flour milling in Hertfordshire as we know it today. The following is a summary of Hertfordshire's surviving major commercial mills.

Allinson

The company S. Edwards and Son was founded by Sylvester Edwards, who built the original Beech Flour Mill at Bishops Stortford in 1901 (Figure 3.1). It was a steam mill from the outset, equipped with roller mills of Edwards' own design, and enjoyed wharfage at the headwaters of the Stort Navigation. This mill lasted until 1935, when it was destroyed by fire. It was replaced by an entirely new mill equipped by Henry Simon Ltd. Power was supplied by a Ruston and Hornsby 200 hp oil engine. An advertisement at that time described the company as flour, corn, cake and meal merchants.[3]

Figure 3.2 The Town Mill complex today under Allinson's ownership.

The current mill was built between 1979 and 1982, the old mill being demolished shortly afterwards. It was designed and equipped by Thomas Robinson and Son of Rochdale. The business remained under the control of the Edwards family until the late Tony Edwards retired in the 1990s (Figure 3.2).[4]

It has been known as the Town Mill, Edwards' Mill or the Beech Flour Mill. It remained a family-run business until it was taken over by Associated British Foods in 1963 as part of its policy of acquiring mills to supply its core bakery business. It introduced the Allinson brand at that time.[5]

At Bishops Stortford the company has traditionally concentrated on locally sourced soft wheat and specialised biscuit flour. Since 1970 the company has expanded its pre-packed flour operation and added an additional plant for that purpose. With a continuing emphasis on the sourcing of the grain locally, it now produces a variety of ready-bagged culinary and bread-making flours for retail outlets.

MILLING IN HERTFORDSHIRE TODAY

Cereform Ltd

Station Mill, at Kneesworth Street, Royston, was built in 1872 as a steam corn mill and run by the Smith family until 1962. It is of yellow brick with four floors. Much of the original mill, apart from the engine houses and chimneys, still exists. Several of the windows have been bricked up, but otherwise it is recognisably the same building (Figure 3.3). It owes its location to the adjacent railway, where there was a goods yard with a siding adjacent to the north side of the mill. It was also located close to the local maltings and brewery.

Station Mill was bought, in 1962, by British Soya Products, who also owned New Mill at Standon and had their head office at Puckeridge. It has been used solely for the production of soya flour ever since. The mill was acquired in 2001 by Garfield Weston to expand the 'Ingredients' portfolio of Associated British Foods with the addition of the Cereform soya milling facility. Station Mill was making heat-treated soya flour, which is suitable for the confectionery business, while the mill at Standon concentrated on enzyme-active flour for the baking industry. In 1998 both activities were concentrated at Royston and Standon's mill was sold for conversion to apartments.[6]

Figure 3.3 The front of Station Mill, Royston, in 1905. Reproduced by kind permission of Cereform Ltd.

Soya flour was an early bread improver, making bread crumb whiter and bread larger in volume. Later it was to become a carrier for other functional ingredients in improvers. The flour produced at Royston is used as a baking additive to improve the stability of the dough. It is high in protein and gluten-free, which gives it several roles elsewhere in the food processing and health food industry. All of the soya is imported from Canada at Tilbury and is strictly non-genetically modified. The soya beans are milled in a plated mill manufactured by Macrof that contains two vertical steel plates, one turning clockwise and the other anticlockwise. The mill has a throughput of 15,000 tonnes (16,500 tons) a year.[7]

Heygates Ltd

Tring flour mill, known as the New Mill, was built in 1875 and is located on the Wendover Arm of the Grand Union Canal, which was designed to supply the summit level of the canal with water. It therefore enjoyed good transport links, allowing for the bringing in of grain from the Thames at Brentford or from the London docks via the Regents Canal, and for the distribution of flour to the London market. Despite its waterside location it was always a steam mill and never a watermill. Such was the

Figure 3.4 Mead's Tring steam mill in 1893, with the windmill in the background and Bushell's boatyard in the foreground. HALS.

success of Thomas Mead's mills business that it was rebuilt in 1875 with the latest millstone installation as a five-storey industrial-style building (Figure 3.4). It was described by *The Miller* as 'what was at that time, a model stone plant'. In 1891 the mill passed from Thomas Mead to his son William, who wisely decided that the future lay with roller mills driven by a steam engine. He ordered E.R. and F. Turner Ltd to install a roller milling plant capable of producing two and a half sacks of flour per hour. This was subsequently enhanced to four sacks an hour.[8]

There were two double sets of rollers 30" by 9" and five sets of break rollers. Power was provided by a compound-condensing beam engine† which was replaced only when electric power was installed in 1946.

The plant earned the unqualified enthusiasm of *The Miller*:

> To Mr W.N. Mead belongs a great credit for his enterprise and business ability, and to Messrs E.R. and F Turner Ltd we tender our congratulations on the result of yet another instance of successful engineering.
>
> A mill which ... for completeness in every detail would certainly be hard to beat, and we rejoice to see such an example of a go-a-headness in a country miller, as well as to find from actual observation that it is possible to have a thoroughly good and complete plant on a comparatively small scale.[9]

This building still survives as part of today's complex. Heygates Ltd, a family-run business with farming and milling interests based at Bugbrooke Mill in Northamptonshire, took over the business in 1944, after the death of William Mead. The company owns a third mill in Downham Market in Norfolk. It is the largest private flour-milling company in the UK, accounting for more than 5 per cent of the total flour output of the country. The New Mill today processes 100,000 tons of wheat a year, or 12 tons an hour, producing baking flour and wholemeal flour for biscuits. This contrasts with the half-ton of flour an hour which had been produced by the windmill whose destruction is illustrated in Figure 1.4.[10]

Heygates also acquired the adjacent Bushell's boatyard in 1952,[11] which is now used as a plant for producing many varieties of pre-packed flour. It concentrates on British wheat, much of it from the company's own holdings in Norfolk, Northamptonshire and Bedfordshire. The company stayed independent during the amalgamations and 'silencing' of mills, and now supplies flours to several specialist bakeries, particularly in London. This accounts for 85–90 per cent of the output. The remaining 10–15 per cent of the output is accounted for by a moderate-sized baking business in Banbury, the Fine Lady Bakery, acquired by the company. Here artisanal type loaves are produced. However, Heygates have never gone in for baking to the extent that other large companies have.

Figure 3.5 Station Mills, Hitchin, as seen from the railway in 1950. Reproduced by kind permission of Jas. Bowman and Sons Ltd.

Bowmans

Bowmans is a family company that was founded by James Bowman in 1857, when he acquired Astwick Mill, just over the county boundary in Bedfordshire. The company eventually had three mills in the Hitchin area: Astwick Mill, Station Mills, Hitchin and Ickleford Mill. Astwick Mill was re-equipped by Whitmore and Binyon with an iron hurst frame and 13 sets of stones. The mill's proximity to Arlesey Station, on the newly opened GNR, transformed the business from a purely local company to a major player in the London market.[12] It was driven by a 20' overshot waterwheel, the largest on the river Ivel. In 1891 James Bowman installed six roller mills to replace some of the stones. It produced three sacks of flour per hour, an output increased to four in 1896. This, however, was the limit of its capacity. It was not as efficient as Bowman's other mills and the company eventually sold it in 1929.

To capitalise on their expanding business Bowmans built a new steam-powered roller mill adjacent to the station at Hitchin, where it was well served by adjacent sidings. It was equipped by E.R. & F. Turner. The company was a major supplier to McVitie & Price from 1905. By 1915 the three mills could produce 14 sacks an hour between them. Station Mills was converted to electric power in 1947 (Figure 3.5). It reached a peak output of 45 sacks of flour per hour but eventually closed in 1981, as production shifted to Ickleford. During the British Rail era goods traffic became less reliable; in consequence, industrialists transferred from rail to road and a lineside

Figure 3.6 A busy scene at Ickleford Mill, c.1910. Reproduced by kind permission of Jas. Bowman and Sons Ltd.

location became correspondingly less critical. Accordingly, Bowmans sold Station Mills and it was redeveloped for retail purposes.

The company had acquired Ickleford Mills just before World War I (Figure 3.6). It was an early nineteenth-century water mill that had been substantially updated at the end of the nineteenth century with roller mills, relying on the limited flow of the river Oughton, installed in 1892. The waterwheel was still being used for raising sacks of wheat and for powering the silo conveyors until World War II, when it was cut up for scrap.

The site enjoyed some surrounding developable land and it was here, in 1969, that Bowmans built a new state-of-the-art mill equipped with machinery by Simon. The old watermill was demolished. Peter Bowman described the new mill as 'fundamentally different in many ways but can be summarised as representing a milestone in British flour mill design and technology. A new exterior shell was erected around a new modern milling plant and equipment as they were assembled.'[13]

George Wright and Sons

Ponders End Mill is the only remaining working mill on the river Lea. It lies on the original course of the Lea, the navigation now bypassing this part of the river. The mill was advertised for sale as Enfield Mill in 1853:

Having a considerable fall and flush of Water, is most eligibly situate on the River Lea, in the neighbourhood of most excellent Markets; it is a substantial and well-arranged Building, partly brick-built, with tiled roof comprising Four Floors. The Mill is divided into Two Portions – The One Side, with Three Pairs of Stones, is worked by Mr Young, the other with Four Pair of Stones, by Mr Farmer, the whole thus containing Seven Pair of Stones in Work, Three Pair of 4-ft. 4, and Four Pair of 4-ft. 6 in diameter, French Burrs, with two powerful breast or undershot wheels.[14]

The present company was founded in 1867 by George Reynolds Wright and the mill has been run by the Wright family ever since. At that time the mill had two breastshot waterwheels and seven pairs of stones, as described above. The fact that all seven sets of stones were the expensive French burrs suggests that the mill was geared towards the London markets and was not catering at all for animal feeds. The mill has been successively modernised, demonstrating the family's appreciation of the need to keep technologically up to date. It was, for instance, one of the first to be powered

Figure 3.7 Ponders End Mill with the loading bay, c.1950. Reproduced by kind permission of G.R. Wright and Sons Ltd.

by electricity, which was installed as early as 1909. During World War II the mill was able to make up some of the shortfall in flour caused by the bombing of mills in the London docks, but by the 1950s worn-out plant needed to be replaced and the mill was re-equipped by Thomas Robinson of Rochdale. Since then new silos have been installed and a new packaging facility has been built to allow a wide variety of specialist flours to be packed in small amounts ready for domestic consumers. Much of the original mill remains, although it is little used and not easily recognised because of a loading bay constructed in front of it (Figure 3.7). The mill house, too, remains.

The company is relatively small and owes its successful survival to a twin-track policy. Firstly, it serves several major customers within a short distance, of which Warburtons is perhaps the biggest (Warburtons, a northern-based baking company, is the largest in the UK without milling facilities of its own. It has opened a new plant in nearby Enfield). Secondly, the company has carved out niche markets with a wide range of pre-packed cake and bread mixes for use in domestic bread-making machines and in small local bakeries. The company also produces flours specifically for constantly evolving markets in ethnic breads such as ciabatta, naan, focaccia and pizza.[15]

The Chorleywood Bread Process

Hertfordshire has a unique claim to fame in the history of milling: it was here that a far-reaching revolution in bread-making took place. The British Industries Baking Research Association (later the Flour Milling and Baking Research Association) was established in Chorleywood shortly after World War II with the aim of creating stronger links between research into bread-making and its practical application to the manufacture of bread in large quantities for the mass market. The emphasis was on the application of science and technology to the baking industry, rather than the craft and artistry which had been the hallmark of local bakeries.

Its most far-reaching achievement was the Chorleywood Bread Process, which was introduced to the baking industry in 1961. This was a watershed in baking, having a profound effect on the direction in which bread-making and baking technology developed. The main innovation of the new process was the continuous mixing of the dough in a single operation without the need for a lengthy period during which fermentation took place. The advantages were that more loaves could be produced to a consistent quality: furthermore, they had a longer shelf life. It also enabled home-grown wheat to be used extensively in the milling business. This was an important consideration at the time, when the balance of payments was a matter of national concern. However, the process also offers significant advantages in terms of the automation and control of a complex process that ensures greater consistency in the final product.[16] It is now used for making 80 per cent of loaves and enables a loaf to be produced in 3.5 hours from start to finish.

Figure 3.8 The new waterwheel being installed at Lemsford Mill in 2005. Reproduced by kind permission of Ramblers Worldwide Holidays.

The Chorleywood Bread Process resulted in technological changes both in improvers and ingredients and in the design of equipment. It also handed an incremental advantage to large industrial plant bakeries over traditional milling businesses, and meant that the market would be dominated by the major milling and baking concerns, Rank Hovis McDougal, Spillers (subsequently Dalgety) and Garfield Weston, all of whom made the decision to move to the Chorleywood Bread Process. Local mills and bakeries were unable to compete with either industrial bread production or the rise of in-store bakeries in the supermarkets. However, the mills described in this chapter have survived and prospered by moving into the upper end of the market, specialising in niche products for increasingly sophisticated customers.

Renewable energy

Hertfordshire also boasts a notable example of the generation of 'green' energy. As part of the refurbishment of Lemsford Mill on the river Lea, Ramblers Worldwide Holidays have installed a new waterwheel which has been generating electricity since 2005 and meeting much of the demand for energy at the company's offices. It was considered that a waterwheel rather than a turbine would be both more appropriate and an attractive feature within the offices. The final design, built by HydroWatt of Karlsruhe, was for a metal wheel 14' in diameter with 24 simple wooden paddles of larch installed in the wheel pit and connected to a generator through a gearbox, although an unexpected difficulty was the need to carry out substantial engineering works to the profile of the wheel pit in order to ensure a tight fit (Figure 3.8). The wheel turns at 7 rpm and consistently generates 11 kilowatts an hour. During the daytime the offices consume 18 kilowatts an hour; outside working hours unused electricity is exported to the National Grid.[17]

References

1. 'Successful country millers', *The Miller* (4 August 1902).
2. Interview with Nigel Bennett, National Association of British and Irish Millers, 2014.
3. *The Herts and Essex Observer Year Book, Directory and Almanac 1935*.
4. A.S. Edwards, *Edwards & Son – a brief history*, unpublished, n.d.
5. Dr Allinson, 1858–1918, celebrated dietician and founder of the Natural Food Company, had set up a mill in Bethnal Green to produce wholemeal flour. His slogan was 'health without medicine'. In 1897 he built a very large watermill, with twenty sets of millstones, at Castleford, on the river Aire in Yorkshire, as his main production centre. It closed in 2002.
6. Interview with Robert Dunderdale and Adrian Seeley of Cereform, 2014.
7. *Soya, the versatile ingredient* (A.B. Mauri, Northampton, 2008).
8. Mills in Britain and parts of the empire rated mill capacities in terms of sacks of flour per hour. The British unit of a sack of flour is 280 pounds: that is, eight sacks equals one

imperial ton of 2240 lbs. A rule of thumb conversion is to multiply the sacks of flour per hour by a factor of four to give an approximate tonnage of wheat per 24 hours: that is, a 60-sack mill would be a 240-tonne mill.

9   'Successful country mills', *The Miller* (4 August 1902).
10 Interview with Paul Messenger, mill manager, New Mills, Tring, 2014.
11 *The Berkhamsted Gazette* (24 December 1954).
12 Bowmans, 'Bowmans Flour technology 1857–2007 millstones and milestones – the story of Bowmans', unpublished, 2007.
13 Bowman, 'Bill, thrift and damsel'.
14 L. Wright, 'The history of G.R. Wright and Sons Ltd, flour millers 1070–1970', unpublished, 1970.
15 C. Lyddon, 'London's last miller', *World Grain* (September 2004), pp.54–9, and J. Lewis, *London's Lea valley* (Chichester, 1999).
16 S.P. Cauvain and L.S. Young, *The Chorleywood bread process* (Cambridge, 2006).
17 Ramblers Worldwide Holidays, 'Reinventing the wheel at Lemsford Mill', unpublished, 2007.

4

The eight accessible mills

The Hertfordshire mills that can be visited are but a fraction of the mills that were once widespread across the county. These eight mills all retain significant amounts of original machinery and provide an insight into both historic industries and the life of the miller in years gone by (Figure 4.1). Hertfordshire enjoys the rare luxury of two traditional working corn mills, Mill Green and Redbournbury, where the whole milling process can be seen. Four others – Kingsbury, Cromer, Moor Mill and Hyde (near Harpenden) – contain complete or almost complete sets of milling machinery but are not operational. The value of these surviving mills is that they demonstrate the technical development of the machinery of corn mills during the nineteenth century. It can be traced from Mill Green and Kingsbury Mills, which show milling in a pure late eighteenth-century form, through Moor Mill, representing the early nineteenth-century millwright's art, to Cromer windmill, which exemplifies the technology of the 1860s. Unusual late nineteenth-century machinery can be seen at Redbournbury and Hyde Mill. The latter has more modern elements characteristic of the late nineteenth and early twentieth centuries: a now empty roller mill plant and an auxiliary steam engine. There are no accessible examples of roller mills, but examples of two industries that once formed the backbone of Hertfordshire's commercial base – the Paper Trail Museum at Frogmore Mill and the Royal Gunpowder Mills at Waltham Abbey – still exist.

The waterwheels at these Hertfordshire mills offer a unique insight into the increasing application of science to their design. Sir William Fairbairn, who was a pre-eminent exponent of this technological progress – a rare survivor of his waterwheels can be seen at the Royal Gunpowder Works – summarised the evolution of the design of waterwheels:

> The substitution, however, of iron for wood, as a material for their construction, has afforded opportunities for extensive changes in their forms, particularly in the shape and arrangement of the buckets, and has given, altogether, a more permanent and lighter character to the machine, than had previously been attained with other materials. A curvilinear form of bucket has generally been adopted, the sheet-iron of which it is composed affording facility for being moulded, or bent into the required shape.

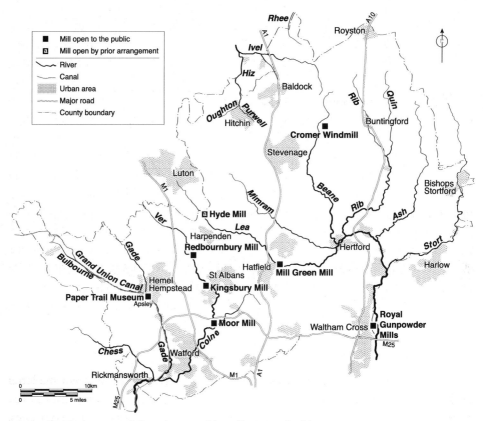

Figure 4.1 The location of the eight accessible mills in Hertfordshire.

> ... in every fall, however low, it is generally found advantageous for the water to act by gravitation and not by impulse, as in the earlier period of the industrial arts.[1]

This progression from waterwheels made of wood through to the most advanced overshot wheels is well illustrated in Hertfordshire. At one end of the spectrum there are the simple wheels at Mill Green and Kingsbury; at the other, there are scientifically designed waterwheels which 'act by gravitation and not by impulse' at Redbournbury, Hunton Bridge (Abbots Langley) and in the Tring Silk Mill.

Mill Green Mill, Bush Hall Lane, Hatfield

Mill Green Mill was the estate mill for the Hatfield House estate (Figure 4.2 and Plate 1). The estate also owned Bush Hall Mill (which was originally a fulling mill and latterly a paper mill), the Cecil sawmill and Essendon Mill. The history of Mill Green Mill can be traced back for 1,200 years, over most of which time the estate has belonged to the Cecils. James I considered the Bishops Palace at Hatfield inadequate

Figure 4.2 Mill Green Mill in the early years of the twentieth century. © HBPT.

and persuaded the Cecil family, then residing at Theobalds Park, to swap the latter for Hatfield Palace. Sir Robert Cecil replaced the Palace with the seventeenth-century mansion still extant today. The mill, therefore, predates the Cecils by several centuries.

In 1911, after more than 800 years, the mill's working life came to an end when the then tenant, along with many others, found that corn milling was no longer economic. It was let to Hatfield Rural District Council in the 1920s, originally to house its district engineer. The buildings gradually deteriorated, but the machinery remained intact apart from the waterwheel, which had in part been removed to reduce the likelihood of flooding. Then, in 1978, Welwyn/Hatfield Borough Council acquired the freehold and instituted a museum service, of which the mill was to be an integral part. The Mill Green Water Mill Restoration Trust was set up and in seven years a full restoration of the mill to working order was carried out by Millwrights International. The completely restored mill was reopened on 8 August 1986. In the meantime, the Hatfield Historical Society had set up the museum at the mill.[2]

What to see at Mill Green Mill

In the medieval period two separate waterwheels on either side of the river drove their own sets of stones, but all under one roof. However, in 1762 the tenant tore out the millwork and installed new machinery, reusing much of the timber for the new hurst frame, which is still there today. There have been very few changes since then. The mill, therefore, offers a rare opportunity to see an eighteenth-century water corn mill

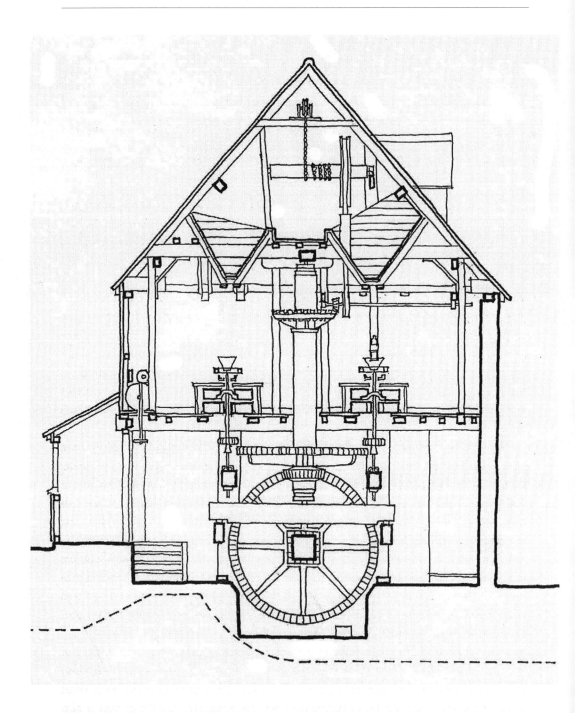

Figure 4.3 Cross section of Mill Green Mill showing, from the top, the bins for the storage of corn, the chutes which fed the corn to the millstones and the drive mechanism through the pit wheel, the wallower, the great spur wheel and the stone nuts. Kindly supplied by Welwyn and Hatfield Museum Services.

at work (Figure 4.3 and Plate 2). The waterwheel is a near replacement of the original wooden wheel. Its main frame is made of English oak and the paddles of elm. It is a simple breastshot wheel with a fall of 3' which, in the words of William Fairbairn, 'acts by impulse', and measures 14' in diameter by 7' 6" wide. The volume of water driving the wheel is controlled by a sluice, the surplus being deflected over a weir and into a bypass channel to the east of the mill. The main flow of the river goes through the mill itself. The great spur wheel† is of cast iron. On the floor above are two sets of French burr millstones with balance weights† inscribed 'Hughes Power Co, London'.

The mill produces flour on a commercial basis. It is sold in the mill shop and supplied to a local bakery, Simmons of Hatfield. The flour sold commercially in the mill shop is a blended imported grain, while that supplied to the bakery is locally grown.

Kingsbury Mill, St Michael's Street, St Albans

This, the estate mill of the Gorhambury Estate, is a Grade II listed timber and brick three-storey mill with weatherboarded gables that lies in the valley of the river Ver, close to the historic heart of St Albans and Verulamium. Since 1982 parts of the miller's house, the ground floor of the mill and a covered area at the rear have been a 'waffle house' restaurant. However, the mill building itself has been left in its original state. The mill is historically important not only for its place in the street scene of St Michael's Hill but also because it contains an almost complete set of traditional milling machinery of early design.

The mill and mill house (which accommodated the miller and his family) share a Georgian brick façade, but the large amount of timber in the construction suggests an earlier date. The right-hand gable of the front elevation houses the mill and the central and left-hand gables are the mill house (Figure 4.4). The mill was last used to make flour in 1936, but continued to produce animal fodder until the 1960s. The Gorhambury Estate Company then took steps to conserve the mill and to restore the machinery with a view to creating a working mill museum. It made a good subject for restoration, as it was complete and intact, allowing the visitor to see what a pre-industrial vernacular mill was like. Sadly, the upper floors – the stone and bin floors with their machinery – no longer meet modern health and safety requirements and are no longer open to the public.[3]

On the ground floor, and still accessible, is the waterwheel. This is an undershot wheel measuring 12' in diameter by 6' wide and of an early design, with cast-iron shaft, spokes and rims. The original wooden floats have been replaced with sheet iron. It revolves whenever flows in the river Ver are adequate. The sluice gear is also visible, beyond which there is a view over the mill pond. The pit wheel† can also be seen, together with the iron wallower†, wooden great spur wheel† and stone nuts† enclosed in the massive timber hurst frame. There is also a fragment of a screw auger†. The flour was fed down from the stones on the floor above. This auger, or 'worm

Figure 4.4 Kingsbury Mill before World War I. HALS.

conveyor', carried the flour to the other side of the mill, from where it was lifted to the floor above for grading. The graded flour then came down individual chutes to be collected into sacks on the ground floor.

On the stone floor are three pairs of under-driven† stones, of which only one has a complete set of stone furniture†. The central shaft, crown wheel and subsidiary drive pulleys have all survived. There is also a purifier†, which allowed for separation of different grades of flour.

The top floor, also known as the bin, or granary, floor†, contains a remarkably complete set of storage bins designed to store the different types of grain: wheat, barley, maize and beans. The grain was fed by gravity from the bins via wooden chutes to the hoppers† on the millstones below. There are two sack hoists†: an internal one driven by power from the waterwheel, which hoisted bags of grain through trapdoors in the floors, and an external electrically driven one in the luccam† at the front of the building.[4]

An industrial-style chimney suggests that there was a supplementary steam engine at one time, but this is long gone. The only surviving evidence is a notice for the sale of the mill in 1892, which is on display and which refers to a 'Horizontal Engine and Boiler'.

This is a very complete and original pre-industrial mill of great character and interest. It is very much to be hoped that it can once again be fully opened up as a working mill museum at some future date.[5]

Moor Mill, Moor Mill Lane, Colney Street, St Albans

The building is a long timber-framed structure dating from the eighteenth century (Figure 4.5 and Plate 3): the exact date of construction is believed to be 1762. It is a fine example of a large watermill with the internal workings almost intact. Although it ceased to operate as a mill in 1939, much of the milling machinery from that time remains. Subsequently it was converted to a restaurant and restored in 1993, after a lengthy planning saga described in Chapter 10. It is extremely fortunate that the mill survived damage from the construction of the nearby M25, and the restoration and conservation of the mill with its machinery intact is down to visionaries who were prepared to see the project through.[6] The renovation is generally considered to have been carried out to a high standard of craftsmanship, with great attention to detail.

What to see in Moor Mill

The two waterwheels, restored to working order, are visible behind glass screens and the millstones, tuns and chutes have all been preserved on the stone floor (Plate 4).

Figure 4.5 Moor Mill in the 1990s. Reproduced by kind permission of Susan Watts.

Redbournbury Mill, Redbournbury Lane, St Albans

This is a rare survivor of a local rural mill, most of which went out of business between 1880 and 1914. It is an eighteenth-century three-storey mill building with a steeply pitched slate roof that is listed Grade II* as a building of more than local interest. Alongside is a two-storey mill house of red brick with a more shallowly pitched tiled roof.

The current building has been rebuilt several times following fires, the most recent of which occurred in 1987. Restoration took over ten years. It is now a well-established working museum and is the only working mill on the river Ver producing stone-ground flour. Not only is the mill a rare survivor, a representation of a long forgotten past, but it is particularly unusual in being a working mill perpetuating some traditional skills and using locally sourced grain to produce stone-ground organic flour. There is also a bakery which produces a range of artisanal loaves, using flour from the mill, for sale on the site.

The mill was modernised in the late nineteenth century with up-to-date milling machinery, including the unusual lay-shaft† layout (Plate 5; although there is also evidence of an earlier, more conventional hurst frame). However, it was equipped with millstones rather than roller mills. The drive is taken through a pit wheel, whence it is transferred from horizontal to vertical by a wallower. At the top of the vertical main shaft a crown wheel† drives the horizontal lay-shaft that powers the three stones, which, unusually, are in line with each other.

The millwork has been described by Kenneth Major, an expert on milling technology, as 'a high point in the design of water driven corn mills'. Major described it thus:

> The waterwheel shaft comes into the mill and on the inside end of this shaft there is an all-iron pit wheel. This pit wheel is 7ft in diameter and was cast in two parts. It engages with an all-iron one piece wallower 2ft 4in in diameter, and this is the first gear wheel on an iron vertical shaft. Above the wallower an upside down crown wheel, 3ft 9in in diameter, is mounted. This crown wheel engages with an iron bevel wheel on the end of the lay shaft which runs the length of the cog-pit, and from which the millstones are driven.[7]

A similar arrangement exists at Sopwell Mill, further down the river Ver.

Like other mills, in its latter days as a working mill Redbournbury Mill was used only for grinding animal feed. This ceased in the 1940s and it stood unused until the death of the owner, Ivy Hawkins, herself a rare case of a female miller. It was offered for sale but only to a buyer who was prepared to restore it to full working order. Happily, this is exactly what has happened since (Plate 6).

What to see in Redbournbury Mill

The cast-iron waterwheel is outside the building, but the sluice which controls the flow of water to the wheel is operated from inside the building. Like several others in Hertfordshire, it is 'overshot': the water is fed to the top of the wheel by a wooden channel known as a launder† (Plates 7 and 18). It needs a head of water, which is achieved by diverting the river water into an artificial leat† raised on an embankment of excavated chalk. The waterwheel measures 9' 6" in diameter and 7' 6" wide and has 60 buckets, or floats, and a 10"-deep rim or shroud that prevents water spilling over the edges, which would result in a loss of power. The wheel was restored in 2009 with stainless steel buckets in place of the original iron ones. The axle and spokes are original and date from the early nineteenth century. A hundred years separates the design of this wheel from that of Mill Green, described above; it is a much more efficient design in which the weight of the water provides significantly more power.

Flows on the river Ver have seldom been adequate and a supplementary steam engine was installed in 1890. It powered the mill by means of a large flat belt across the mill race. Early photographs show the housing for it. It was sold for wartime scrap in 1915 and no details of it have survived. A survey of the mill in 1972/3 concluded: 'There is now, unfortunately, the distinct possibility that there will never again be sufficient water to turn the wheel.'[8] Since then, however, the amount of water abstracted at Friar's Wash (a pumping station to the north) has been much reduced and the bed of the river lined where it leaked. Now the flow has been sufficiently restored for the waterwheel to be brought back into use. The wheel runs whenever the mill is open, but the low flow in the Ver and backwatering in the tail-race mean that it is not capable of producing enough power regularly to run the millstones. Its power is thus augmented by a recently installed second-hand Crossley single-cylinder compression-ignition diesel engine powering an electricity generator.

On the top floor are the sack hoist and grain elevator which brought the grain to the top of the mill to be fed to the bins which used to occupy the floor below. The latter were destroyed by the fire in 1987, along with the purifiers needed for cleaning the grain brought in by local farmers. Today the wheat is supplied ready cleaned and this floor is now used for the display of explanatory material and historic artefacts.

On the stone floor†, adjacent to the wall by the waterwheel, are the three sets of millstones, enclosed in circular wooden tuns in the traditional manner (Plate 8). They bear the supplier's name: W.R. Dell of Mark Lane, London. Two run clockwise and one anticlockwise. Each pair has a complete set of 'furniture': hopper, horse†, shoe† and damozel†. The hopper is fed from a wooden spout and the flow of grain is controlled by a flap at the end of the spout.

When milling is taking place the grain between the stones holds them apart. If the grain runs out the stones will touch and sparks could then ignite the flour dust. To avoid such a situation the tun has a dust extractor to blow the dust outside and the

WIND, WATER AND STEAM

alarm bell warns the miller when the grain in the hopper is getting low. The bottom stone, the bedstone, is fixed to the floor; the stone spindle† projects through it and turns the runner stone. Grain falls through the eye of the runner stone and moves along the furrows cut into the stones. Eventually it reaches the edge of the stones and falls as wholemeal flour through a spout to the ground floor. The flour is then graded into white flour, brown flour, semolina flour and bran in a cylindrical machine of varying mesh sizes. The bagging process takes place on the ground floor.

Hyde Mill, Lower Luton Road, near Harpenden

Hyde Mill has been run by the Cole family ever since the present owner's great grandfather became the miller in 1879. He was born in Stotfold and worked as a baker before becoming miller at Codicote and Kimpton until the abstraction of the waters of the Mimram reduced the capacity of those mills. He then moved to Hyde Mill.

This is an important water-powered corn mill dating from 1835, with a late nineteenth-century steam roller mill extension to the west (see Appendix 4 for a description of the roller plant). The red brick mill buildings with slated luccams form part of a complex of farm buildings (Plate 9)[9] through which runs the county boundary: the mill is in Hertfordshire, while the mill house is in Bedfordshire. The whole complex is listed Grade II*.

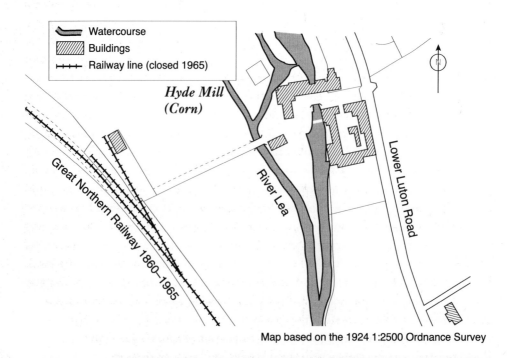

Figure 4.6 The siding and loading bay which used to serve Hyde Mill.

Figure 4.7 The stone floor at Hyde Mill. Three sets of millstones with complete stone furniture.

The roller mill enabled the miller to use imported wheat from Canada and the Argentine. The mill had a private railway siding on the Dunstable, Luton and Welwyn Garden City line until the line closed in 1965 (this is closer to the mill than the Midland main line) (Figure 4.6). The railway line is now the Upper Lea Valley Walk. Flour milling ceased in the 1920s and only animal feed was produced thereafter.

What to see at Hyde Mill

The mill contains an iron breastshot waterwheel 14' in diameter and 8' 6" wide. There are three pairs of stones (Figure 4.7). Some of the arms of the waterwheel have been replaced to prevent it collapsing, but the rims are now in a parlous state. The wheel was rebuilt around the original hub in 1934 by Armfield Engineering. With hindsight, and in view of its short remaining working life, it can hardly have justified the expenditure. Although the millstones are complete, the roller mills (Figure 4.8) were removed in the mid-1950s. They were similar to the Jordans' installation at Holme Mills near

Figure 4.8 Diagram of roller mills at Hyde Mill. Reproduced from The Miller, *1 May 1893.*

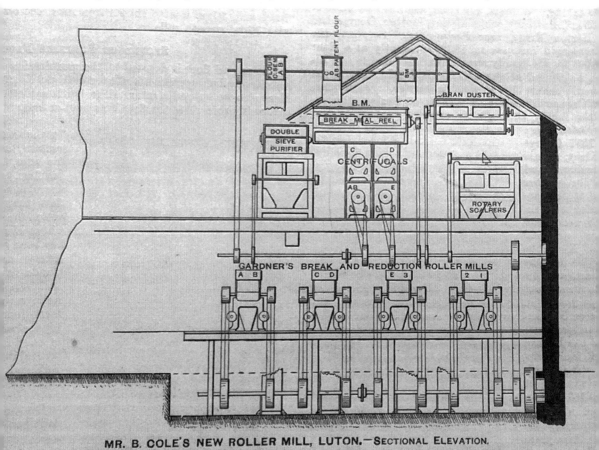

Biggleswade, which is now accessible to the public. Some of the drive system is still in place; there are two stationary steam engines installed by Nathan Vardy of Royston, with ancillary equipment by Tangye's of Birmingham. Flour was distributed by horse and cart to local bakers in Luton and Harpenden. The cart has been preserved in the Museum of Rural England at Reading (see Figure 1.10).

Also at the mill is a sack barrow marked 'G Lewis, Kettering' and scales by Avery. The office contains a comprehensive set of ledgers itemising the various clients with the quantities of the various grades of flour supplied.

Access to Hyde Mill is only by special arrangement with the owner.

Cromer windmill, Ardeley

There has been a post mill† on this site for many centuries. Dendrochronology has indicated that the main post in the mill came from a tree that was felled in the spring of 1679. As a post mill it is typical of the earliest form of windmill, yet its equipment demonstrates the final evolution of the traditional millwright's art. The mill as it is seen today dates from the 1860s, when it was rebuilt following an almost total collapse, and the millwork is typical of that time, having 'patent', or shuttered, sails† and a fantail†, which enabled the whole body of the mill automatically to face into the wind. Several components, including the wallower and windshaft†, are cast iron, indicating that they do not pre-date the rebuilding.

Joseph Scowen was the last miller here, and worked the mill until his death in 1920 (Figure 4.9). He had migrated to New Zealand in 1879, but returned to Hertfordshire following a fire in the mill that he operated in New Zealand. He came from a family of millers and his son became the miller at Watton-at-Stone watermill.[10]

In 1914 the sails and at least one stock were replaced, and presumably it was considered worth the cost of doing so. However, in the mill's later years it was producing only animal feed, and it is believed to have worked for the last time in 1923. Certainly, when the fantail and one sail were lost in storms shortly afterwards the mill was beyond economic repair (Figure 4.10).

In 1931 Stanley Freese wrote:

> ... between Cromer and Cottered ... is a tall and very exposed post mill notable for the elaborate driving gears from the fantail ... The sweeps were intact about four years ago, but I recently found nothing left of them but for a sail-stock, resting on the bank against the round-house and measuring, as far as I could tell by pacing it out, about forty two feet.
>
> The old mill is truly a sentinel of the road, for it stands high upon the bank at the roadside, unprotected by any hedge, and commanding a wonderful stretch of rolling cornfields with scarcely a building or a tree to challenge

Figure 4.9 Cromer Mill, c.1900. Joseph Scowen, seen here with his wife and two daughters, was the last miller at Cromer. Reproduced by kind permission of the Scowen Family.

Figure 4.10 Cromer Mill in a sorry state in 1930. Reproduced by kind permission of Hertford Museum.

its supremacy. The tall body juts out against the sky in all directions, and if it is allowed to go the way of so many other old mills the surrounding countryside will be sadly changed indeed.[11]

In 1938 the mill was described as 'Cromer, gaunt ogee-roofed† sail-less, a great gap in the breast boarding disclosing some of the fine machinery'.[12] But help was at hand. A group of concerned local people reboarded and repainted the buck†, or main body of the mill, which seems to have saved it from complete collapse.[13]

The Cromer windmill has been owned by the Hertfordshire Building Preservation Trust since 1967.[14] The guiding principle in the Trust's restoration has been to return the mill to the state it was in in 1923, when it ceased working. By 1930 the mill had no sails, no fantail and only the remains of the ladder, and without immediate attention would have been a total loss. The restoration has taken place in stages ever since.

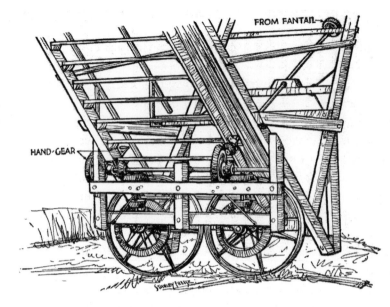

Figure 4.11 Sketch of the elaborate fantail gearing of Cromer Mill from beneath its steps. Illustration by Stanley Freese, from In search of English windmills *(1931).*

Figure 4.12 The recently restored fantail and ladder of Cromer Mill. Kindly supplied by Jane Housham.

What to see at Cromer windmill

The first view of the outside of Cromer windmill shows all the main elements of a post mill (Plate 11). The buck is clad in white weatherboarding, has a black roof and measures in plan some 17' by 13' 6". It is balanced on the vast vertical main post, which is 18' high. This is held in place by a triangulated trestle framework contained within a brick-built roundhouse† (Plate 12). The buck is accessed by a steep ladder to which is attached the fantail, which is linked, through a system of gearing, to the truck wheels at the foot of the ladder. The ladder also supports a sack slide which enables sacks of flour to slide down from the meal floor into waiting carts below. Stanley Freese wrote that the mill was 'notable for the elaborate driving gears from the fantail, an arrangement which I think is self-explanatory from the sketch'[15] (shown in Figure 4.11; see also Figure 4.12).

The sails have a span of 56', weigh 1.75 tons and revolve at 12–15 rpm. There are two rows of shutters†, an arrangement that allows maximum exposure to the wind, harnessing its energy to greatest advantage. The shutters are readily adjustable in a manner analogous to a venetian blind. By pulling a chain at the rear of the mill, the miller can open or close the shutters according to the strength of the wind.

Entering the buck by the meal floor (Plate 13), which is the first of three floors, the great spur wheel can be seen, along with the stone nuts, which can be meshed with the great spur wheel to drive two sets of millstones on the floor above. The chutes that convey the flour from the millstones into waiting sacks below are also visible. Also on this floor are the centrifugal governor†, which compensates for fluctuations in wind speed, and the tentering screws†, immediately below the millstones. These raise or lower the running stone and hence adjust the gap between the stones to ensure an optimum fineness of flour.

The next floor is the stone floor (Plate 14), where the two sets of stones, driven from below, represent the two main types of stone. Monolithic stones, usually from the Peak District, are suitable for the coarse grinding of barley, offals† and beans or animal food, while French burr stones, traditionally from the Marne valley, are used for producing the finer types of flour. The latter were much more expensive than Peak stones: only £5 would have bought a pair of Derbyshire Peaks in Victorian times, whereas £36 would have been needed for a pair of French burrs, which consisted of pieces of hard quartz held together with plaster of Paris and bound with iron hoops to ensure that the runner did not fly apart under centrifugal force.

The top floor is the bin floor. Sacks of grain would be lifted through a series of trapdoors to this floor, where the grain was stored in bins. From here it would be fed into the millstones below. The hollow iron windshaft dominates this floor with its massive brake wheel†, which can control the speed of the sails if they threaten to turn too fast. The other wheel on the windshaft is the pulley, which drove the sack hoist in the roof.

Gearing

In most wind and watermills the transmission of power to the stones is through a two-stage speed-increasing gearing system. The ratio of a pair of gears is that of the numbers of teeth on each gear. The first stage in a windmill is the brake wheel and wallower, and at Cromer the brake wheel has 72 teeth (or 'cogs', in mill-speak) and the wallower 18, giving a ratio of 4:1, so that the wallower turns four times faster than the brake wheel. The second stage is the great spur wheel and the stone nuts for each stone. At Cromer the spur wheel has 64 cogs and the stone nuts 32, which gives a ratio of 2:1. Hence, with the sails at 15 rpm the stones will revolve at 120 rpm. The gear ratio between the fan and the wheels of the fan carriage is approximately 300:1.

Figure 4.13 An aerial view of the full extent of Dickinson's Apsley complex in its heyday in 1939. It has all been redeveloped for housing and retail parks now. It also shows how the Gade valley has become a transport corridor, with rail, road and canal competing with each other. © Royal Commission on the Ancient and Historical Monuments of Scotland. Reproduced courtesy of J.R. Hume, licensor, www.rcahms.uk.

Frogmore Paper Mills, Fourdrinier Way, Apsley

This mill was acquired by John Dickinson in 1809, by which time it had already been converted to a paper mill. Steam power was introduced, together with the Fourdrinier† machine. In 1838 it was producing nine tons of paper a year. By 1888, when manufacturing of paper ceased, it was producing more than double that. The beam engine installed in 1844 was removed in 1888 and the mill was then switched to producing card and envelopes. The mill became part of a very extensive plant in Apsley (Figure 4.13). The waterwheels were removed, but the wheel pits still remain.

Since 2008 the building has been the Paper Trail Museum, the aim of which is to conserve the legacy of the industry. It contains a unique archive of the paper-making industry and offers the visitor the chance to view the early machines which revolutionised paper-making. There is also the opportunity to make individual sheets in the pre-industrial manner.[16] A 1938 Dennis Ace fire engine is a reminder of the constant risk of fire in a situation where both raw materials and finished products were highly flammable. (See also Chapter 7 for a full description of the paper-making industry in Hertfordshire and descriptions of the sites of the mills founded by John Dickinson.)

Royal Gunpowder Mills, Beaulieu Drive, Waltham Abbey

At the point at which Hertfordshire, Essex and the former Middlesex (part of Greater London since 1975) meet a hub for gunpowder and fighting weapons was established at the end of the seventeenth century. Originally a private company, it started producing gunpowder in 1665 as a response to the demand for gunpowder caused by the English Civil War and its aftermath (Figure 4.14). So valuable did the expertise at Waltham Abbey become in its supplying the government with the means of protecting the expanding British trade routes during the next century that it was acquired by the Crown in 1787. The Royal Gunpowder Mills and the Royal Small Arms (RSA) factory, which was established nearby at Enfield Lock for the manufacture of fighting weapons, thereafter became an important complex for national defence.

The Royal Gunpowder Mills was a nationally important and highly secret site which supplied the British military machine first with gunpowder, then with cordite and nitro-glycerine and finally with propellants for rockets. Perhaps its most famous product was Barnes Wallis' bouncing bomb, used in the Dambusters raid.[17] The production of explosives finished only in 1945, when the site was reopened as the Experimental Station of the government's Royal Armament Research and Development Establishment. The site finally closed in 1991 and a visitors' centre was established for what is now one of the most extensive scheduled industrial monuments in the country. The RSA factory was closed in 2000 and much of the site has been redeveloped for housing.[18]

Gunpowder, once it had been manufactured, had to be delivered safely to destinations such as Woolwich Arsenal and the magazines at Purfleet. Water transport

WIND, WATER AND STEAM

Figure 4.14 The Waltham Abbey Powder Mills, by J. Farmer, 1739. The engraving shows a loading basin with stamping mills adjacent in the centre, together with a loading house or controller's office. On the right is a corn mill and to its left there are three horse mills, a coal mill and a composition house. Reproduced by kind permission of Royal Gunpowder Mills.

was safer than carriage by road, where jolting might cause explosions. However, the danger of carrying explosives through built-up areas was all too vividly demonstrated when, in 1874, a barge carrying gunpowder on Regent's Canal exploded. The crew of three were killed, Macclesfield Bridge destroyed and the canal blocked for several days. Damage to surrounding property was less than might have been expected, however, because, fortunately, the canal runs in a cutting at this point. There has also been a history of explosions at Waltham Abbey, culminating in two separate nitroglycerine explosions in 1940 resulting in ten fatalities.[19] The effects were contained within the site, but these explosions were a warning that an increasingly populated area was not the best place for such a hazardous industry. This was one reason for ending the manufacturing of explosives. As there was no actual production, the research processes after 1945 were considered acceptable in an increasingly densely populated urban area.

A complex system of water channels was used for both power and transport.[20] Originally water power from the river Lea was used in the production of gunpowder; in order to ensure a constant supply of water, the Board of Ordnance bought the water rights on the Lea by acquiring the mill streams of nearby Cheshunt and Waltham

Abbey mills and by developing an elaborate canal system to provide a good head of water for the mills. Waterwheels supplied the power for grinding saltpetre, sulphur and charcoal and mixing the ingredients in readiness for grinding with on-edge millstones. This process, which is known as 'incorporating' and was done by on-edge-runner millstones in the Incorporating Mill, improved both the consistency and the stability of the product, making it safer to transport.

The superiority of the product from Waltham Abbey had proved critical at the Battle of Waterloo. However, the Crimean War had revealed that although this technical superiority had been maintained the production facilities for armaments needed to be radically upgraded. From 1856 onwards steam-powered mills were built to power up to six of these millstone assemblies by means of underfloor drive shafts, not unlike the lay-shaft arrangements at Redbournbury and Sopwell Mills. By 1888 there were 40 steam-powered incorporating mills on the site. All the engines have subsequently been removed, but the underfloor drive shafts can still be seen.[21]

Although most of the milling equipment is long gone, significant items from both the water- and the steam-powered periods still exist on the site. Of particular interest is an external waterwheel in the Hydraulic Press House. It has been authenticated as being by William Fairbairn and dates from 1857; as such, it is a rare survival and of considerable historic importance (Plate 15). It measures 14' by 3' 2" and has 40 buckets with deep shrouds. The hatch controls are also a notable example of Fairbairn's design. Finally, within the now roofless building is a hydraulic press driven by a pump. The installation as a whole represents the latest in water technology and design.[22]

Various other sites are related to those described above; these are outlined below.

Cheshunt Mill

In 1805 the mill was bought and demolished by the Board of Ordnance to augment the water supply to the gunpowder mills a mile downstream.

Waltham Abbey Mill

Known as the Cornmill, this too was acquired by the Board of Ordnance. This mill was just downstream of the northern part of the Royal Gunpowder Mills, and was entirely separate from the steam-driven Sun Flour Mill in Sun Street.

Barwick Gunpowder Works

A short-lived gunpowder works known as the Smokeless Powder Company existed at Barwick, south of Standon, from 1889 until 1922. During World War I the government took over the plant for explosives manufacture. After 1922 the plant made explosives for crackers. Since 1946 the site has fulfilled a variety of commercial uses.[23]

References

1. W. Fairbairn, 'On waterwheels with ventilated buckets', Institution of Civil Engineers paper 793 (9 January 1849).
2. Interview with Joe Taylor at Mill Green Mill, September 2013.
3. N. King, *Kingsbury water-mill museum* (Derby, 1993).
4. K. Major, 'Kingsbury Mill', report of the Mills Archive (June 1982).
5. D. Ogden, 'Kingsbury Mill', report of the Mills Archive (October 1969).
6. *Herts Advertiser* (29 January 1982, 16 March 1984, 23 March 1984, 14 December 1984, 22 September 1989, 26 January 1990, 19 April 1990).
7. K. Major, 'Redbournbury Mill', report of the Mills Archive (November 1985).
8. Report of survey by industrial archaeology tutorial class, Dacorum College of Further Education, held by St Albans Museum 1972/3.
9. L. Bonwick, *Hyde Water Mill*, East Hyde, Archaeological Building Survey Report, Bonwick Milling Heritage Consultancy (2007).
10. Information provide by Greg Scowen.
11. S. Freese, *In search of English windmills* (London, 1931).
12. *Hertfordshire Mercury* (22 July 1938), letter from Archibald Jackson.
13. L. Bonwick, *Cromer windmill history and guide* (Hertford, 1999).
14. Interview with Robin Webb, 2012, and K. Major, reports June 1976 and October 1978.
15. Freese, *English windmills*.
16. Interview with M. Stanyon, 6 February 2012.
17. *The Sunday Times* (26 June 1999).
18. *Cheshunt and Waltham Mercury* (24 July 1998).
19. *Cheshunt and Waltham Mercury* (17 April 1998).
20. R. Thomas, *The waterways of the Royal Gunpowder Mills* (Waltham Abbey, 2009).
21. L. Tucker, *The listed buildings and other principal structures at the Royal Gunpowder Mills, Waltham Abbey* (Waltham Abbey, 2013).
22. K. Major, *A waterwheel by William Fairbairn at the Royal Gunpowder Mills, The Mills Archive report* (2004).
23. W. Branch Johnson, *Industrial monuments in Hertfordshire* (Hertford, 1967).

5

Corn milling

Until the middle of the nineteenth century corn millers enjoyed a monopoly position and were notoriously wealthy compared with other workers in the community. For centuries this picture had changed little. However, the revolution in milling described in Chapter 1 opened up the county's mills both to unexpected pressures at home and to competition from abroad. An American miller, visiting the UK in 1875 to locate agents for the importation of American flour, found 'that nine tenths of the flour consumed in England by bakers was much inferior to American varieties'. Prophetically, he also expressed 'an opinion that in the process of time both the Scotch and English markets will furnish a constant outlet for American surplus flour'.[1]

The 'hard' imported grain was better suited to mass bread-making than was the locally grown grain. Moreover, the new roller mills that were making inroads into the traditional forms of milling, based on millstones, were ideal for processing this 'hard' grain. Imported grain was a major threat to English grain, producing a whiter loaf, which, in those days, carried a certain status. Suddenly the monopoly position was gone, and traditional millers, therefore, struggled with the question of whether, in view of the expense involved, to re-equip their mills with roller-milling machinery.

Whereas Chapter 3 concentrated on the success stories of corn milling in Hertfordshire, this chapter documents the decline in the great majority of corn mills and the various fates that awaited them.

Corn milling in the Colne valley

There were only two corn mills on the river Colne itself, but several on the other rivers in the Colne catchment: the Gade, Bulbourne, Chess and Ver (Figure 5.1). Many of the mills on the Gade were made over to paper-making at the beginning of the nineteenth century. However, on the Bulbourne corn milling continued to thrive. In the early years of the twentieth century J.G. Knowles modernised the mill at Bourne End, which worked until 1948. He also built a new industrial mill, Castle Mills, in Berkhamsted. Likewise, the Meads replaced their Gamnel windmill at Tring with a new extension to their existing steam-driven industrial plant.

Of the corn mills in the Colne catchment four have been demolished: Grace's Mill at Akeman Street, Tring, Upper Mill in Berkhamsted, Toovey's Mill at Kings Langley and Hunton Bridge Mill (Abbots Langley). Five have been converted to

WIND, WATER AND STEAM

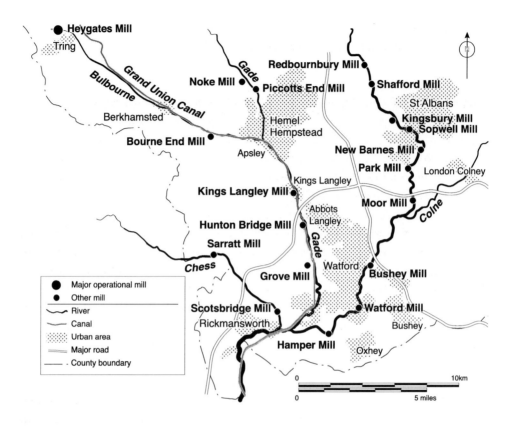

Figure 5.1 The location of corn mills, past and present, within the catchment of the river Colne.

homes: Noake and Piccotts End at Hemel Hempstead, Grove at Watford, Shafford, and Abbey Mill at St Albans; and two, Lower Mill at Berkhamsted and Moor Mill at Colney Street, have been converted to pubs or restaurants. Only one, Sopwell, has remained substantially as it was when it ceased working.

New industrial mills were built at Kings Langley and at New Barnes and Park Street, St Albans. The latter two are now offices and Castle Mill, Berkhamsted, has been converted to flats. Kings Langley and Castle Mills survived as working mills until after World War II.

Corn mills on the river Colne

Bushey Mills, Bushey Mill Lane, Watford (Plate 24)

There are few surviving details relating to the date of this mill complex's construction or demolition, and it does not appear in the Hertfordshire HER. One part was a paper mill and the other a corn mill. An advertisement for a new tenant in 1838 described the mill as follows:

The Mills now consist of a one Vat paper Mill with all its gear – work, Presses, Engine, and all other requisites for making paper.

Also a Corn Mill with two pairs of Stones, 4 dressing Mills, and other tackling will be included in the above disposal, both mills are worked on the same head, and capable of great improvement, having a strong stream of water equal to drive two powerful Wheels, carrying 6 Engines or six pairs of Stones, and at no time of the year is short of water, and near 7 Feet fall; the whole may be converted into a Paper or Corn Mill as may be required: in addition to which there is a Beautiful spring of clear water which produces the finest colours.[2]

'Capable of great improvement' would seem to be estate agents' speak for a dire condition. A further negative is that the advertisement refers to the mill being 'two miles from the Navigation', presumably at Watford. In view of what has already been said about the importance of good transport links, this attribute was hardly appealing. It probably failed to attract a new tenant, as it does not appear on the tithe map of 1840. Ominously, the advertisement concludes with the phrase, 'Rough timber for repairs will be found'.

Watford flour mill, Lower High Street, Watford (Figure 5.2)
Built in 1826, it is described in the Hertfordshire HER as tall and plain, and towering over its neighbours. It had two waterwheels and seven pairs of stones. It was destroyed by fire in 1924 and demolished in 1938.

Figure 5.2 The Watford flour mill in 1903, showing the results of a summer flood of the river Colne. HALS.

Figure 5.3 Noake Mill in the 1950s. Reproduced by kind permission of David Jones and the Mills Archive.

Figure 5.4 Piccotts End Mill in 1955, before its destruction by fire and subsequent rebuilding as apartments. © HBPT.

CORN MILLING

Corn mills on the river Gade

Noake Mill, Water End, Hemel Hempstead (Figure 5.3)
A small mid-nineteenth-century red-brick three-storey mill with a high-pitched roof, this is the highest mill on the river Gade. The overshot waterwheel measures 12' by 6'. It has been converted to a private house.

Piccotts End Mill, Riverbank, Hemel Hempstead (Figure 5.4)
This was a large timber-framed three-storey weatherboarded watermill that burned down in 1991 and has since been rebuilt as apartments with surrounding residential development.

Site of Toovey's Mill, Waterside, Kings Langley (Figure 5.5)
This steam corn mill belonged to the Toovey family, who produced 'Golden Spray' flour. It was an important commercial mill that survived until after World War II. Its grain silos were a dominant feature beside the Grand Union Canal and the river Gade. Lewis Dean's 1971 article 'The History of Kings Langley Mill' provides a comprehensive description of what such a large mill was like:

Figure 5.5 Kings Langley Mill with the grain silo, built in 1948, dominating the Grand Union Canal. © HBPT.

The Kings Langley Mill had four pairs of break rolls and about sixteen pairs of smooth rolls and from the time the wheat started to feed into the first break rolls it was at least ten minutes before you were able to collect the final product.

Thomas Toovey in about 1916 installed a new Woodhouse and Mitchell steam engine which survived until 1956. Coal for the boilers was brought in from the Midlands by boat, on the Grand Junction Canal which had opened in 1800. Occasionally English corn from Dagnall was brought by boat, but this ceased in about 1913 when he introduced Foden steam lorries which also replaced the 30 to 36 horses which had previously been kept for deliveries. In 1921 the old breast wheel which was about 12 feet in diameter, was taken out and two magnificent Swiss turbines installed in its place. Instead of letting the water flow as it would, it had to leave the turbine through a circular streamlined flume.

At Kings Langley we were too near London to compete with the port mills and we were not far out enough in the country because houses were continually being built where wheat used to grow. And so it was that in 1938 we took the difficult decision to stop making flour.

After the war in 1946 the mill was in a very poor condition. As the Grand Union Canal Company, who were the owners, would not spend any money on it, I offered to buy it from them. To my astonishment they agreed, and so exactly

Figure 5.6 Hunton Bridge Mill in c.1890. Reproduced courtesy of Abbots Langley Local History Society, Parish Archives, from the David Spain collection.

one hundred years after my great-grandfather had sold it, I bought it back again, for considerably less than Thomas Toovey had received for it in 1846.

> The mill was driven by a curious combination of water and steam power. At one end of a long shaft was the steam engine, with its great flywheel, its power transmitted by long cotton ropes. The shaft went right through the mill with many counter-drives from it … a set of spur gears transmitted the drive from the larger turbine to the main shaft. So the steam engine was pushing at one end and the turbine at the other.[3]

The mill was demolished in 1978 and the site redeveloped for housing. The mill house survives. A further description from *The Miller* is provided in Appendix 5.

Site of Hunton Bridge Mill, Old Mill Road, Abbots Langley (Figure 5.6 and Plate 16)
This was a large rural traditional flour mill until the 1920s and was used as a small munitions factory during World War II. It was demolished shortly afterwards, probably to improve visibility on a blind bend in Old Mill Road.

Only the external waterwheel has survived, but it is in an inoperative state. It is a very wide overshot wheel of five bays with an estimated total of 200 buckets. Its diameter is approximately 10' and its width is some 13'. Its sophisticated design suggests that efforts may have been made to update the mill at the end of the nineteenth century with a significant investment in more efficient milling equipment. However, no record of the mill's other machinery has come to light. The formidable power suggested by the form of the waterwheel would have been augmented by

Figure 5.7 Grove Mill, Watford, before World War I. Reproduced by kind permission of David Huggins.

harnessing the combined falls of the adjacent Hunton Bridge upper and lower locks on the nearby Grand Union Canal. These amount to more than 11'. The half-buried iron pit wheel also survives.

Grove Mill, Grove Mill Lane, Watford (Figure 5.7 and Figure 10.1)
This was a three-storey watermill dating from 1875 which has now been converted into flats. The luccam has been retained. A significant portion of a turbine, visible from Grove Mill Lane, survives.

Corn mills of the river Bulbourne

Grace's Mill and Maltings, 15 Akeman Street, Tring
This was a two-storey part sixteenth- and part seventeenth-century building which remained in use as Francis Carter, Maltsters, Corn Merchants and Canvas Weavers until 1920. From then until 1945 it produced animal feed. It was powered originally by horses, and then by steam; finally, it relied on a Crossley Gas Engine, which is now at the Pitstone Green Museum. There were plans to restore the mill and create a local museum; however, in 1977 Dacorum Borough Council took the view that the building and the adjacent mill house were beyond economic repair and should be demolished. The site has since been redeveloped for housing.[4]

Bourne End Mill, London Road, Berkhamsted (Figure 5.8)
J.G. Knowles was an enterprising miller who sought to keep abreast of technological developments. In the early years of the twentieth century he not only updated the Bourne End Mill but also built Castle Mill in Berkhamsted, running the two as a single enterprise. Although the Grand Junction Canal ran right past Bourne End Mill there never seems to have been any attempt to use it for importing grain, whereas Castle

Figure 5.8 Bourne End Mill at the turn of the twentieth century. Reproduced by kind permission of the Hemel Hempstead Local History and Museum Society.

Mill was deliberately sited to take advantage both of the canal and of the adjacent London and North Western Railway. These developments were enough to keep the mills in business until after World War II, when they, along with other medium-sized mills, could no longer compete with the big industrial mills.

Until Knowles took a long lease in 1893 Bourne End Mill contained three pairs of stones driven by water and three pairs driven by steam. Knowles installed a roller-mill plant consisting of four double sets of rollers 'on the latest and best lines, and entrusted the work to Messrs Turner, who have executed the contract in an excellent manner'. Power was provided partly by the overshot waterwheel, 9' in diameter by 8' wide, and partly by a Cundall 12 hp oil engine. There was also a Howes combined smutter and brush, a double Turner purifier and an offal-dividing sieve.[5]

The mill, a two-storey weatherboarded building with luccam, ceased operating in 1945. Following a fire in 1970 it was redeveloped as the Watermill Motel with part of the building extending over the Bulbourne. The waterwheel has been retained.[6] Appendix 6 contains a description of the mill in 1911.

Castle Mill, Lower Kings Road, Berkhamsted (Figure 1.12)

This corn mill was built in 1910 by J.G. Knowles and Son and operated until 1948 for the production of animal feeds. It is constructed in red–grey brick on four storeys with a five-storey silo, and has a wharf to the canal. It was converted first to offices and subsequently to apartments. Appendix 6 contains a description of the mill in 1911.

Site of Upper Mill, Mill Street, Berkhamsted (Plate 10)

This was a rural vernacular mill which must have been obsolete when it was demolished in 1926 to make way for extensions to Berkhamsted School. The mill itself was of timber with a tiled roof. Next to it was the miller's house, a long cement-faced building. A Latin inscription on a plaque in Mill Street commemorates the mill:

> in hac ripa molae steterunt mille per annos alimentumque praebuerrunt donec utilitatibus scholae aeque altricis cesserunt.
>
> (Here for a thousand years the old mill stood and gave us bread. Here now our school in rival motherhood feeds minds instead.)

The site of the waterwheel can still be seen and two millstones have been retained in the school grounds.[7]

Lower Mill, London Road, Berkhamsted

Much of the complex survives, but without any machinery. It has been converted to the Old Mill restaurant.[8]

Figure 5.9 Shafford Mill today.

Corn mills on the river Ver

In contrast to other Hertfordshire rivers, the Ver has retained much of its milling heritage. There is a working watermill at Redbournbury and a preserved watermill at Kingsbury (both described in Chapter 4), as well as fairly complete sets of machinery at Sopwell and Moor Mills and waterwheels at Park Mill.

Shafford Mill, Redbourn Road, St Albans (Figure 5.9)
Shafford Mill, the estate mill for the Childwickbury estate, had an internal iron breastshot waterwheel and two pairs of stones with hoppers. There was also a steam-powered 6 hp engine and a vertical boiler housed in an extension on the west side. These drove pumps which pumped water from a nearby well to a water tower one mile away in Bush Wood in order to supply the mansion and estate houses, farm and cottages with water. It was replaced in 1923 by a gas engine. The estate was sold off piecemeal in 1978 and the mill was damaged by fire in the subsequent year, with the loss of the bin floor. It was then converted to a private house and extended upwards by one floor in the 1980s. The ribs of the waterwheel, measuring approximately 14' by 4', survive, together with the mechanism of the sluice, as do the pit wheel, wallower, great spur wheel and some of the gear for the stone nuts.

CORN MILLING

Dixon's Flour Mills, 23 St George Street, St Albans
This was a nineteenth-century steam mill (later converted to gas) known as City Steam Flour Mills. Owned by A.J. Dixon and Co, it was a corn, seed and forage merchant business. It stood beyond the end of the yard at the rear of the site and burned down in 1924. A small electric-powered mill which replaced it has survived. The warehouse on the street frontage survives, as does the mill manager's house.

Sopwell Mill, Cotton Mill Lane, St Albans (Figure 5.10 and Plate 17)
This is a Grade II listed building and is a near-complete example of a late nineteenth-century water-powered corn mill with attached dwelling. The mill and conjoined house, a three-storey brick building with a slate roof, date from 1868, following a fire. The mill ceased working in 1939, but much of the original machinery remains. The external breastshot mill wheel, measuring 13' in diameter by 6' wide, is essentially

Figure 5.10 The lay-shaft arrangement at Sopwell Mill.

Figure 5.11 The pit wheel, wallower, great spur wheel and stone nuts are all visible in this historic photograph of Park Mill taken in 1983. Reproduced by kind permission of St Albans Museum.

complete except for the wooden brackets supporting the buckets, which have rotted. The head leat no longer exists, but a pipe allows a flow to the wheel pit. Nothing remains on the bin floor, and the tuns and hoppers of the millstones are missing. However, the three millstone sets, one Peak and two French burrs, are still in place and bear balancing weights inscribed 'Clarke and Dunham, Mark Lane, London'. The mill machinery includes a pit wheel and lay-shaft drive similar to that at Redbournbury Mill. There is also a separate drive-chain from a now-missing steam engine. The sluice in the launder was controlled from inside and there is a governor for the steam engine drive-chain. A stone quern has been found in the riverbed nearby.

New Barnes Mill (also known as Cowley Mill), Cotton Mill Lane, St Albans
The present mill, a four-storey brick building with a turbine and roller mills, dates from a reconstruction in the 1890s. From 1920 it was used by the British Flour Research Committee, after which it passed to the CWS. Since 1957 it has been a business centre.

Park Mill (also known as Corville Mill), Park Street, St Albans (Figures 5.11, 10.8 and 10.9)
Park Mill, a fairly typical Victorian industrial-style mill building, was built in its present four-storey form in 1846 and was a corn mill until 1920. There is no record of the internal machinery, but the likelihood is that it was in a modern industrial style. However, the available documents refer to millstones but not to rollers.[9] It would seem, therefore, that the millwork was never updated. Since 1920 the building has had a chequered history. The next owner clearly saw no future for corn milling and converted the mill to crush animal bones for glue, a process which cast an appalling smell over the neighbourhood. The conversion involved removing all the corn-milling equipment and installing a steam digester to convert the bones into glue. The waterwheels were henceforth redundant. The building was then taken over by scrap-metal merchants during World War II. The mill house (but not the mill) was demolished in 1959 for road widening. Writing in 1981, B.D. Adams of St Albans Museum said, 'At the moment the mill is being used as a store for scrap metal. The interior is crowded with junk and it is very difficult to see any historical development there.'[10]

By 1984 it was in a very poor state. In that year permission was granted for a change of use to offices, which, in planning terms, was a great improvement over the scrap yard. The conversion, which includes three dummy 'luccams' on the south side, was carried out to a high standard. The waterwheels have been enclosed by glass screens. Both approximately 12' in diameter, one is 6' wide and the other 10'. They are overshot and would seem to date from the time when the mill was built. They both have close-set and steep-angled floats, as befits overshot wheels. The larger wheel lacks several floats, but the smaller one is reputed to turn. The headstock of the former is still in place. The leat is now dry, but it can still be seen how the waters of the Ver once powered the mill. There is a 4' Peak stone between the wheel arches on the north side.

Corn milling in the Lea valley
From the point where the Lea enters Hertfordshire to the head of navigation at Hertford the corn mills are in traditional vernacular style. There are two in a good state of preservation – Hyde (Harpenden) and Mill Green – and conversions at Batford, Wheathampstead, Lemsford and Essendon. In Hertford itself four rivers converge: the Lea, Mimram, Beane and Rib. There are seven mill sites within or close to the borough. Downstream of Hertford are large late Victorian industrial mills: Allen and Hanburys (now Glaxo Smith Kline) Ware Town Mill and Stanstead Abbotts Mill.

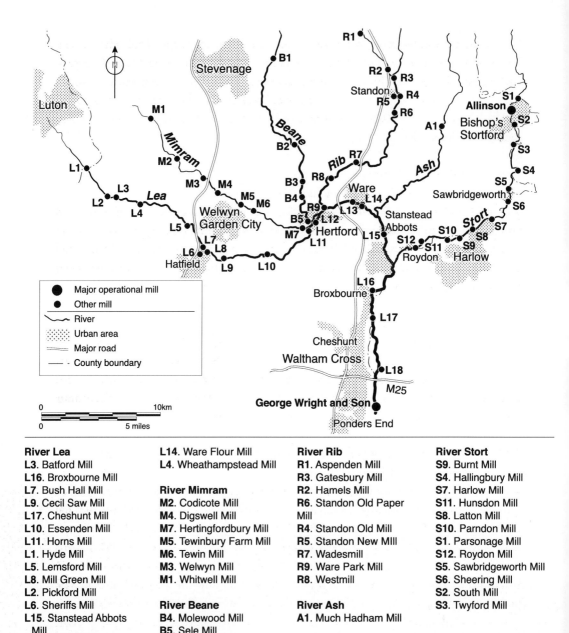

Figure 5.12 The location of corn mills, past and present, within the catchment of the river Lea and its tributaries.

Of the vernacular mills, most have been demolished: Pickford Mill, Harpenden; Town Mill and Dicker Mill, both in Hertford; and Broxbourne Mills. Others – Batford and Lemsford – have been converted to offices, Wheathampstead to shops and Essendon to residential. Two have survived intact: Mill Green as an unmodernised eighteenth-century mill and Hyde as a mill updated at the start of the twentieth century (Figure 5.12).

Corn mills on the river Lea

Site of Pickford Mill, Coldharbour Lane, Harpenden
This mill had been used for paper-making from the mid-eighteenth century and was still so used in 1851, when Philip Weedon was the paper-maker. Flour milling resumed in the 1870s and 1880s under George Bates, who by 1886 had introduced steam power. In 1897 it was converted to a latex factory. The mill has since been demolished and the site redeveloped as an industrial estate.[11]

Batford Mill, Lower Luton Road, Harpenden (Figure 5.13)
Both Batford and Wheathampstead Mills (see below) were owned and run by the Titmuss family. The mill building at Batford was built in 1857. George Titmuss bought it in 1886 and installed a roller mill and steam power. Thenceforth Batford Mill produced up to 200 sacks of flour a week. Competition of lower-priced flour milled in East London rendered the mill uneconomic, however, and flour milling

Figure 5.13 An historic view of Batford Mill from the upstream side. Reproduced by kind permission of Harpenden Local History Society.

Figure 5.14 Lemsford Mill, in 1935, from the downstream side. © *HBPT.*

Figure 5.15 Lemsford Mill today, from the upstream side.

ceased in 1928, the mill being sold at that time. The mill was used before World War II for making fertiliser and, more recently, for the manufacture of plastics.[12] The building was restored in 1983 and now houses individual small-business units.

Wheathampstead Mill, High Street, Wheathampstead (Plate 22)
This is a Grade II listed mill of rural vernacular style in a pleasant setting. The three-bay timber-framed building, which is remarkable for its length, dates back to at least the eighteenth century. The wheel, believed to have been manufactured in Kilmarnock and dating from 1895, was undershot or low breastshot; there were two sets of stones.[13] The water that powered the mill wheel ran beneath the mill. The High Street runs immediately in front of the mill over the mill tail race.

The Titmuss family owned and ran the mill from 1882. It was a provender mill from about 1900 onwards and was also used for seed cleaning and dressing for agricultural purposes. It could not compete with more modern flour mills in the London docks and in 1986/7 it was converted to a variety of business and retail uses. All machinery has been removed.[14]

Lemsford Mill, Lemsford Village, near Welwyn Garden City (Figures 5.14 and 5.15)
Lemsford Mill, which was the flour mill of the Brocket Hall estate, was rebuilt in 1863 in the form in which it appears today: a four-storey flour mill, part yellow brick, part weatherboarded. It operated as a flour mill until 1911, after which time the building was left empty. The waterwheel is believed to have generated electricity for the mill house. The river Lea flows beneath the building, with a drop of 5' 9" to the mill race. A horizontal turbine was installed in about 1895.

Its first use after its days as a mill was to house a small family business manufacturing electro-magnetic control equipment. The mill building was then refurbished in 2005 by Ramblers Worldwide Holidays.[15] The work included installing a new waterwheel to generate electricity by hydropower. It is a metal wheel with simple wooden paddles which has provided electricity for the needs of a modern office, any surplus being fed into the grid.

Sherriff's Mill, Great North Road, Bull Stag Green, Hatfield
Sherriff's Mill was a steam mill built in 1899 in the then open countryside to the north of Hatfield, adjacent to the GNR. There was a siding to which deliveries of seed, coal and fertiliser were made. It was a grist† mill with three pairs of under-driven stones which were removed at an unknown date and replaced with hammers. At first it was a gas-fired steam mill, the gas for which was produced by an anthracite coking plant. In 1950 the coal business was sold off and the building used as an agricultural store until the company moved to Royston in the 1980s.[16] The building burnt down just before it went to auction. The site is now a housing development.[17]

Figure 5.16 Essendon Mill. HALS.

Essendon Mill, Low Road, Essendon (Figure 5.16)
This is a seventeenth-century watermill and an estate mill of the Cecil estate. It survived as a corn mill until 1925, after which it was used for pumping water to Essendon Water Tower until 1945. The mill building is of three floors with weatherboarded luccam and gabled sack hoist. The estate sold it in 1959, after which it was converted to residential use. No wheel or machinery remains.

Hertford Town Mill, Mill Bridge, Hertford (Figures 5.17 and 5.18)
The mill was demolished in 1967 to make way for a new theatre and arts complex, The Castle Hall (now Hertford Theatre). Few details have survived: at one time it is said to have contained a Poncelet† wheel.[18]

The Old Waterworks, Hartham Lane, Hertford
Paper Mill Ditch seems to have been a mill stream for a mill on the site that became the Hertford Waterworks, but this is the only evidence that a paper mill ever existed here.

Site of Dicker Mill, Mill Road, Hertford East (Plate 30)
The mill was rebuilt after a fire in 1840 as a seed-crushing mill for oil cake. A steam engine was installed in 1858/9. The mill could be served both from the river Lea and from a rail connection. Milling ceased in 1924 and the site is now part of an industrial estate.

CORN MILLING

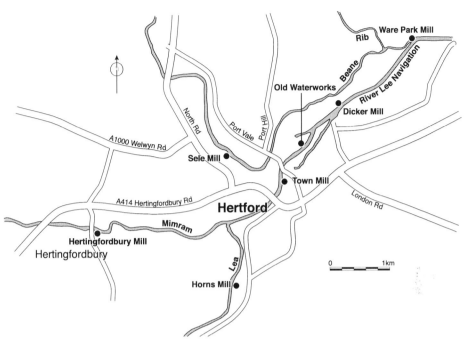

Figure 5.17 Four rivers converge on Hertford, powering several mills.

Figure 5.18 Town Mill, Hertford in 1954. Reproduced by kind permission of David Jones and the Mills Archive.

Figure 5.19 The edge-runner millstones raised from the river in 1982 at Ware Town Mill. Reproduced by kind permission of Glaxo Smith Kline.

Town Mill, Priory Street, Ware (Figures 5.19 and 5.20)
The year 1897 saw the two mills in Ware change hands and their sites redeveloped. J.W. French and Co. bought the mill in Amwell End from Augustus Brown and sold the lease on the mill in Priory Street to Allen and Hanburys Ltd, the well-known pharmaceutical company then based in London. The Priory Street site was owned by the New River Company, which had an interest in diverting water from the Lea into the New River. A new factory was built in 1897 as a production centre for pastilles, capsules and baby food to complement Allen and Hanburys' research facility in Bethnal Green. Two water turbines produced 30 hp of electricity. The millstream runs under the building and rejoins the river in front of Ware Priory. In due course a Thorneycroft steam lorry plied the route between the two centres, carrying baby food and pharmaceuticals.[19]

Allen and Hanburys sold out to Glaxo Smith Kline in 1958.[20] In 1982 three millstones were recovered from the river Lea.[21] They each weigh between 1.5 and 1.75 tons and are 4' 6" in diameter and 15" thick. It has been suggested that two of the stones revolved end-on over the base stone and were used for grinding chemicals. This would suggest that they were used in the 1897 mill before being discarded in the river. They are now on display at the Priory Street premises.

Figure 5.20 A Hertfordshire Mill. *Are these the same stones as at the Ware Town Mill? This pencil drawing by Beatrix Potter shows in remarkable detail the drive train for turning edge-runner millstones.* © *Frederick Warne and Co. 1955.*

Ware Flour Mills, Amwell End, Ware (Figure 5.21)

In 1859 Augustus Brown bought this flour mill in Amwell End. It had a basin with access from the river Lea for unloading grain from barges.[22] The mill had been built in 1851 with five sets of French stones powered by a 16 hp steam engine by Wentworth and Sons. Lacking rollers, the mill went into decline in about 1881/2.

Figure 5.21 Ware Flour Mills today.

John Whyman French built a new and much larger steam-driven roller mill to the north of this mill. The new mill had a luccam on the east side from which sacks of grain could be hoisted direct from barges to the top floor. Power was supplied by a 4 hp electric motor. This plant had about 18 roller mills equipped by Simon Engineering, three purifiers and three plan-sifters, and could produce 40 sacks of flour an hour, equating to approximately 160 tonnes (176 tons) of wheat processed in 24 hours. The mill prospered, producing 'Frenlite' flour, until Spillers bought out J.W. French and closed the mill. Most of the mill complex, including the grain silos and the 1851 mill building, was demolished in 1987 to make way for a new housing development,[23] and the water access was filled in. The later mill building was converted into apartments and a new block of apartments was built on the site of the concrete silos.[24]

Stanstead Abbotts Mill, Roydon Road, Stanstead Abbotts (Figure 1.7)

Stanstead Abbotts Mill is the last before the confluence of the rivers Lea and Stort, and is situated just below the point at which the river Lea turns southwards onto its course through London's East End. This corn mill is an industrial-style watermill built in 1865, following the destruction of its predecessor by fire. It was constructed adjacent to a lengthy mill stream once owned by the New River Company and now by the Environment Agency. Originally it had an external waterwheel on the north side. Steam power was introduced in 1890, but marks remain in the brickwork to show where the wheel once was. Subsequently a turbine was tried, but appears not to have been a success. The tail race has a cast-iron beam dated 1865. The mill is a handsome four-storey yellow-brick building with a slate roof and five arcaded bays on the flank walls and four on the end walls. Various extensions were added, including a boiler house and chimney on the east end which powered a steam engine to provide auxiliary power. These have now all been removed.

In the mid-1890s an unusually long luccam was added. This extended over the mill stream, allowing corn and flour to be raised and lowered between mill and barges as well as grain to be unloaded from horse-drawn carts in the normal way. The fact that grain could be unloaded from barges implies that imported grain was being brought from Surrey Docks direct to the mill and flour was being taken back to supply the London market.

After the mill ceased working in 1926 it was used as a glass factory until 1991. All the machinery was removed at this stage. In 1995 planning permission was granted for conversion to offices and for a new office extension. The permission was conditional on the retention of certain features, including the main bearings of the waterwheel.

On the south side there is an extensive range of maltings belonging to French and Jupp, who now also own the mill building.

Figure 5.22 Broxbourne Mill in 1905. HALS.

Site of Broxbourne Mill, Mill Lane, Broxbourne (Figure 5.22 and 1.9)
This was a handsome four-storey mill, not unlike Ponders End Mill, with a ground floor of brick and timber and weatherboarded upper floors. The site is on a long mill stream which neatly separated millers' and bargemen's interests and thus avoided the disputes that could occur between these parties (as discussed in Chapter 2). The mill is believed to have contained two sets of stones, which ceased working sometime during the 1890s, and was powered with an undershot wheel with elm paddles. It became an engineering works, using the wheel to generate power. The mill was destroyed by fire in 1949, and only some of the ground-floor brickwork survives. The ruins remained untouched until 1977, when the Lee Valley Regional Park Authority began the restoration of the low breastshot waterwheel and sluices. A few walls and the wheel chamber survive. Alongside, in a separate chamber, are the remains of a water turbine.[25]

Corn mills on the river Mimram

The river Mimram is some 12 miles long from its source in the Chilterns, near Whitwell, to its confluence with the Lea at Hertford, over which distance it falls some 120' and flows through Whitwell, Old Welwyn, Digswell, Tewin and Hertingfordbury. There are records or tangible evidence of 12 mills along it, with a concentration in its upper reaches. Most are named after villages. The villages in the area tend to be some distance from the river, and thus the watermills' locations are often quite remote. Some of them have no remains, but the sites are identifiable. These include Pann Mill, Knebworth Mill and Ayot Mill. Kimpton, Codicote, Digswell and Hertingfordbury

Mills have all been converted to dwellings. The latter survived as a corn drying plant throughout the 1950s, a decade of notably wet summers. Mill houses have survived at Whitwell, Old Welwyn and Tewin, although the mills themselves have gone. Waterwheels have survived at Whitwell and Tewinbury.

Whitwell Mill, High Street, Whitwell
The mill house survives. The mill ceased working in 1920 and the building was demolished in 1970. There remains an overshot cast-iron waterwheel measuring 6' 6" in diameter by 6' wide.

Kimpton Mill, Kimpton Road, Codicote (Figure 5.23)
This mill comprises an eighteenth-century vernacular building with a seventeenth-century mill house. The mill stopped working in 1933 and was converted to a dwelling. The waterwheel was in the arch under the building.

Codicote Mill, Codicote Bottom, Welwyn
This mill was worked by the Garratt family, of Sele Mill fame, for most of the nineteenth century, and then by Ben Cole of Hyde Mill in the twentieth century. It was described as a 'steam and water mill' in 1886. The original mill building was demolished in about 1900, leaving little evidence of its existence.[26]

Figure 5.23 Kimpton Mill before conversion to a house. © HBPT.

Site of Welwyn Mill, Mill Lane, Welwyn (Figure 5.24)

The mill was demolished and the waterwheel removed in 1921, but the mill house remains.

Digswell Mill, Digswell Lane, Welwyn Garden City

Digswell Mill is a two-storey vernacular brick building which was converted into a house early in the twentieth century. The last miller did not install rollers, as he considered there was not enough scope for the business to justify the outlay. The wheel was housed in an arch under the house. Until conversion the mill supplied flour to the Three Counties Asylum, which had its own station on the GNR, just north of Letchworth, on the Hertfordshire–Bedfordshire border.

Figure 5.24 The miller and workers at Welwyn Mill shortly before it closed down in 1910. Kindly supplied from the Tony Rook collection.

Figure 5.25 Walkern Mill in the interwar years, showing the mill building, which has since been converted to apartments, and the grain silos, which have been demolished. Reproduced by kind permission of the Mills Archive.

Figure 5.26 Watton Mill in 1912 showing the miller on the stone floor ready to lower sacks of flour onto a wagon. Also clearly visible is the luccam. Reproduced by kind permission of Alan Rattue.

Tewin Bury Farm, Hertford Road, Tewin
Only the waterwheel and parts of the sluice remain under cover and within the grounds of a hotel.

Site of Tewin Mill, Hertford Road, Tewin
This was a substantial mill with four sets of French burr stones, dressing machines and a screw auger for distributing wheat to the appropriate bins, and dust-extracting equipment. It was demolished in the 1970s.[27]

Hertingfordbury Mill, Hertingfordbury Road, Hertingfordbury (Plates 19, 20 and 21)
A former industrial-style steam corn mill dating from 1839, it is of yellow/grey brick with weather-boarded luccam. Milling ceased in 1933 and from the middle of World War II it was used as a corn-drying store. Planning permission was granted in 1992 for conversion to offices and in 1996 for conversion to dwellings. The latter was implemented. Driers and dressers were in place at the time of the conversion, and some elements of grain chutes remain. There is no record of machinery before 1933. The sluice control gear, by Joseph J. Armfield of Ringwood, Hampshire, has been remounted in the front porch.[28]

Corn mills on the Beane

Walkern Mill, High Street, Walkern (Figure 5.25)
Mr A. Pearman acquired the mill in 1855. In 1881 it passed to his son G.D. Pearman, who made substantial alterations in 1900, including the installation of a roller plant by E.R. & F. Turner. There was also a tandem-compound condensing engine, for which an engine house and chimney were built. A grain silo was erected in the 1920s.

This updated equipment was clearly intended to utilise imported grain. It is not known whether the grain came via the Lea to Hertford and then on the well-managed Watton turnpike to Walkern,[29] or whether it came by rail to a siding at Stevenage Station.

The mill prospered until production ceased in 1937. The fabric deteriorated until the mill's acquisition by the present owners, who converted it into three flats between 1979 and 1981.[30] Appendix 8 contains a description of the mill in 1906.

Site of Watton-at-Stone Mill, Mill Lane, Watton-at-Stone (Figure 5.26)
This was a four-storey yellow-brick building dating from 1830. Milling ceased 100 years later and the building was demolished in 1968.

Sele Mill, North Road, Hertford (Figure 10.2)
Sele Mill has an important place in English history, as it was here, towards the end of the fifteenth century, that John Tate became England's first paper-maker. After his death in 1507 Sele Mill reverted to grinding corn. The present buildings date from the

mid-nineteenth century. Steam later supplemented water power and a chimney still stands in the yard.

The mill burnt down in 1890 and was rebuilt and re-equipped by Whitmore and Binyon. Cast-iron columns stamped with that company's name support the floor with all the heavy roller mills, which were supplied by Simon Engineering. The parapet displayed the words SELE ROLLER MILLS in coloured brick. At the same time the waterwheel was replaced by a turbine. A steam engine was installed, although the turbine had ceased to be used by World War II.

The mill's production was approximately two tons per hour. Around 1936 the mill was remodelled and roller mills by T. Robinson and Sons of Rochdale were installed, with an increase in output to three tons per hour.[31] Wheat was by then brought by lorry from Tilbury.

Thomas Garratt bought the mill in 1867 and sold it to his younger brother George in 1877. It remained in the family until it was sold in 1988. The buyers, Spillers, ran the mill for only a few years before closing it down and applying for permission for conversion to flats. All the machinery was sold to developing countries; this was common practice, as it was well made and would last for a long time in its new role.

Corn mills on the river Rib

Braughing Mill, Station Road, Braughing (Figure 5.27)

This was a nineteenth-century steam corn mill dating from around 1870. It worked until 1938, when it was demolished. Sited next to Braughing Station, it enjoyed direct access from a siding.

Figure 5.27 Braughing Mill. A steam mill, owned by Haslers, a corn and seed company based at Dunmow in Essex, enjoying a lineside site. It was demolished in 1938. Kindly supplied from the S. Ruff collection.

Figure 5.28 Standon New Mill in 1913, with the station in the background and a wagon of the Great Eastern Railway adjacent to the internal loading bay. HALS.

Figure 5.29 Wadesmill deteriorating in the 1960s, before conversion to apartments. © HBPT.

Buntingford Mill, Luynes Rise, Buntingford

This is a small watermill with a Grade II* listing on the headwaters of the Rib. The mill is now incorporated into a mill house, where a considerable amount of the original machinery remains.

Gatesbury Mill, Puckeridge

Demolished in 1906. The mill house remains.

Standon Old Mill, Mill End, Standon

Standon gained a charter for a market and achieved a pre-eminence over adjacent towns such as Puckeridge and Buntingford. This may account for its having three watermills and becoming a centre for milling.

Standon Old Mill, a former water-powered corn mill, stands on the east bank of the river. In 1901 the waterwheel was supplemented by steam power, which also powered the new mill on the west bank of the river (below). The waterwheel is gone, but the chimney remains; however, only one wing survives following a fire in 1961.

Standon New Mill, Mill End, Standon (Figure 5.28)

New Mill was built on the site of an earlier mill,[32] of which no details survive, by Messrs Chapman Bros between 1901 and 1905. It was a corn mill of yellow stock bricks with a slated mansard roof and was steam-powered from the start, with a chimney 100' in height. The outdated style is thought to have matched the old mill on the other side of the river. The building had been re-equipped in 1913 with a 'new and up-to-date milling plant',[33] and although a serious fire in 1914 destroyed that part of the building containing silos the milling machinery was undamaged because of a substantial 14" dividing wall. A sale notice of 1936 gives an indication of the power sources and shafts and pulleys, but not of the flour-milling equipment; presumably the mill was equipped with rollers. The notice does show that it enjoyed a private rail siding – off a branch line of the Great Eastern Railway which ran from Hertford to Buntingford and was closed following the Beeching report – which terminated in a loading bay and enabled imported grain to be brought right into the building. At the time the mill was let to British Soya Products Ltd, a newly founded company that had its headquarters on the north side of Puckeridge, and produced several varieties of soya flour until 1994. British Soya Products Ltd acquired Station Mill at Kneesworth Street in Royston in 1960 and subsequently phased out production at Standon (see Chapter 3). It was converted into flats in 2005.[34]

Wadesmill, Ermine Street, Thundridge (Figure 5.29)

This mill was owned by Augustus Brown, who also built the original mill at Amwell End. He sold it to Charles Adams & Co, who ran it until it became

Figure 5.30 Ware Park Mill, at the confluence of the rivers Lea and Rib, showing the external housing for the overshot waterwheels at the turn of the twentieth century. Reproduced by kind permission of the Mills Archive.

economically unviable. In the immediate post-war period it was in a dilapidated and dangerous condition. It has since been converted to apartments, preserving much of its original appearance.[35]

Ware Park Mill, Ware Park Road, Bengeo, Hertford (Figure 5.30)

Adjacent to the existing mill house was the eighteenth-century estate mill for Ware Park mansion, demolished between 1830 and 1840. It was then owned by J.W. French. The mill house was built around 1800, and in 1823 construction began of a new mill to the east. The lower three storeys were of brick and the top two of weatherboarding. A luccam is also apparent in Figure 5.30. The mill was fed by a lengthy leat from the river Rib, turning two 28'-diameter overshot waterwheels that backed onto a substantial retaining wall. They represented 'the pinnacle of waterwheel technology' and would have been very powerful. Steam power, however, was introduced in 1864. The mill building is thought to have been demolished in 1924[36] (see also Chapter 10).

CORN MILLING

Corn mill on the river Ash

Mardock Mill, Wareside
Mill converted to house.

Corn mills on the river Stort

The river Stort rises near Clavering in Essex. It enters Hertfordshire at Bishops Stortford, flowing some 12 miles to its confluence with the river Lea at Rye Meads. From Bishops Stortford it is a navigable waterway which forms the boundary between Hertfordshire and Essex. Some of the mills are in one county and some in the other. In the interests of providing a complete picture of milling on the Stort, some of the more interesting Essex mills have been included below.

Over its navigable distance the river drops some 93' through 15 locks. This relatively steep rate of fall ensured plenty of power for the 13 mills on the river. However, none of these mills had a mill pond and they relied entirely on the water in the pounds between locks to power the waterwheels; the potential for disputes

Figure 5.31 Parsonage Mill, Bishops Stortford, towards the end of the nineteenth century. Kindly supplied by W. Wright from the Ed Goatcher collection.

Figure 5.32 South Mill, Bishops Stortford, in 1905. Kindly supplied by W. Wright from the Ed Goatcher collection.

between millers and bargemen over the use of water was thus particularly acute on the Stort. The management of the river was taken over by the Lee Conservancy in 1902 and the old turf-sided locks rebuilt with modern concrete chambers. This investment was justified by the amount of malting and flour milling taking place primarily in Bishops Stortford and Sawbridgeworth.

All the mills were built of timber on brick foundations and all were powered by breastshot waterwheels. There are surviving mills at, from north to south, Twyford, Hallingbury, Harlow, Latton, Parndon, Hunsdon and Roydon. Those that have been demolished include South Mill in Bishops Stortford and mills at Sawbridgeworth and Sheering. Many of the technical details have been lost, but a letter written in 1949 by Harry Burton of Sawbridgeworth Town Mill provides an indication of the equipment in each of these lost mills.[37]

Parsonage Mill, Cannons Mill Lane, Bishops Stortford (Figure 5.31)
The mill has been demolished but the mill house remains and the site is occupied by a housing estate. The mill had a waterwheel driving, probably, not more than two sets of stones.

South Mill (also known as Garratt's Mill), Mill Street, Bishops Stortford (Figure 5.32)
It had seven bays and a weatherboarded timber frame. There were three pairs of stones driven by a waterwheel. It was demolished around 1910.

Twyford Mill, Pig Lane, Thorley, Bishops Stortford (Figure 5.33)
Twyford Mill operated as a corn mill until World War II and was converted into flats in 1954. It is a three-storey building of rendered brick with a slate roof. The mill race runs under the building. The general outline remains, but neither waterwheel nor machinery has survived.

Figure 5.33 Twyford Mill in 1910. Kindly supplied by W. Wright from the Ed Goatcher collection.

Figure 5.34 Harlow Mill towards the end of the nineteenth century, before conversion. Kindly supplied by W. Wright from the Ed Goatcher collection.

Figure 5.35 Hunsdon Mill, probably in the 1890s, showing corn being delivered both by barge on the Stort Navigation and by farm cart. Kindly supplied by the Hunsdon Local History and Preservation Society.

Hallingbury Mill, Old Mill Lane, Little Hallingbury, Essex
The current building dates from 1874 and worked through until 1952, when production ceased. Although most of the more modern machinery was removed, all the essentials have survived and the mill is in working order. This mill provides an excellent model of how the Stort mills must have been. The low breastshot waterwheel measures 16' in diameter and 7' wide, has 48 buckets and weighs 15 tons. The pit wheel is 14' in diameter and has 160 hornbeam cogs. There were originally four pairs of stones, but only one complete set with appropriate tun and horse and stone furniture remains.[38]

Sawbridgeworth Town Mill (Burtons), Mill Lane, Sawbridgeworth (Figures 1.2 and 2.5)
This was an eighteenth-century timber-framed and weather-boarded corn mill that was rebuilt in 1880 when it was converted to steam power. It was owned by three generations of the Burton family, Thomas, Harry and Owen. It had a tiled roof and luccam, and was still operating in 1970. The surviving eighteenth-century mill house is of similar construction, but has a slate roof; it was built around the buck of an old windmill brought from Harlow between 1820 and 1830. The mill itself was equipped with roller mills. Originally there were two buildings, each with four pairs of stones: six for flour and two for farmers' grist. The waterwheel was replaced by a turbine in 1904, the remains of which can still be seen. The sluice gear, by Ransome and Rapier, is also still in place. The adjacent early nineteenth-century three-storey malt house and granary, of brick with a slate roof, is now a private house. The mill was sold to Garfield Weston in 1962 and stopped working in 1970.[39] It was destroyed by fire in 1977.

Sheering Mill, Sheering Mill Lane, Lower Sheering, Essex
The mill was located on the island between the lock and the weir. It was a typical timber Stort mill which last worked in 1891/2. There is a 9' fall and was a correspondingly large breastshot waterwheel which drove four pairs of stones. The mill was acquired by the Lee Conservancy in 1913 in order to reopen the navigation and rebuild the lock. The mill building was demolished in 1917.

Harlow Mill, Cambridge Road, Harlow, Essex (Figures 5.34)
This mill stopped working in about 1890, when it could no longer compete with roller mills. It is now converted to a hotel. As at Sheering, there was a 9' fall that powered four sets of stones.

Hunsdon Mill, Hunsdon Mead, Hunsdon (Figure 5.35)
This was a tall three-storey weather-boarded mill on a brick base, straddling the river. It was still working in 1902, with roller mills, but was demolished in 1908. An unusually large waterwheel was powered by a 9' fall. Barges were loaded at the river frontage, while farm wagons charged and discharged their loads close to the house at the other end.[40]

WIND, WATER AND STEAM

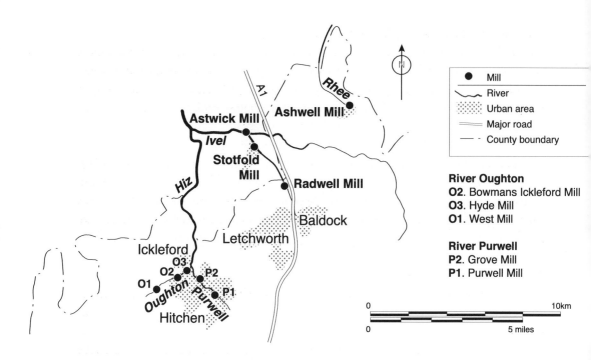

Figure 5.36 The location of corn mills on the tributaries of the Great Ouse.

Figure 5.37 Oughton Head, or West Mill, Ickleford, in the 1930s. Kindly supplied by R. Freeman.

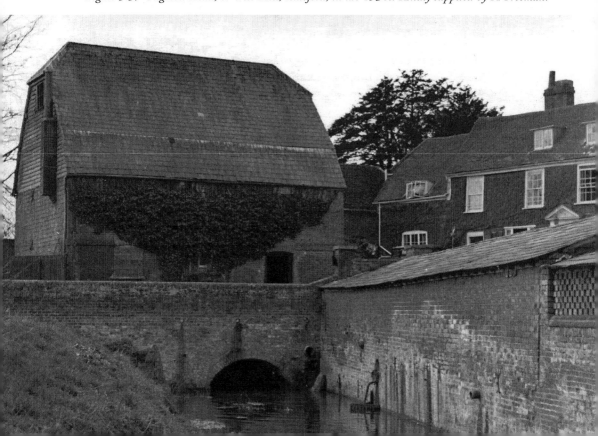

Roydon Mill, High Street, Roydon, Essex

The mill is a four-storey building with a slated mansard roof. The lower two storeys are built in yellow stock brickwork while the upper part is a timber frame clad in plain weatherboarding. A projecting luccam is supported on arched braces over the waterway. A turbine remains, although other machinery, including the roller mills, has been removed.[41]

Corn mills on the rivers Ivel, Hiz, Oughton and Rhee

There are several mills or mill sites on the tributaries of the Great Ouse (Figure 5.36). Most have been converted to houses. The best legacy is on the Oughton Brook and includes Bowman's Ickleford Mill, described in Chapter 3. The brook is barely two miles long, yet it powered three corn mills. However, by the 1860s flows of water were becoming depleted because of the abstraction of groundwater and mill owners were obliged to look for alternative sources of power.

Oughton Head Mill (also known as West Mill), Westmill Lane, Ickleford (Figure 5.37)

This was a two-storey brick and weather-boarded watermill which continued to operate until the 1920s. After this date it became derelict, and was burnt down in 1959. It had an overshot wheel. It appears to have been a very typical rural mill. Phebe Glaisyer recalled in the 1820s what life in this mill was like: 'Sometimes I went into the mill and watched my cousin Stafford chipping away at the great mill stones, or placed my hands under the hopper where warm soft flour was pouring down.'[42]

Hyde Mill, Old Hale Way, Ickleford (Figure 5.38 and Plate 29)

This mill lay at the confluence of the Oughton Brook and the Hiz. The mill house and mill were demolished in the 1930s and 1940s respectively, and their sites have been the subject of a recent archaeological investigation.[43] The positions of the waterwheel, sluice and pit wheel are clearly visible. Parts of the waterwheel have survived, which has made it possible to produce a 'virtual' reconstruction of the mechanism of the mill (see Appendix 3).

Purwell Mill, Purwell Lane, Hitchin (Figure 5.39)

This is a substantial brick-built early nineteenth-century mill which has been converted to dwellings.

Ashwell Mill, Mill Street, Ashwell

This mill was powered by the headwaters of the Rhee, a tributary of the Cam. The mill and mill house are under one roof. The miller went bankrupt in 1895 and his successor installed a steam turbine in an attempt to keep the mill going, but it had ceased working by 1898. The mill section collapsed in the 1960s, but has been rebuilt with a waterwheel from Fordham's Brewery. The remains of a turbine are on site.

Figure 5.38 Hyde Mill, Ickleford, c.1880, with a covered wagon similar to that shown in Figure 1.10. Kindly supplied by R. Freeman.

References

1. 'The direct American flour trade with Europe', *The Miller* (5 July 1875).
2. J.B. Nunn, *The book of Watford* (Watford, 2003).
3. Dean, 'The history of Kings Langley Mill'.
4. P. Ward, 'Corn milling in Dacorum', *Hertfordshire Past*, 29 (1990), pp. 3–14.
5. 'Messrs J.G. Knowles and sons, Bourne End Mills', *The Miller* (4 March 1901).
6. J. and R. Hands, *Bourne End and Boxmoor, old and new* (Boxmoor, 2013).
7. J. Sherwood, 'The changing face of Mill Street', *Berkhamsted Review* (July 2008), pp. 14–15.
8. J. Hunn and B. Zeepvat, 'The Old Mill, Berkhamsted: archaeological investigations', *Hertfordshire Archaeology and History*, 16 (2009), pp. 97–109.
9. 'History of Head Office Building', The Orchid Group.
10. B.D. Adams, 'Park Mills, Bury Dell Lane, Park Street', paper held at St Albans Museum.
11. I. Freeman, *The old order changeth*, The History Publishing Society, Book 5 (Wheathampstead and Harpenden, 1991).
12. P. Titmuss, 'History of Wheathampstead Mill', undated notes.
13. 'John Mathews at Wheathamstead Mill', undated notes from the Wheathamstead History Society.

Figure 5.39 Purwell Mill today. Kindly supplied by Jane Housham.

14 Interview with Peter Titmuss, 18 January 2013.
15 Ramblers Worldwide Holidays, *Reinventing the wheel at Lemsford Mill*.
16 Interview with L. Sheriff at Mill Green Mill, 1983.
17 E. Barber, 'The making of a family business', *Hertfordshire Countryside*, n.d.
18 'Hertford Mills', 2010 leaflet by Hertford Museum.
19 *Hertfordshire Mercury*, 'Peeps into the past' (28 October 1977).
20 *Hertfordshire Mercury*, 'Company Centenary a winning formula' (20 June 1997).
21 *Hertfordshire Mercury*, 'Millstones lifted from river' (10 September 1982).
22 Burgess, 'Amwell End Mill and House'.
23 *Hertfordshire Mercury*, 'Homes at old flour mills?' (5 July 1985).
24 *Hertfordshire Mercury*, 'Old flour mill's future is plain' (8 January 1988).
25 B. Barwick, 'Millstream meanders through Broxbourne', unpublished, 2011.
26 W. Branch Johnson, 'Trouble at Codicote Mill led to Star Chamber', *Hertfordshire Countryside* (June 1968).
27 Inventory of contents of Tewin Mill, 1882.
28 'Men of mark in milling mechanism – Mr Joseph J. Armfield', *The Miller*.
29 G. Curtis, *A chronicle of small beer* (Chichester, 1970).
30 J. Currey, *A mill on the Beane* (C. & J. Currey, Walkern, 2011).
31 Telephone interview with Simon Garratt, 13 February 2013.
32 *Hertfordshire Mercury*, 'Improvements at Standon Mill' (9 February 1895).
33 *Hertfordshire Mercury*, 'Serious fire at Standon' (11 July 1914).
34 Hertfordshire Archaeological Trust, 'The New Mill, Stortford Road', Standon Archaeological Desk Based Assessment and Historic Building Recording 2002 (HCC Ref RNO 1227).
35 *Hertfordshire Mercury* (2 February 1979).
36 S. Wilcox, *The Mill House and Ware Park Mills, Hertford* (BEAMS, 2004) (HCC Ref RNO 1979) and K. Fairclough, 'James Fordham and the construction of Ware Park Mills', *Hertfordshire's Past*, 47 (1999).
37 Transcript of interview with Owen Burton, 30 November 1985.
38 Hallingbury Mill, descriptive pamphlet.
39 Letter from Harry Burton dated 28 March 1949 and *Harlow Citizen*, 'The last bag of flour has been ground at Burton's Mill' (30 January 1970).
40 Essex County Council, 'Hunsdon Mill House', Archaeological desk-based assessment and site inspection, HER 6362.
41 John Samuels, Archaeological Consultants, 'An archaeological survey and record of the corn mill, Roydon Road, Stanstead Abbots', 2000.
42 J. Lucas, *Phebe's Hitchin book* (Hitchin, 2009).
43 Ickleford Parish Council, *The mills of Ickleford* (Ickleford, 2014).

6

Hertfordshire's windmills

'Time and changing economic conditions bid fair to rob us of this hitherto active outstanding landmark.' So wrote Percy Archer in 1923.[1] He was writing about Goff's Oak windmill, but he could equally well have been writing about virtually any other of Hertfordshire's windmills. The county has never been noted for its windmills because of the prevalence of fast-flowing rivers down the dipslope of the Chilterns as an alternative, and more reliable, source of power. Compared with neighbouring counties, Hertfordshire does not, therefore, have a sizeable windmill heritage. Stanley Freese has noted that Hertfordshire had not fared well in the preservation of its windmills,[2] the emphasis being always on watermills. The point is made in a notice of sale of the Barkway smock mill in 1866 that the viability of a windmill depended on its 'distance from Water Power': in other words, windmills were only used in areas where no suitable streams or rivers existed. In 1889/90, for example, Hertfordshire had only 18 windmills, compared with 22 in the smaller county of Bedfordshire and 111 in Cambridgeshire.

The county could, however, boast two of the most spectacularly large windmills in the whole of England. These were the smock mill at Stanstead Abbotts and the tower mill at Much Hadham. Unfortunately, not only have they gone without trace but very little technical information or, indeed, photographic evidence of them has survived. This is greatly to be regretted, as it would have been a source of endless wonder to see how these enormous windmills, which were seven storeys, and over 100' high, were operated.

A concentration of windmill sites exists in the upland parts of the north and east of the county, where there are fewer rivers and streams (Figure 6.1). However, apart from Cromer windmill, described in Chapter 4, there is very little of this heritage to be seen today. Windmills, universally relying on millstones, started to become technologically obsolete from about 1860 onwards. This was not obvious to contemporaries, as several of the most sophisticated tower mills date from then. The decline of windmills in Hertfordshire is similar to that seen in other counties in the South East, and so many have disappeared without trace, unable to compete with the industrial scale and efficiency of steam-driven roller mills.

Such, however, had been the misplaced level of confidence at the time that six new tower windmills were constructed between 1859 and 1861; these were at Goff's Oak,

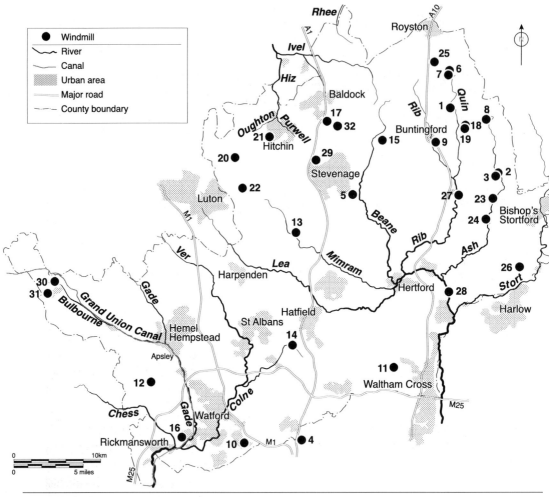

1. Albury, Patmore End, demolished tower mill
2. Anstey, Lincoln Hill, demolished post mill
3. Anstey, Snow End, demolished smock mill
4. Arkley, existing tower mill
5. Aston smock mill, demolished
6. Barkway, Newsells Smock Mill, demolished
7. Barkway, Rokey Post Mill, demolished
8. Brent Pelham, existing smock mill
9. Buntingford Post Mill, demolished
10. Bushey Heath, Smock Mill, demolished
11. Cheshunt, Goff's Oak tower mill, demolished
12. Chipperfield Common Smock Mill, demolished
13. Codicote Heath Smock Mill, site of
14. Colney Heath Tower Mill, converted
15. Cromer Post Mill
16. Croxley Green Tower Mill, converted
17. Gravely Smock Mill, site of
18. Great Hormead post mill, site of
19. Great Hormead Smock Mill, site of
20. Great Offley Tower Mill
21. Hitchin, Lucas Windmill, Gaping Hills, site of
22. King's Walden, Breachwood Green Tower Mill
23. Little Hadham Smock Mill, site of
24. Much Hadham Tower Mill, site of
25. Reed, Mile End Tower Mill, converted
26. Sawbridgeworth, High Wych Post mill, site of
27. Standon Smock Mill, demolished
28. Stanstead Abbots Glenmire Smock Mill, site of
29. Stevenage, Corey's Mill, site of
30. Tring, Gamnel End Tower Mill, site of
31. Tring, Goldfield Tower Mill, converted
32. Weston, Lannock Tower Mill, converted

Figure 6.1 The location of Hertfordshire's windmills. The majority are concentrated in the north-east, where there are few rivers.

Figure 6.2 Goff's Oak tower mill towards the end of its life in 1900, boarded up and missing fantail and shutters. Reproduced by kind permission of Hertford Museum.

Breachwood Green, Patmore Heath, Great Offley, Croxley Green and Weston. These mills embodied the latest technology and were correspondingly expensive investments. Although they represent the final evolution of the windmill, their dependence on millstones meant, as already noted, that they were obsolete within a very short time. They can hardly have repaid the initial investment and there are several examples of millers who ran windmills going bankrupt during this period. In the latter part of the nineteenth century windmills were less and less able to provide sufficient income to support a family. Cyril Moore quotes the case of the Rayson family of Goff's Oak (Figure 6.2):[3]

> One cannot resist commenting that it would be extremely unlikely that a windmill in the last quarter of the 19th century would provide a living for such a household plus 3 employees. Indeed, whoever owned the mill in 1885, was declared bankrupt and the windmill ... put up for auction on 18th May that year.

In his book *Hertfordshire windmills and windmillers*, published in 1999, Cyril Moore has traced the decline of Hertfordshire's windmills. He listed 46 windmills and concluded, describing the situation in 1862, that 'there were at least thirty four windmills in use that year'. Indeed, up until 1875 several new mills were built and others rebuilt, and there are many instances of the installation of portable steam engines and gas engines from 1870 onwards. This had the advantage of avoiding the expensive maintenance of the sails and drive systems while enabling millers to obtain some residual use from obsolete millstones, if only for providing animal feed. But from then on decline was rapid. Moore reports that in 1876 only 25 windmills were still in use, and ten years later this figure had shrunk to 17, four of which were then steam-powered. In part this decline occurred because the tower and smock† mills built in the 1850s were much more efficient than the small post mills that they had displaced. However, by 1899 only 13 were still working, and in the next three years those at Patmore Heath, Anstey (two), Bushey Heath, Goff's Oak, Croxley Green and Breachwood Green stopped working. Only those at Cromer, Arkley, Colney Heath, Weston and Tring (both Gamnel and Goldfield) were still in use. By 1914 Hertfordshire had only seven windmills still working. The intervention of World War I meant that imported grain was in short supply and the soft English wheat was again in demand. In consequence, five windmills enjoyed an Indian summer: Arkley, Cromer, Little Hadham, the smock mill at Great Hormead and Patmore Heath. This respite was short-lived and by 1930 no windmills were in use. Little Hadham, the last working windmill in the county, ceased work when a sail blew off in 1929. A report for the Society for the Protection of Ancient Buildings in 1932 showed that the few survivors were no longer using wind power: 'only the smock mills at Little Hadham and Much Hormead (*sic*) (both damaged and mutilated in gales a year or two earlier) and the tower mill at Weston, also without sails, were occasionally grinding for grist by mechanical means.'[4]

The aim of this chapter is to give an impression of Hertfordshire's windmill heritage by concentrating on those mills for which there is some evidence – often incomplete – of their existence. They illustrate the technological advances in the construction of windmills, their shortcomings and their rapid decline over a relatively few years.

The earliest windmills, post mills, were fairly simple structures that could be bodily moved, as in the case of the Lucas windmill at Gaping Hills, just to the west of Hitchin (see below). Several were updated in the 1860s with patent sails and tail rotors. Cromer windmill remains the outstanding example of a post mill: indeed, no others have survived.

A post mill is so called because the whole of the large wooden body, or buck, including the machinery and sails, can rotate on a large central post, allowing the sails to face into the wind. Although only Cromer windmill survives, evidence for the exterior of many post mills exists in the form of photographs and paintings by such artists as Samuel Lucas (1805–1870), James Wilcox (1778–1865) and Sidney Massie (1801–1891), all in Hertfordshire collections, which give a good impression from the pre-photographic era of what the primitive post mills were like.

Despite the paucity of windmills in the county, a good selection of smock mills – timber structures on a brick base – did exist, typically spanning the period from the late eighteenth century until the 1860s. They were cheaper to build than tower mills (below). Of these, only Brent Pelham Mill survives. Finally, there were the tower mills, many of which were obsolete almost before they were built. A static brick tower with a revolving frame at the top carrying the sails, the tower mill was the technologically superior successor of the post mill. The earliest ones date from the 1820s, and no more were built after the 1860s apart from the extraordinary example at Much Hadham. Several of the masonry towers have survived, but without their vulnerable caps and sails. The only surviving tower mill in a reasonably complete state is at Arkley, once in Hertfordshire, now in the London Borough of Barnet. Several other towers do remain, some of which, such as those at Weston, Reed, Colney Heath, Tring (Goldfield) and Breachwood Green, have been converted into houses.

Fading memories
Hertfordshire's post mills
Site of post mill, Downhall Field, Windmill Hill, Buntingford (Plate 25)
Lying to the south-east of Buntingford, off the London Road, this was a very basic post mill with four common† sails and an open trestle. It burnt down in 1885. Clearly, at that stage, there would have been no case for replacing it.

Site of Lucas windmill, Gaping Hills, Hitchin

The Lucas family were farmers, maltsters and brewers. The family also included several artists, who produced a number of detailed pictures of windmills. The windmill at Gaping Hills, to the west of Hitchin, was a simple two-storey post mill initially with an open trestle. Samuel Lucas painted the mill twice. The first of his paintings shows an open trestle; the second that the mill had acquired a roundhouse. It had four common sails and a tail post. It was destroyed around 1850.

In 1820 the mill was moved some 450 yards to a more exposed site. An interesting insight into how this was achieved is provided by George Beaver:

> In former days there was a windmill, the property of Messrs Joseph and William Lucas, the Brewers, of those days;- standing in the open field land between the 'Manly Highway and the Offley Road', at about 100 yards from the south west corner of the Mount Pleasant Plantations: About the year 1820 or 1821 (date not certain) this mill was removed, bodily, to a new site on Gaping Hills (a distance of about 450 yards, or say ¼ mile) whole as it stood, in full working order; stones, machinery and sails – the motive power was 36 horses, viz (six abreast and six ahead), it was raised bodily by screw jacks, and a frame and on 4 wheels, built under it:- then bound again onto its frame-bed, and removed by these 36 horse power:- the ground from point to point was cleared of all fences, banks or ditches, to such a width as was requisite, and the mill gradually drawn to and safely deposited on, its new foundation. The removal took place on a Saturday, and we boys in Mr Billinghurst's Academy, as also those in 'Jacky Newton's' School, both in Tilehouse Street, had a whole days holiday purposely to go see this wonderful feat. The Engineer or conductor of the operation was one 'Martin' a working millwright then living in Back Street, Hitchin …[5]

Site of Corey's post mill, Corey's Mill Lane, Stevenage (Plate 26)

Lying in what are now the grounds of Lister Hospital at the northern extremity of Stevenage New Town, this was a post mill with four common sails and a thatched roundhouse. It burned down in 1878. This mill, too, was the subject of a painting by Samuel Lucas (see cover). As was commonly done, he has exercised a degree of artistic licence with the background: in this case, a broad navigable river has appeared to the north of Stevenage! However, the detailing of the windmill appears to be authentic. It shows a primitive post mill, which could be turned to face the wind by using its tail pole†. The mill has plain sails, two of which are under repair. One has the sail cloth furled and one has it spread. The miller is repairing the laths† and his wife is working on a new sail cloth. Sidney Massie's painting corroborates the detail of the Lucas painting, with furled cloth sails. However, she has omitted the tail pole and included a porch at the rear of the mill.

Plate 1 (above)
Mill Green Mill today.

Plate 2 (left)
The great spur wheel and stout timber hurst frame at Mill Green.

Plate 3 Moor Mill in 1990, before its conversion to a restaurant, with the embankment of the M25 just visible in the background. Reproduced by kind permission of Susan Watts.

Plate 4 The stone floor at Moor Mill before conversion. The millstones and much of the machinery have been retained in the conversion. Reproduced by kind permission of Susan Watts.

Plate 5 The unusual lay-shaft arrangement at Redbournbury. Reproduced by kind permission of Justin James.

Plate 6 Redbournbury Mill today.

Plate 7 An axiometric representation of the machinery at Redbournbury. Reproduced by kind permission of J. Brandrick.

Plate 8 The stone floor at Redbournbury. Reproduced by kind permission of Justin James.

Plate 9 Hyde Mill, on the upper reaches of the river Lea.

Plate 10 Upper Mill, Berkhamsted, around the turn of the twentieth century. Reproduced by kind permission of Dacorum Museum.

Plate 11 Cromer Mill today.

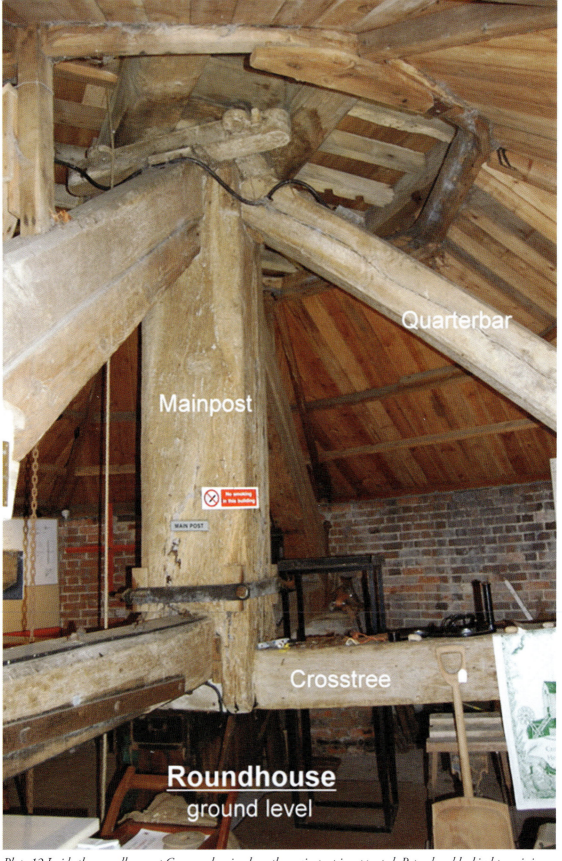

Plate 12 Inside the roundhouse at Cromer, showing how the main post is supported. Reproduced by kind permission of R. Webb.

Plate 13 The meal floor at Cromer, showing the 'stone nuts' which drive the 'underdriven' stones and the chutes that deliver flour from the millstones into the sacks below. Reproduced by kind permission of R. Webb.

Plate 14 The stone floor at Cromer, showing the brake wheel, wallower and millstones. Reproduced by kind permission of R. Webb.

Plate 15 (left) The 'Fairbairn' waterwheel at the hydraulic press house at the Royal Gunpowder Mills.

Plate 16 (below) The waterwheel at Hunton Bridge Mill.

Plate 17 (left) The mill wheel at Sopwell Mill in 1990. Reproduced by kind permission of Martin Watts.

Plate 18 (above) The waterwheel at Redbournbury today.

Plate 19 (left) Hertingfordbury Mill before conversion in 1990. Reproduced by kind permission of Susan Watts.

Plate 20 (below) Hertingfordbury Mill after conversion.

Plate 21 (above) The preserved controls for the penstock at Hertingfordbury Mill.

Plate 22 Wheathamstead Mill today.

Plate 23 Roydon Mill today. Kindly supplied by Chris Howes.

Plate 24 (above) The Water Mill, c.1815–20, a watercolour of Bushey Mill by William Henry Hunt (1790–1864). Reproduced by kind permission of the Trustees of the Cecil Higgins Art Gallery, Bedford.

Plate 25 (right) Buntingford Windmill, *1843, a watercolour by James Wilcox. This was a basic post mill with plain sails and an open trestle. Reproduced by kind permission of Hertford Museum.

Plate 26 Corey's Mill, Stevenage, *1850, by Sidney Massie. Reproduced by kind permission of Stevenage Museum.*

Plate 27 Welch's Windmill, Gaping Hill, *1840–65, by Samuel Lucas. This picture poses a mystery. The windmill on Gaping Hills was a post mill and not the smock mill shown here. Was there a plan to transfer Welch's Mill at Codicote to Gaping Hills? Reproduced by kind permission of North Hertfordshire Museum Services.*

Plate 28 (above) Rowley's Mill, Ickleford, *1864*, by Samuel Lucas. Reproduced by kind permission of North Hertfordshire Museum Services.

Plate 29 Ickleford Mill, *1880, by E.M. Seebohm.*

Plate 30 Sailing Barge at Dicker Mill, Hertford, *a late nineteenth-century painting by Edgar Wigram (1864–1935). Reproduced by kind permission of the Hertford Museum.*

Site of Barkway post mill (also known as Rokey Mill), Windmill Close, Barkway (Figure 6.3)

This mill, built in about 1819/20, stood at the end of Windmill Close, to the north-west of the village. It had an octagonal roundhouse and was described in auction particulars as:[6]

> A newly erected substantial POST MILL well situated for wind in every direction at the north end of the town of BARKWAY containing a capital pair of French stones, 5 feet high, with all other necessary going gear and tackle in the most complete order with Miller's Cottage plus about 1 acre and 2 roods of rich land.

It appears to have been demolished in about 1903.

Figure 6.3 Barkway post mill in 1905, shortly before demolition. From the state of the sails it had been out of use for some time. Kindly supplied from the Tom Doig collection.

Figure 6.4 Hertfordshire's 'Jack and Jill'. The post and smock mills at Great Hormead c.1928: out of use, but before serious decay had set in. Reproduced by kind permission of Hertford Museum.

Site of Anstey post mill, Lincoln Hill, Anstey
Lincoln Hill lies to the west of the village of Anstey. This was a post mill of similar design to those at Cromer, Chishill (in Cambridgeshire) and Barkway, with an octagonal roundhouse. It featured the less common clockwise sails. It worked until 1902 and was demolished in 1920.

Site of Great Hormead post mill, off Anderson's Lane, Great Hormead (Figure 6.4)
This was one of a pair of windmills, one post mill and one smock mill, which stood in a remote location on an exposed ridge to the north of the village. The post mill dated from the late eighteenth or early nineteenth century. It had a white painted buck with an unusual 16-sided weatherboarded roundhouse, two pairs of French stones, one in the breast and one in the tail, and four single-sided shuttered spring sails, but the mill was turned by the traditional tail pole. This would suggest that the mill was partially upgraded in the 1860s, when windmills still appeared to have a future. It ceased working in 1924/5. It was described in 1938 in the following terms: 'Hormead, disused weatherboards clinking and sails perishing, but internally in good condition, the last specimen of a complete Hertfordshire post mill.'[7] It collapsed in the 1940s.

Figure 6.5 High Wych windmill in 1870, shortly before the mill was removed to Little Dunmow. Kindly supplied by W. Wright.

Figure 6.6 The smock mill at Little Hadham in 1927. Reproduced by kind permission of Hertford Museum.

Site of High Wych post mill, High Wych Road, Sawbridgeworth (Figure 6.5)
The mill stood at the junction of Broadfields and High Wych Road. The photograph of this windmill shows an entirely unmodernised mill, clearly in good condition, just before the bad harvests of the 1870s undermined the viability of such mills. Indeed, at the time it must have had sufficient value to justify its removal to Little Dunmow, some 15 miles away. There were four common sails and it is shown with the cloths furled. The covered wagon also points to the operation of the mill being firmly anchored in the past. The adjoining mill cottage survived until the 1920s, but there is no evidence of the mill today.

Hertfordshire's smock mills
At one time the north-east of the county was noted for a fine collection of smock mills. At the peak of corn milling at the end of nineteenth century the county had around 12 examples. The only one to survive, and that only in part, is at Brent Pelham.

Site of Glenmire smock mill, Glenmire Terrace, Stanstead Abbotts
Cyril Moore suggests that this must have been the largest smock mill in the county and the second largest of all Hertfordshire's windmills. It was a seven-storey smock mill built around 1760–70. Four storeys were of brick and three of timber. It was presumably modernised, as it had four double-shuttered sails controlled by a chain from a gallery on the third floor and a fantail. It was situated on the wharf on the mill cut, from where the flour would be taken by barge to the London markets.

Richard Hunt wished to sell it in order to concentrate on the Much Hadham estate, where he built the tower windmill described below. The sale notice in 1891 stated:

> WINDMILL FIELD, situate in High-Street, with six floor WINDMILL fitted with crown wheel and two pairs of stones. Wheelwrights' and Carpenters' shop etc. A large proportion of the land is adapted for and ripe for building purposes.[8]

It was reported to be in a poor state of repair in 1921 and demolished about that time. No trace remains and there is very little photographic evidence of it.

Site of Little Hadham smock mill, Standon Road, Little Hadham (Figure 6.6)
This fine smock mill stood to the north-west of the village, north of Standon Road and west of Albury Road. A planning appeal in 1980 against the local authority's decision to refuse permission for its demolition, and the subsequent public inquiry, yielded much detailed information about it. It was built in the late eighteenth century and was a five-storey smock mill with four spring sails which were blown off in 1929. It last worked in 1941. Stanley Freese wrote: 'There was a very fine smockmill with

spring sails and a very wide gallery working at Little Hadham till 1928 when a windshaft broke in a gale and the sweeps were hurled to the ground.' One witness at the public inquiry described it in glowing terms:

> I was profoundly impressed by the superb craftsmanship, proportions, full extent of internal machinery, and its position in relation to the village. Undoubtedly the general external appearance is poor, but this is certainly not the worst example of dereliction that I have seen, and many mills have been saved from a comparable condition, and with far worse structural problems …
>
> The construction shows craftsmanship of unsurpassed quality. The great majority of the framing is oak, and no mill that I have seen includes a more thorough attention to detail and arrangement for a complete flour milling complex. This is a typical, but now exceptionally rare example. Nearly all of the prime and auxiliary machinery remains, complete with mill stones and a good deal of everyday clutter of a mill which is so important in considering whether an old mill is worth preserving.[9]

The appeal against the decision of East Hertfordshire District Council to refuse permission for demolition of the mill was dismissed in July 1981. The inspector's report read:

> I am of the opinion that the appeal building is of historic and architectural importance and, if restored, would make a significant contribution to the character and appearance of Little Hadham. I am of the view that no sufficiently compelling reasons have been advanced to justify its demolition.
>
> No attempt has been made to seek financial or other assistance, and I consider that, until such avenues have been explored, the demolition of the remaining structure would be premature.[10]

Restoration was estimated at £100,000 and negotiations had been proceeding for the mill to be re-erected at the Chilterns Open Air Museum at Chalfont,[11] but the mill was destroyed by fire shortly afterwards and only the red-brick base remained. The Hertfordshire Constabulary was unable to determine whether the fire had been caused by accident or by a criminal act.[12]

Chipperfield smock mill, Windmill Hill, Chipperfield Common
Built in 1820, this five-storey smock mill ceased grinding corn by wind power in 1864.[13] A notice of sale on 4 August 1828 describes it as:

Figure 6.7 Bushey Heath smock mill in 1904. The site was in Windmill Lane. Kindly supplied by the Mills Archive from the Max Hoather collection.

Figure 6.8 An early photograph of the smock mill at Graveley. Kindly supplied by the Mills Archive from the Harry Meyer collection.

Figure 6.9 Brent Pelham smock mill today.

> Excellent newly-erected four story smock windmill
> With Stones, Gears, and Apparatus complete

This is followed by more details:

> The Property comprises a capital brick and timber built Smock Windmill in excellent repair, having been erected within these few years at a very considerable expense, with two pairs of Stones, dressing Machines and all requisite Apparatus, in complete order; containing 5 Floors (including the Ground Floor), and all other necessary Conveniences, together with Desirable Plot of Ground surrounding the same containing in the whole about One Acre, upon which is a stable and Cart Hovel.

The mill was demolished during the 1880s or 90s.

Site of Bushey Heath smock mill, Windmill Street, Bushey Heath (Figure 6.7)
This was a five-storey smock mill with a two-storey octagonal roundhouse. There were four single-shuttered patent sails and an external staging at second-floor level. The mill was demolished in 1910. The site is now a housing estate.

Site of Graveley smock mill, Jacks Hill, Graveley (Figure 6.8)
This was a smock windmill located in open countryside some distance to the north of the village on the old Great North Road (now the B197). It was built around 1825 and burned down around 1884.

There were probably four common sails. Figure 6.8 shows that two have been replaced with double-shuttered sails, possibly at the same time that a steam engine was installed in 1880. There were two pairs of millstones. The cap was turned by an inside handle.

Brent Pelham smock mill (Figure 6.9)
Situated to the north of Cole Green Farm, this is the sole surviving smock mill in Hertfordshire. A stone above one of the doorways suggests that the mill was built in 1826 by William Halden, who owned the Brent Pelham estate. It is quite a small mill, with an octagonal brick base and a timber structure above. In 1860 there was a petition to erect a steam engine which, however, was never built. It appears that the mill was not well sited for exposure to the wind. Milling ceased around 1890, and the mill was subsequently converted to a feed store above which was a water tower supplied by a wind-driven pump. However, mains water was supplied in 1947 and the need for the water tank ceased. The corrugated-iron cladding dates from about 1900 and seems to have preserved the structure well. The inside is clad with tongued and grooved boarding, meaning that it is not possible to see the structural timbers, but

Figure 6.10 Snow End smock mill, Anstey, shortly before demolition in 1889. Kindly supplied from the Tom Doig collection.

all the machinery is long gone and a grain hopper on the ground floor may date only from the time of its use as a feed store. In 1938 a Gloucester Gauntlet aircraft is said to have collided with it, to the detriment of the plane.

Site of Great Hormead smock mill, off Anderson's lane, Great Hormead
This was a small octagonal four-storey smock mill of tarred weatherboarding on brick footings. It stood next to the post mill at Great Hormead (see above). Its exact date is not known, but it appears to have been built in the mid-nineteenth century, at the same time that the adjacent post mill was upgraded, reflecting commercial optimism. There were four single-sided patent sails, an eight-bladed fantail and two pairs of stones. It appears that poor access may have hastened the decline of both mills.

These mills were both operated by Joseph Scowen of Cromer windmill in 1907/8. Unsuccessful attempts were made to sell both mills in 1908, and by 1929 they were reported to be in poor condition. In 1930 a gale removed the cap, sails, windshaft and brake wheel of the smock mill, which continued to be used for a short time afterwards powered by a steam tractor.

Site of Barkway smock mill (also known as Newsells Mill), Royston Road, Barkway
This smock mill was sited to the north of the village between the Cambridge and Royston roads. It was described in a sale notice of 1866 as:

> Having Storage for 150 quarters of corn, with Patent Sails, driving 2 pairs of capital French Stones, Flour Machine and Hoist, Iron Shafting and Gearing, driven by 5 horse power portable steam engine (put in new 3 years since), the whole in good working order.[14]

The sale was successful, perhaps on the basis of an 'established grist trade', and the mill changed hands for £360. However, by 1900 it had closed for business and it had ceased working altogether by the time of World War I.

Site of Anstey smock mill, Snow End, Silver Street, Anstey (Figure 6.10)
This smock mill, situated to the south of the village, was built in 1860, struck by lightning in 1919 and demolished in 1921. No technical details appear to have survived.

Standon smock mill, Hadham Road, Standon
This was a three-storey octagonal timber-built tower on brick footings. It had a boat-shaped cap with two common and two spring sails. It stood to the south of the village, off the Hadham Road. There is no evidence of its construction date. It is believed to have had two pairs of stones and a fantail. During the nineteenth century there was a combined corn-milling and bread-baking business here.

Figure 6.11 Reed tower mill in 1910, in a derelict state. Kindly supplied from the Tom Doig collection.

The mill continued to work until 1895. However, the addition of steam power to the watermills in Kents Lane meant that the windmill ceased to be competitive from 1880 onwards. By 1918 it had lost its sails and by 1930 it had been demolished.

There are two other sites in Standon that may have been smock mills but for which there is no conclusive evidence.

Site of smock mill on Codicote Heath
Cyril Moore believes that there may have been a smock mill with a date of 1840 to the east of Codicote and north of the river Mimram. He suggests that it was owned by the Garratts of Sele Mill, Hertford, and leased to George Welch from 1855. Could this be the Welch's Mill shown in the picture by Samuel Lucas (see Plate 27)? Was there a proposal to move it to Gaping Hills, which is clearly the view painted by Lucas?

Site of Aston smock mill, Brookfield Lane, Aston
There is said to have been a smock mill at Aston with two pairs of stones which stopped working by 1871. It appears to have been destroyed shortly afterwards.

Hertfordshire's tower mills
The Windmill, Mile End Farm, Reed (Figure 6.11)
The name of the farm derives from the mill's location one mile south of Royston. The mill was built *c.*1820 and described in an advert for a tenant in 1886 as 'A large brick tower WINDMILL, consists of two pairs of mill stones, 4 ½ feet, in good condition.' It had double-sided patent sails and a conical roof and operated until 1890. In 1970 it was described by Arthur Smith as being in very poor condition, with no sails. It was converted as part of a house in the 1970s, when the top storey was removed.

Site of Gamnel End tower mill, Tringford Road, Tring (Figure 6.12)
Built in 1826, beside the Wendover Arm of the Grand Union Canal, this six-storey tower mill had a stage gallery at second-floor level. The latest technology of the time was used, including double-shuttered patent sails and fantail. It was powerful enough to drive three sets of millstones. The output would have been impressive in 1830, but was no match for its new neighbour, Mead's steam mill (see Figure 3.4), by 1900. It was used until 1911, when it was pulled down to enable the roller-mill building to be extended (see Figure 1.3).

Arkley tower mill (also known as Barnet Gate Mill), Barnet Road, Arkley (Figure 6.13)
Built in 1826, this is a four-storey brick-built tower. A steam engine had been installed by 1895. Originally with four sails, it ran on two until 1914, when it ceased working for good. It fell into disrepair and by 1930 the mill was in 'a very bad condition', according to a report by Rex Wailes, the noted molinologist. The new owner, Cecil

Figure 6.12 The Gamnel End windmill beside Mead's steam mill, Tring. HALS.

Figure 6.13 A postcard from c.1900 shows the Arkley windmill in a derelict state. HALS.

Figure 6.14 Goldfield windmill, Tring, with a complete set of sails, showing the fantail and gear for turning the cap manually. HALS.

Figure 6.15 The mill at Breachwood Green, showing the aperture created to remove the machinery and timbers. © HBPT.

Harmsworth, carried out the restoration of the cap, fantail and gallery. New sails were added in 1960. An estimate at that time from R. Thompson, Millwright and General Engineer of Alford, Lincs, detailed the costs of the restoration.

One new sail Back in Columbian pine	£180.00
Two new common sails	£160.00 each

Further restoration was carried out in 1984/5 and two more sails added. Otherwise, machinery is missing except for the great spur wheel, iron windshaft, wallower and one pair of stones.

Goldfield tower mill, Icknield Way, Tring (Figure 6.14)

This four-storey mill dates from the late 1830s. It had four double-shuttered patent sails, a fantail and a mechanism for winding† the mill by hand. A sale notice of 1876 indicates that it had three pairs of stones. Despite its elevated position, it does not seem to have been very successful, apparently operating beyond its economic life with support from the Rothschilds, as was the case with the Tring Silk Mill. The sails were removed around 1906–8, when it was converted to steam power, and it worked on until the 1920s. It was derelict at the time of Arthur Smith's survey in 1970. Little survives of the machinery except the wooden great spur wheel, a single stone nut and some of the caster wheels for the cap. It was converted into part of a house in 1970 and the replacement cap contains windows which take advantage of the views across the Vale of Aylesbury towards Mentmore.[15]

Remains of tower mill, Luton Road, Great Offley

Built on the site of a post mill in 1855, this mill had five storeys and four double-shuttered patent sails. It ceased grinding by wind in 1895. Of red brick with a conical roof, it has since been reduced to two storeys.

Breachwood Green tower mill (also known as Darley Hall Mill), King's Walden (Figures 6.15 and 10.5)

Located to the north of The Heath, this tower mill, built in 1859/60, was approximately 45' high. Grinding corn by wind power had ceased by 1900. It was described by Branch Johnson in 1967[16] as a derelict empty shell open to the weather and by Arthur Smith in 1970 as being close to collapse. A large opening had been made, allegedly by explosives, in order to extract the timbers and remaining machinery. The ogee cap was removed, leaving the remains of curb, frame and portion of fantail structure in position.

Nevertheless, Grade II listed status was accorded in 1978. In 1986 Millwrights International carried out a survey and recommended minimal restoration to make it weather-tight by providing a new cap, at a cost of £10,000.[17] It was then consolidated

Figure 6.16 Croxley Green windmill in 1970 © HBPT.

but remained an empty unroofed shell without sails until it was converted to a house in the 1990s.

Croxley Green tower mill, Windmill Drive, Croxley Green (Figure 6.16)
Located to the north of Scots Hill, this mill, a red-brick four-storey tower 50' high, dates from the 1860s. A deed of 1877 refers to a steam engine and steam boilers. The sails were lost in 1880 and from then on it was powered by steam until 1898, when the comparative weakness of millstones rendered the whole operation uneconomic. It was then converted to a house, a fairly typical fate for a Hertfordshire windmill.[18]

Lannock tower mill, Hitchin Road, Weston (Figure 6.17)
Built in 1860, this was – and still is – a very fine 60' tower mill of five storeys, described, when it was advertised for sale by auction on 10 September 1887, as 'one of the best windmills in the county'. It has an ogee-shaped cap with a ball-topped finial and four large round-headed windows with cast-iron frames in each of the second, third and fourth floors, with one in the fifth. It had four single-shuttered patent sails and an eight-bladed fantail. There were three pairs of stones on the second floor and a small pair of stones on the first, which were driven by a 10 hp auxiliary steam engine.[19]

It worked by wind power and gas engine until 1924. The sails and machinery were removed in 1928 and the cap in 1946, when a concrete roof was installed. It then remained derelict until it was converted into a house.

Colney Heath tower mill, Coursers Road, Colney Heath (Figure 6.18)
Built around 1860, this brick tower is 30' high and capped with a rendered-brick dome. It was advertised for auction in 1890, when the sails had been removed and it was run by steam. Working ceased in 1910. It was gutted of all machinery, but the tower was described as being 'in remarkably good condition' when surveyed in 1970. It is Grade II listed, and has now been restored and converted into part of a dwelling.[20]

Site of tower mill, Orchard Way, Goff's Oak, near Cheshunt
Built in 1860 on the site of a post mill to the north-west of the village, 'on a commanding elevation' 430' above sea level, the mill was six storeys and 85' high. Following the bankruptcy of the owner, it was put up for sale in 1885. The undated sale particulars indicate that it had two pairs of French stones, one pair of Peak stones, patent sails and a double fantail. There was also a 'capital dwelling house' and 'large yard containing therein – two stall stable, chaise house, hay and wagon barn, piggery and fowls' house'. The mill last worked at the turn of the twentieth century. In late 1918 one sail blew off, and for safety the other three, each 35' long and 9' wide, were at once dismantled; the cap was lost in 1921 and the mill was finally demolished in 1953/4.[21] There was also a steam mill in the village on Cuffley Hill. This was shown on the 1873 Ordnance Survey

Figure 6.17 'One of the best windmills in the county': Lannock Mill, Weston, c.1920s. Reproduced by kind permission of the Mills Archive from the Harry Meyer collection.

but otherwise no details appear to have survived. It was believed to have been built to supplement the Goff's Oak windmill during windless periods.

Site of Patmore Heath tower mill, Albury

Built in 1857 to the north of the village, this was a tall slender six-storey brick tower mill believed to have had three pairs of stones, four double-shuttered patent sails and an ogee cap with ball finial and fantail. A lightning strike in 1919 downed one sail, bringing its working life to an end, and the mill was demolished in 1921. Very little in the way of technical details or even good photographic records of the mill have come to light; however, a press report does illustrate the hazards of a working windmill:

> A fatal accident occurred at the windmill at Patmore Heath near Albury which resulted in the death of the proprietor Mr Julius Holder. The mechanism of the sails was out of order and Mr Holder mounted to the top of the structure to do the repairs although his wife earnestly entreated him to leave the work until daylight. Whilst so engaged a pulley which was sustaining him snapped and he was thrown to the ground falling a distance of sixty feet. When picked up he was in a dying condition and expired in a short time.[22]

Figure 6.18 Colney Heath windmill before conversion. © HBPT.

Figure 6.19 A rare photograph of the tower mill at Much Hadham, c.1900, near the end of its very short life. Kindly supplied from the S. Ruff collection.

Site of Much Hadham tower mill, Millers View, Much Hadham (Figure 6.19)

'A new windmill for driving mill stones is, we hear, now in course of erection at Hadham, Hertfordshire' stated *The Miller* in 1893.[23] No doubt this was a considerable surprise, as no new windmills had been built in the previous 30 years. The rationale for building this huge windmill, standing to the south-west of the village, adjacent to the site of Much Hadham station, is not clear. Richard Hunt, a wealthy retired miller and the owner of the giant smock mill at Stanstead Abbotts, commissioned it. Was it just a whim or folly? It could hardly have hoped to compete against modern roller mills and had a very short working life.

It appears to have been the last corn windmill to be built in the country and one of the tallest, at 115' to the top of the finial. It had eight patent sails built by Saunderson's of Louth. The company's records have all been destroyed, leaving uncertainty about its machinery. It probably had four sets of stones, but apparently there was no auxiliary power. The sails were removed in 1905/6 after a dispute with the Great Eastern Railway, because they allegedly overhung the railway line. The internal machinery is likely to have been of similar design to that found in the existing six-sailed mills in Sibsey and Waltham in Lincolnshire, which had been built in 1877 and 1879 respectively.

References

1. Archer, *Historic Cheshunt*.
2. Freese, *English windmills*.
3. Moore, *Hertfordshire windmills and windmillers*.
4. *Hertfordshire Mercury*, letter from Archibald Jackson (22 July 1938).
5. Journal of George Beaver, Hitchin Museum.
6. Cockett and Nash auction papers, Cambridge County Record Office, CRO296/B673/6.
7. *Hertfordshire Mercury*, letter from Archibald Jackson (22 July 1938).
8. *Hertfordshire Mercury* (2 May 1891).
9. Proof of evidence of David John Nicholls, Director of Millwrights International Ltd, 12 November 1980.
10. *Bishops Stortford Observer* (2 July 1981).
11. *Bishops Stortford Observer* (6 August 1981).
12. Letter from Hertfordshire Constabulary, 22 October 1981.
13. H.D. Liddle, *Notes on Old Chipperfield* (privately published, 1948).
14. Cockett and Nash auction papers, Cambridge County Record Office, CRO296/B900/10.
15. Letter from J.P. Mullett, *Hertfordshire Countryside* (May 1981) (re Goldfield).
16. Branch Johnson, *Industrial monuments*.
17. File on Millwrights International held at Mills Archive.
18. *Rickmansworth Historian* (Spring 1966).

19 J. Kenneth Major, 'Weston Windmill, Hertfordshire', report (29 April 1976); letter from Harry Meyer, *Hertfordshire Countryside* (Winter 1950–51); and letter from H. Stratton, *Hertfordshire Countryside* (Spring 1952).
20 Martin Watts, 'Colney Heath Windmill Tower', report (May 1996) and 'The Mill Tower, Coursers Road, Colney Heath, St Albans', Archaeological Solutions Ltd report (May 2012) (RNO 3067).
21 D. Hutchin and R. Mott, *We ploughed the fields and scattered* (privately published, 2005).
22 *Hertfordshire Mercury*, 'Fatal fall from windmill on Friday evening' (15 October 1887).
23 *The Miller* (1 April 1893).

7

Paper mills

Hertfordshire has a long history of paper-making. The first specific record of a paper mill relates to Sele Mill in Hertford and dates to 1495. However, there are no records of paper-making in the county for the next 150 years. An isolated and short-lived paper-making industry existed at Sopwell Mill in 1649, but this had reverted to corn milling within 50 years. During the eighteenth century, before the full effects of the industrial revolution had been felt, paper was produced in a number of mills across the county, at Standon, Sarratt, Redbourn, Hemel Hempstead, Wheathampstead, Watford and Bushey. Paper-making was established at Bush Hall Mill, Hatfield, from the seventeenth century and lasted until 1849. It also took place in the Chess valley. At Standon, the paper mill had a working life of 45 years from 1810 and not only had an important role in the local economy, as it employed from 40 to 50 people at any one time, but was also the county's most significant producer of paper during the eighteenth century.

There were some 21 mills producing paper at various times in the county. These generally produced high-quality paper and the makers would have been familiar names throughout the English paper industry at the time. In the middle of the eighteenth century the paper-milling industry developed in and around Rickmansworth, in no small measure because of the plentiful supply of clean water available there.[1] Additionally, many of the corn mills in the area were becoming redundant and were available for conversion to paper-making. Solesbridge, Scotsbridge, Mill End, Batchworth and Loudwater Mills were all producing paper for journals, in particular for the *Illustrated London News*. Its proprietor, Herbert Ingrams, built the mansion Glen Chess (now converted to flats) in Loudwater. Clearly he found the area well-endowed with adequate supplies of water, an attractive place to live and close enough to London. However, when chlorine was introduced into the paper-making process it led to pollution of the river Chess and resulted in legal action under the Rivers Pollution Act, one of a number of permissive Acts of Parliament in the 1870s that enabled local authorities to improve the living condition of the expanding urban population. This appears to have precipitated the decline of the Rickmansworth and Chess mills which, in any case, suffered from relatively poor access compared with the paper mills in the Gade valley. However, Mill End Mill switched to producing blotters from 1888 to 1905, when the mill was closed and demolished. Scotsbridge

Figure 7.1 A continuous paper-making machine at Croxley Mills. HALS.

specialised in producing photographic paper and dyeline paper (which enabled several copies of maps and plans to be produced) until 1927. This marked the end of the paper industry in Rickmansworth.

From 1800 onwards these isolated paper-makers began to be eclipsed by the sheer concentration of paper-making in the Gade valley. Production had previously been entirely by hand, and gradually these mills were overtaken by Dickinson's mechanised 'endless web' mills in the Gade valley and, subsequently, at nearby Croxley. Then, at the beginning of the industrial revolution, there was suddenly a huge demand for paper, particularly from London, generated mainly by the flourishing newspaper industry but also by parliament and the legal profession. In turn, there developed an expanding role for commercial stationers, who commanded enhanced markets for paper products. The importance of the proximity of London, only 30 miles away, cannot be overestimated. These markets had a great potential for expansion and the Gade mills were ready to meet it.

In the nineteenth century paper-making was, arguably, the most important of the county's industries. The industry depended on water not only for power but also for the processing of the pulp for paper. The Gade provided an adequate supply of water for the paper-making process itself and also had a sufficient gradient to supply power to drive waterwheels and, subsequently, turbines. This was where the huge international paper industry was born. It resulted in a demand for skilled and well-paid labour and it fed a growing demand for books and newspapers for an increasingly educated and literate middle class.

A whole range of reasons, some already mentioned, favoured the Gade valley for paper-making, foremost among which were the potential advantages of the newly completed Grand Junction Canal. It allowed the easy delivery of the raw material – rags and cotton waste – by barge from London (rags had a significant value, and there are several instances of mill workers being taken to court for the theft of rags). Barges laden high with esparto grass would proceed up the canal from Brentford to Apsley and Croxley. On the return journey Dickinson's barges delivered the finished product to his wharf at Paddington and, thence, to the London markets. As the Gade paper mills switched over to steam power, the canal also enabled coal to be delivered straight to the mills.

A technological revolution in paper-making took place during the nineteenth century. In 1800 all paper was hand-made, one sheet at a time; by 1850 90 per cent was machine-made (Figure 7.1). The combination of the latest technology and new forms of transport spelled the end for older paper mills that did not enjoy these facilities. Most had gone by the beginning of the twentieth century.

The rise of John Dickinson and Company, Ltd

Although Britain and France were at the time at war, a prototype continuous paper-making machine was imported from France in 1801 through diplomatic channels, and in 1804 the Fourdrinier brothers set up their own first commercial machine at Frogmore. This was the most significant advance in paper-making technology and has assured Hertfordshire a unique place in the history of paper-making. This machine, known as 'the endless web', produced rolls of paper on a 4'-wide continuous wire mesh.[2]

Coming from a company of wholesale printers, John Dickinson realised the desirability of having a paper mill of his own. There were already many established corn mills with waterwheels that could be acquired and converted without the need for additional infrastructure. Dickinson purchased the corn mill at Apsley in 1809 and the adjacent Nash Mills two years later. These mills were ideally sited next to the Grand Junction Canal and subsequently to the London and North Western Railway.[3]

Aware, too, of the advantages of the Fourdrinier machine for making continuous rolls of paper at Frogmore Mills, Dickinson developed his own version, which proved to be very successful. His Apsley Mill had, by 1815, steam power sufficient to work three machines, making Dickinson pre-eminent among English paper-makers of the period 1810–60. Steam engines and machines were installed, and during the next 20 years the firm started to work three other mills in Hertfordshire: Batchworth was taken over as a paper mill and used to make 'stuff' (pulp for paper-making) and Home Park Mill was newly built in 1825 and Croxley in 1830, both on sites where hydraulic power was available. By 1838 Dickinson's mills were turning out 40 tons (36 tonnes) of paper a week. Productivity had increased many times over, output had expanded and both costs and prices were greatly reduced.[4]

The company was able to patent a whole range of emerging technologies. These included, in 1806, machinery for the manufacture of continuous paper and, in 1824, a card-cutting machine. Then there was a cylindrical drum for purifying pulp (1832) and, lastly, magnets for removing iron particles in pulp. These advances enabled new forms of paper, such as cartridge paper developed specifically for use in cannon cartridges, to be produced. This development, patented in 1807, in the middle of the Napoleonic wars, obviated the problem of accidental explosions and was very valuable to Wellington's armies. Paper for copperplate printing was patented in 1817. And, finally, there was the surface colouring of paper.

As the scale of Dickinson's business expanded so the limitations of water supplies from the Gade for production and transport became more apparent. The mills started to supplement water power with steam. This required regular inputs of coal, which was delivered by canal from the Midlands. As the railway system developed it offered opportunities to expand the business to new markets. The final plant at Croxley (Figure 7.2), initially still served by the canal, was significantly closer to the London markets and the company's own depot at Paddington. There were 13 fewer locks to negotiate than was the case for Frogmore, higher up the valley. However, by 1899, the

Figure 7.2 The extensive site at Croxley in 1865. HALS.

Figure 7.3 One of the locomotives used at Croxley Mills. HALS.

new mill, with its own internal rail system (Figure 7.3), was connected to the national rail network. This connection lasted until the closure of the site in 1981. It was served from the Watford–Rickmansworth branch of the London and North Western Railway (now a public path and cycleway called the Ebury Way). This allowed for trainloads of raw materials to enter the site, including coal, china clay, esparto grass, wood pulp and fuel oil. By 1947 100 tons (90 tonnes) of finished paper products were leaving the mill daily.

In about the year 1870 the firm of John Dickinson, now one of the largest in the country, was working seven mills in Hertfordshire, five of which (described below) were making paper on a total of 14 machines. An idea of the impact of these printing mills is given in J.C. Bourne's *Drawings of the London and Birmingham railway*:

> The adjacent mill (Nash Mills) belongs to Messrs Dickinson and Longman, the paper makers. At this and other mills in the neighbourhood, they manufacture large quantities of the finest printing and plate papers by machinery and mechanical processes, which have been brought to great perfection by the science and perseverance of the first mentioned gentleman. Till within the last few years, the process of making paper was slow and tedious and performed chiefly by manual labour; now, in a very few hours, a continued sheet, two or three feet in width, and a hundred feet or upwards in length, can be made from the pulp and rendered fit for immediate printing.

Figure 7.4 Croxley Mills being demolished in 1982. HALS.

Figure 7.5 Nash Mills House surrounded by the paper mill in 1955, during a period of redevelopment of the mill site. HALS.

> Not only the rapidity of manufacture, but the quality of the paper has been materially improved by the scientific mode of workmanship employed.[5]

The success of John Dickinson and Co. was founded in part on the willingness of the company to embrace the latest technology and in part on the company's sensitivity to the potential demands of both the wholesale stationery market and the publishing industry. The company could supply all the requirements of stationers and commanded a very extensive international trade.

Production from the Dickinson paper mills has now entirely ceased, leaving little trace of an important industry. The mills were closed in the 1980s in the face of both cheaper production costs in Eastern Europe and increasingly stringent controls on watercourse pollution (Figure 7.4). Trading conditions became increasingly difficult and the IT revolution occasioned a decline in the stationery business. The Gade valley sites have been redeveloped to meet the housing requirements of Dacorum Borough Council and the Croxley site has become partly a housing estate and partly a business park. All that remains is an excellent museum, the Paper Trail, at Frogmore Mill. Here the original pits for the two waterwheels, the only surviving evidence of the power that drove a major industry, can be seen. The museum includes many original artefacts, including examples of 'the endless web' continuous paper-making machines.

Nash Mill House, the home of Sir John Evans (1823–1908), a polymath who wrote on water supply and geology, also survives (Figure 7.5). It has been restored as part of the redevelopment of the site of Nash Mills.

Frogmore Paper Mills, Fourdrinier Way, Apsley

Originally a corn mill, known as Covent Mill, it was adapted as a paper mill in 1774. In 1803 it was acquired by the Fourdrinier Bros and produced the first commercial continuous paper. Towards the end of the nineteenth century it specialised in 'half stuff' (partly prepared pulp) and recycled paper. The site has been redeveloped in part but includes the Paper Trail Museum of paper-making.

Apsley Paper Mill, London Road, Apsley

Converted from a corn mill in the eighteenth century, this mill was making paper by 1774. It was bought by John Dickinson in 1809. Steam power was introduced in 1845 to augment the waterwheels when river flows were low – the waterwheels were entirely removed in 1929. In 1888 production of card and envelopes was concentrated here, with a weekly output, in 1896, of 150 tons (135 tonnes).[6] In 1911 2,000 people were employed in what was then the largest factory of its type in Britain, covering more than 30 acres. It closed in 1999 and the site is now a retail park.

Nash Mills, Apsley
This mill was acquired by Dickinson in 1811 and was rebuilt after a fire in 1813. In 1879 the mill was comprehensively rebuilt, with turbines replacing waterwheels, although the old waterwheels were not removed until 1927. The building contained the smith's, carpenter's and fitter's shops. The mill was used for producing fine plate, duplex and silk thread papers. The site was cleared in 2006 and a housing estate has been built there.

Home Park Paper Mills, Home Park Mill Link Road, Kings Langley
This was a purpose-built factory, constructed in 1825 by Dickinson specifically for paper-making. From 1878 it specialised in coloured paper. Dickinson combined the fall of two locks to increase the head of water at the wheel, but in 1890 turbines replaced waterwheels. Larger than Apsley or Nash Mills, it was producing 10 tons (9 tonnes) a week in 1838, and by 1840 the colouring of paper was started. It closed in 1980 and was demolished in 1992, and the site is now an industrial estate.

Croxley Mills, Blackmoor Lane, Croxley Green
Croxley Mills was a purpose-built paper mill constructed in 1830 and the last built by John Dickinson. It represented a major initiative on a grand scale. Completed in 1830, it was destined to rank among the most important paper mills in the country, and was soon producing 18 tons (16 tonnes) of paper a week. The mill took advantage of a hitherto untapped 14' hydraulic gradient: the adjacent Common Moor Lock has a fall of over 9', which, combined with the fall at Lot Mead lock of 6', meant that the mill had an impressive head of water. In 1881 the business was substantially reorganised to take over all the paper production from the other Dickinson mills and a new steam engine was erected. The beater house and machine house were rebuilt and four American 'Hercules' turbines were installed, replacing the waterwheels. The mill contained two Dickinson cylinder machines and eight Fourdrinier machines. All the better types of paper were produced from rags, esparto grass and wood pulp.

Hertfordshire's other paper mills
There is evidence for some 16 other mill sites where paper has at various times been made, but none have survived as paper mills because in the late nineteenth century paper-making on a small scale rapidly became too expensive.

Mills on the river Bulbourne
Two Waters paper mill, Two Waters Road, Hemel Hempstead
This corn mill was acquired by the Fourdrinier brothers for paper-making in 1792. It was destroyed by an explosion in 1919 when it was being used for the extraction of fats from wool.

Bourne End Mill, London Road, Bourne End

There is evidence from fire insurance policies that it was used for making paper for a short time in the latter half of the eighteenth century.

The Rickmansworth paper mills on the rivers Chess and Colne

On the Buckinghamshire stretch of the river Chess there was an extensive and profitable paper-making industry from the 1760s until the 1860s. Several mills were used for paper-making for limited periods, notably Weirhouse Mill, Blackwell Hall Mill and Bois Mill. So successful was this industry that Bois Mill was equipped with two Fourdrinier machines in 1807 and was converted to steam working in 1830. However, quite suddenly they were no longer profitable. Stanners' *The Mill's Tale* explains: 'Competition from John Dickinson's manufactories in Apsley, combined with the lack of convenient rail or canal transportation, meant that paper-making all along the Chess became costly and largely unprofitable.'[7]

At Sarratt the Chess flows into Hertfordshire with the following sequence of mills.

Sarratt Mill, New Road, Sarratt

Originally a corn mill, this was converted to a paper mill in *c.*1740. There was an extensive range of buildings over the millstream, all of which have been demolished. The river upstream had been straightened and embanked, enabling an overshot waterwheel to be installed. The mill was modernised in the 1850s, with new paper-making machinery and the installation of a steam engine. At the time it employed 55 workers from the village, indicating that this was a large paper-making process. However, this investment was in vain. Competition with the Dickinson mills, coupled with poor access, with a steep and narrow hill to the nearest main road from Rickmansworth to Amersham, made it uneconomic. By 1861 it was employing only 44 people, and it closed in 1862. It was advertised for sale as a going concern, but by that time it was obsolete and attracted no offers. It was acquired instead by the duke of Bedford as a fishing lodge.[8] Original sluice gear survives on one of the bypass channels, but otherwise there is no hard evidence of the mill's paper-making history.[9]

Solesbridge Mill, Solesbridge Lane, Rickmansworth

This was an eighteenth-century mill that made paper from 1746 until 1888, when it closed because of bankruptcy. In 1851 it had four beating engines and employed 35 people.

Scotsbridge Mill, Park Road, Rickmansworth (Figure 7.6)

This mill operated as a paper mill from 1757 until 1881. Both Scotsbridge and Loudwater Mills made paper for the *Illustrated London News*, which had been launched in 1842. After closing for a time, it latterly produced 'half stuff' from esparto grass.

Figure 7.6 Scotsbridge Mill today.

Legal action relating to pollution of the river with chlorine closed both mills. Much altered, it is now a restaurant. The waterwheels were internal and their location is enclosed by glass screens, so that the waters of the Chess can be seen, and heard, by diners.

Loudwater Mill, Loudwater Lane, Rickmansworth
This was a corn mill that was converted to paper-making. It was bought in 1748 by Herbert Ingrams, who built Glen Chess house nearby. An illustration from the *Illustrated London News* shows an imposing three-storey building with seven beating machines.

Mill End Mill, Uxbridge Road, Rickmansworth
This paper mill operated from 1755 to 1905, towards the end of its life making blotting paper. It was sold in 1905 and then demolished.

Batchworth Mill, London Road, Rickmansworth
This mill was used for paper-making from 1775 to 1887. Dickinson acquired it in 1818 for the production of half-stuff to supply other mills; however, rationalisation in 1887 meant that the lease was given up. It now houses the offices of Affinity Water.

Mills on the Colne and Ver
Redbourn Little Mill (also known as Dolittle Mill), St Albans Road, Redbourn
This mill was converted to a paper mill in 1753 by John Vowles, who was a stationer

from London. It lasted in this role until 1783, when it was destroyed by fire. It then reverted to corn milling. It was demolished in the early 1950s for the widening of Watling Street.

Sopwell Mill, Cotton Mill Lane, St Albans
In 1649 this corn mill became a paper mill producing fine white paper, but by 1691 it had reverted to grinding corn. It was rebuilt in 1890 and used until World War II (see Chapter 5).

Bushey Mills, Bushey Mill Lane, Bushey
While this mill was equipped for making paper, there is no evidence that it was ever a significant producer.

Hamper Mill, Hampermill Lane, Bushey (Figure 7.7)
This mill was described in 1776 in the *London Evening Post* as 'a cornmill and paper mill newly erected but not completely finished'. It produced high-quality paper with a watermark. The owner was awarded a silver medal from the Royal Society of Arts for the paper's suitability for copperplate. Following its rebuilding after a fire in 1793, William Lepard acquired it for his stationery business in the City so that he could make his own paper. It was described in 1806 as a 'two vat mill with presses, waterwheels and compleat drying rooms and warerooms'. In the 1830s a Fourdrinier machine was installed and steam power introduced; until then, water power had been adequate to drive the beater engines. A turbine was installed and a steam engine subsequently built. Decline had set in by the 1880s, and it could not compete with Croxley Mills. There was a fire in 1895, but production lasted until 1908. Today the mill house, turbine house, original wheelhouse and part of the vat house survive.

Figure 7.7 Hamper Mill, c.1910. Reproduced by kind permission of D. Huggins.

Mills on the Lea and its tributaries
Pickford Mill, Coldharbour Lane, Harpenden
Thomas Vallance of Cheapside, a wholesale stationer, acquired an interest in the mill in 1775 in order to produce paper for his business. It was taken over in 1833 by Edward Jones, another City stationery wholesaler, who continued to use it until 1849. Latterly it specialised in gummed paper. All the buildings were demolished *c.*1990 and the site is now part of an industrial estate.

Bush Hall Mill, Chequers, Hatfield
The site of this mill lies a short distance upstream from the better-known Mill Green Mill. It was converted from a fulling mill to a paper mill around 1672: fulling stocks can readily be used for mashing rags for paper-making. Damaged by fire shortly afterwards, it was rebuilt by Thomas Vallance, who ran the mill until he concentrated his paper-making activities at Pickford Mill after a considerable amount of industrial unrest at Bush Hall. It was then run by a Thomas Cressick, a wholesale stationer, who manufactured paper, card and board. In 1838 paper-making ceased when Cressick removed the machinery after litigation between himself and the landlord, the marquis of Salisbury, as to who was the rightful owner of the machinery. The buildings were subsequently damaged by fire and demolished.

The Old Paper Mill and sawmill, Paper Mill Lane, Standon (Figure 7.8)
Standon had a thriving paper-making industry dating back to the eighteenth century. This mill was converted from a corn mill to a paper mill by 1713 and formed a substantial enterprise making durable brown wrapping paper which employed between 40 and 50 people in the early nineteenth century. It had the advantage of good access to London, as the turnpike passed close by. However, decline set in in the 1840s as a result of competition from technically superior mills and the development of steam power, and employment had fallen to 14 by 1849. The last miller, James Whitaker, discontinued paper-making by 1855 because water power alone was not sufficient to make it profitable and the trend against hand-made paper meant that it was not worth investing in steam power.[10] The mill was put up for sale, along with five farms, a blacksmith's shop and substantial agricultural holdings. It was later used as a sawmill before being converted to residential use.

Branch Johnson's survey in 1965 records that the industrial part of the site consisted of two large weatherboarded sheds and an undershot waterwheel with an estimated diameter of 12', largely disintegrated and with spokes remaining on one side only (Figure 7.9). In the adjacent lean-to there were vertical and horizontal iron gear wheels, probably of late nineteenth-century date.

The waterwheel, originally under a roof, was made of wood and, after attempts to restore it came to nothing, was removed altogether as part of river-management

Figure 7.8 The Old Paper Mill at Standon, showing the waterwheel before it was removed to alleviate flooding. HALS.

works. Only the axle now survives, but not in situ. The iron pit wheel (Figure 7.10) and spur wheel survive, together with a number of pulley wheels.[11]

Sele Mill, North Road, Hertford

This, the first paper mill, was founded by John Tate on the river Beane and was producing paper in 1495. The site of the original paper mill may have been a little to the north of the present building (see Figure 10.2), where there is a 'Paper Mill Ditch'. As Tate's father was lord mayor of London it is reasonable to suppose that, even at this early date, paper was being produced for the London market. It does not seem to have lasted for much more than ten years, however; although the quality of the paper seems to have been good it could not match foreign competition in terms of price.[12]

References

1. G. Cornwall, 'The paper mills of Rickmansworth', *Watford and District Industrial History Society Paper Journal*, 4 (1974), pp. 41–51.
2. J. Evans, *The endless web: John Dickinson and Co Ltd, 1804–1954* (Jonathan Cape, London, 1955).
3. M. Stanyon, *Railways – the John Dickinson connection* (Apsley Paper Trail, 2011).
4. J. Lewis Evans, *The firm of John Dickinson and Company Ltd* (Chiswick Press, London, 1896).
5. J.C. Bourne, *Drawings of the London and Birmingham railway* (Ackerman and Co. Facsimile by David and Charles, Newton Abbott, 1970).

Figure 7.9 The waterwheel at the Old Paper Mill, Standon, shortly before its removal in the 1990s in the interests of alleviating flooding. Kindly supplied by J. Philpotts.

Figure 7.10 Preserved pit wheel at the Old Paper Mill.

6 E.T. Finerty, 'The history of paper mills in Hertfordshire', *The Paper-maker and British Paper Trade Journal* (April–June 1957).
7 C. and R. Stanners, 'Chesham Bois: the mill's tale', *Journal of the Chess Valley Archaeological Society* (2006), pp. 19–23.
8 A. Coleman, 'The compleatest mill on the stream. A concise history of Sarratt Mill on the river Chess', *Chess Valley Journal* (2009), pp. 22–6.
9 G. Ray, *The book of Chorleywood and Chenies* (Barracuda Books, Buckingham, 1983).
10 P. Bower, 'British paper mills: Standon Mill, Hertfordshire', *The Quarterly* (April 1996)
11 J. Thomas, 'A kindly employer', *Hertfordshire People* (2013).
12 R. Bennett, 'Hertford and its paper mills', *Hertfordshire Past*, 26 (Spring 1989).

8

Silk mills

Hertfordshire is not normally considered to be a textile-manufacturing county. However, a silk-throwing industry began to develop in the south-west of the county in the late eighteenth century and enjoyed a century of success. The arrival of Huguenot refugees from France, many with silk-throwing skills, triggered the development of the industry. Local production was further spurred by the fact that importing silk from its traditional centres in France and Belgium had become impossible during the Napoleonic wars. The county was particularly favoured for processing raw silk. It was close to both the London docks, where it was imported, and to the London markets. It was also cheaper to produce the thread outside London. The production of silk started at the Rookery Mill, on the Colne just outside Watford, in the 1760s, and by 1800 it provided a new prosperity in Hertfordshire. The first half of the nineteenth century was also profitable and justified substantial investments in industrial-style mills in Watford and Tring.

The most important silk mills in Hertfordshire were Rookery Mill in Watford, Tring Silk Mills on Brook Street, the Abbey Mill at St Albans, Woollam's Silk Mill in Redbourn and, for a while, Batchworth Mill and a mill in High Street, Rickmansworth (Figure 8.1). The Watford, Tring, Redbourn and Rickmansworth mills were purpose-built silk mills. Watford and Tring were four- and five-storey mills which clearly represented large investments, but others – Grove Mill, Hitchin, and Abbey Mills, St Albans – were converted corn mills. Hallingbury Mill on the River Stort is sometimes referred to as 'the silk mill', although there is no concrete evidence that it was ever used for this purpose. Apart from the Rookery Mill, Watford boasted other silk mills, whose exact location is not known, in Beechen Grove and in Aldenham Road, Bushey. Indeed, for a period 'silk throwing was the principal manufacture of the town'.[1]

The Hertfordshire silk mills were concerned only with silk-throwing; the finished thread was taken to centres specialising in weaving, notably Macclesfield. Silk-throwing is the process by which raw silk is turned into a useable thread which can then be woven into cloth. It involves washing the silk, removing knots and twisting the fibres to form a strong thread. It was a labour-intensive industry relying heavily on women and children, many of whom were recruited from workhouses and orphanages in London. The silk industry began, therefore, to be organised on factory rather than cottage lines. At its peak the Tring Mill employed 140 women and 320 children.

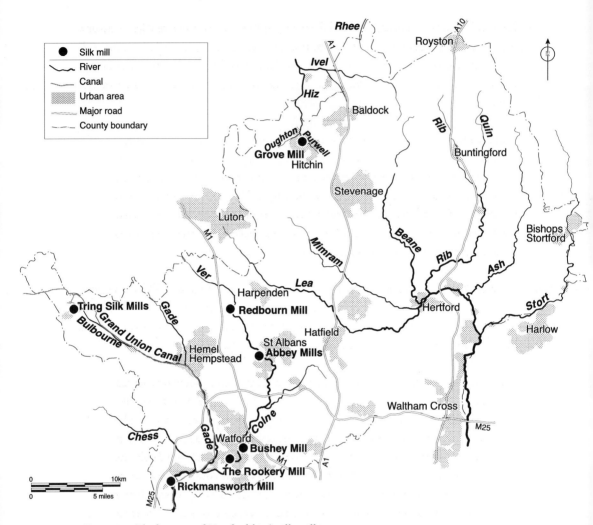

Figure 8.1 The location of Hertfordshire's silk mills.

Despite their working a 12-hour day the Board of Governors and Directors of the Poor reported that 'The employment is not laborious and can in no way be prejudicial to health.'[2]

From 1815 silk production enjoyed protective tariffs, but as these were progressively removed it became less profitable. The worst blow came in the form of the 1860 Cobden-Chevalier Treaty, which placed a 30 per cent duty on the export of English silk while allowing the import of French silk duty free. This effectively destroyed the economic basis of silk production, and by 1890 only John Woollam's two silk-throwing mills were still in production. His mill at Redbourn was constructed as late as 1857 and, although it continued to produce silk until 1938, there is evidence that the number of workers employed fell sharply at the turn of the twentieth century, clearly indicating a substantial fall in production. In covering the sale to Messrs J. Maygrove and Co of Woollam's silk mills at St Albans Abbey Mill and Redbourn in 1905, a report in *The Herts Advertiser* set out the background to the decline of silk throwing:

> Today these two mills are the only survivors of the numerous establishments of their kind which once flourished in the county of Hertford, notably at Watford and Tring, where the process of silk 'throwing' was carried on, the reason assigned for the decline of the industry within the county as well as in other parts of the country being the free importation of 'thrown' silk, the product of cheap Italian and other foreign labour, and the high duties placed upon our exports to foreign countries.

This report foretold the reasons for the subsequent success of the Messrs J. Maygrove and Co., which was achieved by a subtle shift out of the primary process of 'throwing' and into the specialist manufacturing of high-quality threads required in those parts of the furnishing trade which catered for the London markets:

> … it is probable that in addition to the industry of silk 'throwing', which has been followed here for many years, the manufacture of sewing silks and fringes and other silken materials used for furnishing purposes, will be introduced. For such a trade an admirable foundation has been laid, for, in spite of the general decline, the work accomplished at the Abbey Mills has retained its high standard and has continued to command the best prices in the market. The coalition of an important manufactory conveniently situated in the Home Counties with their London business, with their excellent facilities for the despatch of orders large and small, will probably, in the course of time, reinstate the St Albans Mills in the important position which they occupied.[3]

That the business survived into the late 1930s must be considered to be a major achievement.

The county's silk-throwing heritage has survived better than much of the rest of the county's mills, with tangible evidence of five of the seven sites surviving until today.

Grove Mill (also known as Shotling Mill or Burnt Mill), Grove Road, Hitchin

The mill building dates from 1814 and was operated as a corn mill on the Purwell river by Joseph Ransom. Phebe Lucas visited the newly rebuilt mill in the early 1820s, which she regarded as 'a very great treat'.[4] For a few years in the late 1820s Ransom

Figure 8.2 The aftermath of a fire at Grove Mill, Hitchin, in 1889. Reproduced by kind permission of the North Hertfordshire Museum Services.

diversified into silk throwing. There is evidence that local schoolgirls aged ten or under would leave school early to work in the silk mill. It also appears that a silk weaver was employed at this time, so Ransom may have been trying to weave silk as well as throw it. It seems that this enterprise did not succeed, because the mill had reverted to corn within ten years. In 1889 the mill burnt down (Figure 8.2) and, when rebuilt, was used for dressing chamois leather.

The Silk Mills, Brook Street, Tring
The silk mill in Tring was built in 1824 by William Kay, who came from a family who ran a silk mill in Macclesfield. The most significant problem he faced was the securing of a water supply to power the mill, which is situated near the highest point on the Chiltern escarpment but adjacent to the spring line, meaning that there was no watercourse of any size to power the mill. A very large mill pond adjacent to the mill is supplied by two balancing ponds, the Dundale and Miswell lakes, that are connected to the millpond by unlined underground conduits through solid chalk. The water from the waterwheel was discharged by way of a lengthy 'feeder' into the Wendover Arm of the Grand Union Canal, thereby helping to top up its summit level.[5] That

installing this complex and costly hydraulic system was considered worthwhile gives a good idea of how profitable the silk industry was (Figure 8.3).

In 1836 fire broke out:

> The mills are of vast extent, and raised to a height of five stories, and at the time of the accident, trade being very brisk, as many as 800 workpeople, of whom a large proportion of young girls, were kept in constant employ. At noon, as usual, the workers left for their dinner. All was then apparently safe, and also on their return and resumption of their work.

> At 1 o'clock the housekeeper who occupies a cottage adjacent to the mill, on going outside her door saw thick smoke rising from the upper part of the factory. An alarm was instantly given, but before any means could be taken to ascertain the nature of the danger, flames burst forth, and spread with great rapidity along the fourth floor of the mill and thence to the floor above.[6]

Figure 8.3 The scale of the underground conduits to provide water to Tring Silk Mill and the length of the feeder to take it away to supplement supplies to the summit level of the Grand Union Canal give an idea of the profitability of the silk industry for much of the nineteenth century.

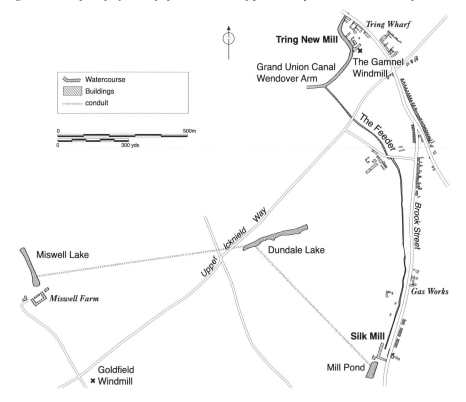

In 1876, following the collapse of the British silk industry, the mill was put up for sale. Unsurprisingly, there were no prospective purchasers and it was acquired by Nathan, Lord Rothschild of Tring (1840–1915), largely for philanthropic reasons (Figure 8.4). The mill finally closed in 1898. During Rothschild's lifetime the buildings were used as the estate office for Tring Park, providing employment for some at least of the redundant silk workers. The building was reduced in height during the Rothschild period, allegedly to improve the sight line between Tring Park and Ascott House at Wing for semaphore communications between these two Rothschild homes. In 1940 the silk mill was sold on again following the death of Lionel Walter, the second Baron Rothschild (1868–1937). During the war it was used by the Royal Mint and possibly for munitions manufacturing. After the war it declined and was almost derelict when the present owner acquired the site in 1979. It has since become home to several light industrial companies.

The mill still contains the largest waterwheel in Hertfordshire, an overshot wheel largely below ground level that is 22' in diameter by 6' wide (Figure 8.5). A wheel of large diameter and small width allowed the limited supply of water to be used to maximum effect. After the mill closed down, the waterwheel was subsequently used to power a sawmill and a dynamo which provided electricity to Tring Park. However, tantalisingly, it is currently not accessible for safety reasons, although the owners have from time to time looked into the possibility of restoring it. At one time a steam engine and chimney existed, but these are now long gone.

Figure 8.4 The predominantly young workforce at the Tring Silk Mill in the 1880s. Reproduced by kind permission of Tring Local History Museum.

Figure 8.5 The 22-foot waterwheel at Tring Silk Mill. Reproduced by kind permission of Tring Local History Museum from the collection of the late Ron Kitchener.

Figure 8.6 Abbey Mills, St Albans, at the turn of the twentieth century. Reproduced by kind permission of the Mills Archive.

Abbey Mills, Abbey Mill Lane, St Albans

This was originally a monastic corn mill. In 1802 John Woollam acquired it and converted it to a silk mill powered first by water and then by steam. So successful was it that he built a second mill alongside (Figure 8.6). The business was sold in 1905 by the Woollam family to John Maygrove and Co., a London firm, who ran it until 1938. The 'new' mill was demolished in 1955, but the original Georgian building survives and has been converted to apartments.[7]

Woollam's Silk Mill, Redbourn Common, Redbourn

John Woollam, who had converted the Abbey Mill in St Albans to silk throwing, went on to build the Redbourn silk mill in 1857. This was a steam-driven mill specifically built for silk throwing. Employment reached a peak in the 1890s, but fell off rapidly thereafter.[8] Like the previously described mill, it was also bought by Maygrove in 1906 and operated until 1938, when demand for silk thread fell in the face of competition from artificial fibres. The buildings were used by Brooke Bond until 1960, when they were demolished and replaced. Most of the site was redeveloped in the 1990s for housing, but the manager's house remained and became a local museum in 2000.[9]

Rookery Mill, Riverside Road, Oxhey, Watford

An advertisement for the tenancy of Rookery Mill was placed in the *Manchester Mercury* in 1768:

> A Silk Shop, or Throwstery, in extreme good Repair, being but lately built, containing twelve double Engines, to wind both long and short Silk, and ten Pair of Mills to throw the same, all of them worked by Water in the same Manner as the mills at Derby, Macclesfield, Stockport, etc. with many improvements.
>
> Watford is a very agreeable Market Town, fifteen miles from London, very populous, and in it great Numbers of Hands, that work at very reasonable Rates, and who have some Years been employed in the Silk Manufactory, and many of them in the above Shop.

From this it seems clear that a very substantial investment had been made in the mill. In order to obtain a good return someone with skills in the silk industry and familiarity with the market for silk was required, and it seems that these attributes were not likely to be found in Watford.[10]

The mill, which was powered first by water and then by steam, consisted of a complex of buildings typical of the industrial hamlets attached to industrial enterprises. A very large concern, it employed up to 500 people until 1881, when it fell into disuse 'from depression of the silk trade', causing widespread unemployment and hardship. The buildings were taken over by Watford Steam Laundry Company.[11] They were demolished in 2000 and nothing remains.[12]

Batchworth Mill, London Road, Rickmansworth

Silk weaving was carried out between 1759 and 1818, when J. Dickinson bought the mill for paper-making.

171 High Street, Rickmansworth

This was a steam-driven silk mill run by Thomas Rock Shute, who also owned the Rookery Mill, until 1898, when the building was taken over by Franklin's Mineral Waters after the silk industry had succumbed to French competition. The 1898 Ordnance Survey map shows the building as a 'Mineral Water Works'. It was a substantial three-storey building with engine, boiler house and chimney, and was a major local employer. It was demolished in 1991 to make way for a Marks and Spencer food store.

References

1. W. Austin, *Tring silk mill* (privately published, 2008).
2. E. Wallace, *Children of the labouring poor* (Hatfield, 2010).
3. *Herts Advertiser* (29 April 1905).
4. Lucas, *Phebe's Hitchin book*.
5. S. Savage, *A short history of Dundale* (Tring, 2009).
6. *Buckinghamshire Herald* (30 January 1836), reproduced by Tring and District Local History Society (March 2004).
7. St Albans Teachers Centre, *Know St Albans: three St Albans watermills* (St Albans, 1976).
8. A. Featherstone, *The mills of Redbourn* (privately published, 1993).
9. A. Featherstone, *Silk mill to museum* (Redbourn, 2010).
10. J. Young, *Silk throwing in Watford* (Watford, 1986).
11. M. Ward, 'Working in Silk Mills', *Hertfordshire People* (2005).
12. G. Longman, *Mystery of Watford's short-lived silk industry* (Watford, 1985).

9

At the margins of milling

So far this book has covered the main traditional forms of milling: corn, paper, gunpowder and silk. This chapter completes the picture with some of the lesser-known uses to which milling technology has been put in Hertfordshire: that is, fulling, leather-working, cotton manufacture, timber production, cement-making and water management.

Fulling mills

Foremost among these more obscure aspects of milling was the process of fulling, which is the cleaning and degreasing of raw wool before it is spun into yarn. During the thirteenth century woollen cloth was produced locally across the country, with several pronounced concentrations in Hertfordshire, among which Codicote was prominent. The road name Fulling Mill Lane in Codicote is a reminder of this long-gone industry. Several water-powered corn mills were converted for the fulling process, which involved removing the lanolin from wool with fullers' earth and water by pounding the cloth with mechanically driven tilt hammers powered by the waterwheel, raising the nap with teasel heads and stretching it on wooden frames with iron tenterhooks. By the seventeenth century both the West Country and East Anglia were specialising in cloth production. The Hertfordshire cloth industry died out and the fulling mills reverted to grinding corn except for the fulling mill at Waltham Abbey which was converted to the production of gunpowder. In consequence, very little of the fulling mill heritage has survived.

The most important fulling mills were at St Albans, Codicote and Hertford. The place-name 'Walkern' means a fulling mill, but there is no other evidence of the village's mill being used for this purpose. Of all the uses to which mills were put, fulling seems to be the one with the least documentation.

Codicote fulling mill, Fulling Mill Lane, Welwyn (Figure 9.1)

This was a fulling mill until sometime in the seventeenth century, but was recorded as a corn mill in 1740. A steam mill was added at the end of the nineteenth century. An advertisement for the sale of the mill by auction on 23 June 1881 describes it as having

Figure 9.1 The former fulling mill at Codicote in 1967. HALS.

Figure 9.2 Fulling stocks at Horns Mill. Reproduced by kind permission of Hertford Museum.

A 12 horsepower high pressure beam engine by Cotton and Hallen; and a Cornish boiler 16ft long and 5ft diameter, by Horton and Son; together with three pairs of French Burr stones, 4ft diameter and mill gear complete for driving the same; the whole being in good working order, as now fixed in the Fulling Mills.[1]

The adjacent mill house is early Victorian and Grade II listed.

Planning permission was granted in 1990 for the conversion of the then empty former industrial building to offices. The white cladding was replaced by black (Figure 9.1).[2]

Horns Mill, Hornsmill Road, Hertford

Horns Mill, once a corn mill, then occupied by a firm of seed-crushers and oil-cake manufacturers, was bought in 1891 by Webb and Co. Ltd, leather dressers. Their equipment included a battery of five fulling stocks dating from the first half of the nineteenth century (Figure 9.2). These were used to beat and compress newly woven woollen cloth to turn it into felt, but were rendered obsolete by the invention of the rotary fuller. Webb and Co. also used them to impregnate sheep and lamb skins with cod liver oil to produce chamois leather.

Most of the complex dated from 1858. It was a large group of buildings comprising the main mill, the engine mill, an engine house, store houses, loading bays and a detached mill house. They were built of yellow brick with weatherboarded upper floors (Figure 9.3). Power was provided partly by a waterwheel and partly by steam. There was a chimney 100' in height. The site was cleared in 1972 and redeveloped for housing; only the street names Tanners Crescent and Glovers Close are a remainder of the industry that once existed here, although photographs of the fulling stocks remain.

There was a railway connection to the Hertford–Hatfield line which was subsequently closed under the Beeching plan. The 1898 Ordnance Survey 1:2,500 survey shows this lengthy rail connection (Figure 9.4).

Cotton milling

The cotton mill, Cotton Mill Lane, St Albans (Figure 9.5)

Another short-lived enterprise was cotton milling. The cotton mill, on the river Ver, had an eclectic career. It was originally a diamond-polishing mill in the eighteenth century. It then made cotton wicks for candles until about 1848, when it turned to making 'Berlin' wool for needlework. However, by 1900 it was grinding flour. The site was subsequently developed as a swimming pool.

Sawmills

Many of the large estates had sawmills to deal with timber grown on their land.

Figure 9.3 Horns Mill before demolition in 1972. © HBPT.

Figure 9.4 The rail connection and loading bay which used to serve Horns Mill.

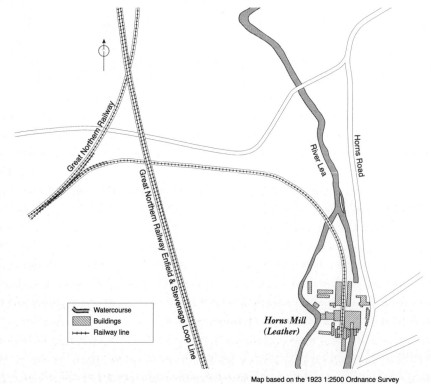

Figure 9.5 The cotton mill at St Albans, by an unknown artist. Reproduced by kind permission of St Albans Museum.

Figure 9.6 The Hatfield estate Cecil sawmill in 1954. Reproduced by kind permission of David Jones and the Mills Archive.

Figure 9.7 Foster's sawmill at Boxmoor shortly before it was destroyed by fire in 1967. HALS.

Figure 9.8 The horse-drawn mill at Broxbourne for the manufacture of 'Pulhamite' artificial stone. D. Housham.

Pre Mill, St Albans
The turbine house, part of the Gorhambury Estate, survives. It contained two turbines, one of which is still in place. It originally powered both a Tangey water pump, which provided water for the estate, and a sawmill in an adjacent building, which has since been demolished.

Hatfield sawmill (also known as the Withy Mill or the Cecil Mill) (Figure 9.6)
The Cecil sawmill dates from the 1830s and closed in 1888.[3] It is a four-storey yellow-brick building with a water turbine, which from 1888 was used to generate electricity, then newly introduced to Hatfield House.

Foster's sawmill, River Park, Boxmoor (Figure 9.7)
This sawmill dated back to 1700 and stood on the bank of the Grand Union Canal. Originally powered by a waterwheel on the Bulbourne, it acquired a steam engine in 1834. From 1850 until 1930 Henry Foster's company supplied timber to the building trade and apparently even to makers of musical instruments. It was destroyed by fire in 1967. The site has been redeveloped as flats known as River Park Gardens.[4]

Miskins' sawmill, Romeland Hill, St Albans
Miskins' steam sawmill, behind Nos 5 and 6 Romeland Hill, dates from the nineteenth century and closed in the middle of the twentieth. Its owner Christopher Miskins moved to St Albans in the late 1850s, created a building and timber business and became lord mayor of St Albans in 1885. This mill was a steam-powered sawing and joinery works. The site is now a housing development.

Oil cake production
Dicker Mill, Hertford (Plate 30)
Relocated from its original site, Dicker Mill was converted from a corn mill to the production of oil cake in the latter part of the nineteenth century. It enjoyed a siding connecting to the national rail network at Hertford East Station. It closed in the early 1920s and the site has since been developed as an industrial estate.

Pulhamite
Broxbourne Terra Cotta and Artificial Stone works, off Station Road, Broxbourne (Figure 9.8)
Pulhamite was an artificial stone used extensively for rock gardens. It was named after its inventor, James Pulham, who set up a plant for producing it in Broxbourne. The material was used at the Royal Horticultural Society's gardens at Wisley, for the Mappin Terraces at the London Zoo and at both Buckingham Palace and Sandringham. It was said that no prestigious garden in Hertfordshire was without it.

Pulham's works consisted of a horse-drawn mill with on-edge stones used for grinding the local claystone.[5] It was demolished in 1968.[6]

Water pumping

Many Victorian country estates used water-powered pumping systems to raise water from the nearby valleys to mansions that were usually sited in commanding positions above the valleys. Hertfordshire has several examples of such installations serving, for instance, Cassiobury, Panshanger, Childwickbury, Hatfield House, The Grove (Watford), Langleybury,[7] Chaulden House, Chorleywood House,[8] Tewin Water, Tring Park and Marden Hill House (Figures 9.6–9.16).

The company Green and Carter developed a range of pumps for this purpose, notably waterwheel pumps and hydraulic rams. They are known to have been installed at Panshanger and Hertingfordbury for Earl Cowper and at Tewin Water for Otto Beit. At Panshanger there are three installations on the estate of the former mansion, which was demolished in 1956. The brick bases of all three remain, but the superstructures are missing and the machinery is all in the open air.

The arrangement at Cassiobury was described in the following terms: 'From this point the supply is pumped by a three-throw horizontal pump actuated by the Turbine into a tank situated at the top of the Tower of the Mansion, which in turn overflows into a tank situated over the laundry.'[9] By 1956 the pump house at Cassiobury was

Figure 9.9 The pump that supplied The Grove, Watford, with water. By kind permission of Peter Eyre.

Figure 9.10 The 'Turbine House' that supplied water to Cassiobury Park. Reproduced from the catalogue for the sale of the mansion in 1922 by kind permission of David Huggins.

Figure 9.11 A whimsical pump house, shaped like a tower and constructed in flint and brick, that was built to supply Chaulden House, Boxmoor, at the turn of the twentieth century. No details of the machinery appear to have survived. It was demolished in the 1960s. Reproduced by kind permission of the Mills Archive.

Figure 9.12 Small waterwheel at Tewin, believed to have served Marden Hill House. The brick base remains and most of the machinery is intact. Reproduced by kind permission of A. Stoyel.

Figure 9.13 Panshanger. A waterwheel measuring 3' 6" wide by 7' in diameter powering a reciprocating pump manufactured by Horsefields of Leeds. It was located in the former boat house, which is long gone.

Figure 9.14 A waterwheel and syphon at Panshanger. The waterwheel measures 2' wide by 5' 6" in diameter. It is unmarked but believed to be by Green and Carter.

Figure 9.15 Hidden in undergrowth beside the towpath of the Grand Union Canal are the remains of a waterwheel which pumped water to nearby Langleybury. The wooden waterwheel has gone, leaving the axle and iron pit wheel amid remnants of the pump house, a corrugated iron structure.

Figure 9.16 This pump house, built over a channel from the river Chess, contains a small waterwheel 10' in diameter by 2' wide with 30 buckets and a three-throw pump, all in a reasonably complete state. It pumped water to nearby Chorleywood House until the late 1960s.

considered to be in a dangerous condition and was demolished by Watford Borough Council. Only a concrete arch of the mill race remains today to mark where the building once stood.

Several installations known to have existed at Shafford Mill have disappeared without trace, such as a steam engine that powered four Haywood-Tyler pumps moving water to a water tower a mile away at Bush Wood on the Childwickbury estate. It was replaced by a Blackstone Spring Injection diesel engine in 1923 which ran until 1957, when mains water was supplied to the estate. The engine has been removed from the site and is occasionally displayed at local steam fairs.

At Hertingfordbury a 'water house' was located on the river Lea (not to be confused with Hertingfordbury Mill, on the river Mimram). It appears to have pumped water to the ornamental water gardens at Roxford. It was re-equipped in 1888 with a Green and Carter three-throw plunger pump driven by a horizontal turbine. The building was demolished during the middle years of the twentieth century.

Finally, water from the Lea was supplied to Hatfield House itself 'by a sophisticated arrangement of pipes'.[10]

References

1. *Hertfordshire Mercury* (11 June 1881).
2. M. Graham, 'Fulling in Hertfordshire', *Hertfordshire Countryside*, 54/479 (1999).
3. M. Ashby, *The book of the river Lea* (Barracuda Books, Buckingham, 1991).
4. Hands, *Bourne End and Boxmoor*.
5. K. Major, *Animal powered engines* (Batsford, London, 1978).
6. E.A.R. Trout, *Traditional milling technology in the English cement industry, 1796–1899* (The Mills Archive Trust, Reading, 2015).
7. R. Smith and B. Carr, *A guide to the industrial archaeology of Hertfordshire and the Lea valley* (Association for Industrial Archaeology, Leicester, 2004).
8. A.J.C. Boswell, 'Chorleywood House Estate – Powerhouse at River Chess', notes (29 March 2000).
9. From the catalogue of the sale of Cassiobury House in 1922.
10. Ashby, *River Lea*.

10

Reflections on the restoration and preservation of Hertfordshire's mills

The preceding chapters have revealed some of the sweeping changes that have taken place in Hertfordshire's economy, with well-established industries, particularly the paper-making and silk-throwing industries, either losing their pre-eminence or disappearing altogether and others, such as corn milling, contracting and centralising. The fall-out has been that many historic mill buildings have become redundant. This has posed challenges relating to the future of those buildings, be it their preservation where possible or their adaptation in ways that are acceptable to both the owners of the buildings and the local planning authorities.

Conservation and preservation issues

Owners of mills, faced with the problem of an obsolete asset requiring substantial maintenance costs, have often thought it best to divest themselves of the liability and to demolish these historic structures in order to realise the full redevelopment potential from their sites, the value of which may be significant, and is often more than that of the building on it. Mill owners are not alone. From the 1920s onwards many owners of stately homes saw them only as liabilities whose retention made no economic sense. Maintaining and repairing such buildings could incur costs out of all proportion to any potential for generating enough income to cover these costs. Cassiobury and Panshanger are prime examples of mansions that have been demolished for this reason. It is little wonder, then, that development pressures have meant that there is a strong temptation for mill owners to pull out the machinery, realise its scrap value and convert the usually sound building to other, usually residential, uses. This has certainly been the case with the big industrial mills: Ware Town Mill, Sele Mill at Hertford and Grove Mill, Watford (Figure 10.1) have been converted to residential use, while Stanstead Abbotts and Park Mill, St Albans have been converted to offices.

The restoration and preservation of the county's milling heritage involves issues almost exclusively economic in character. Restoration is an invariably expensive process involving skilled, labour-intensive engineering and the manufacture of individual parts on a one-off basis. The number of potential contractors for such work is very limited. Mill machinery is not unique in this, as organisations concerned with preserving industrial heritage more widely face the same problems. The preservation

Figure 10.1 Grove Mill, Watford, today.

of mills in their original form entails foregoing a more profitable use of often well-constructed mill buildings. The problem is aggravated by the fact that while the buildings may be listed the milling machinery seldom is. Furthermore, the machinery, however obsolete, often commands a scrap value or, in the case of roller mills, can be sold on, often to developing nations.

Finding alternative uses for the buildings and carrying out sympathetic conversions is rarely easy, posing issues in terms of preserving the essence of the building while adapting its spaces to a new economic use. The core part of the mill is the machinery, and the building exists simply in order to accommodate that; the structure itself may be of no great intrinsic merit. The listing of buildings is usually concerned with the exterior of the structure and its setting, both of which may be considered to be more important than the interior. With mill buildings, in contrast, it is the mill in its entirety, both the building and its machinery, which is important. Furthermore, the conversion of mill buildings to residential use and the preservation of machinery are often incompatible, and only a handful of mills remain with a significant amount of their original machinery. Notable examples in Hertfordshire include Cromer windmill and the watermills at Hyde near Harpenden, Redbournbury and Sopwell.

The conversion of mills to houses (Figure 10.2) has, however, been going on for much of the twentieth century, as at Noake, Essendon, Digswell, Codicote, Ware Flour Mills, Twyford, Purwell, Kimpton and Abbey Mills in St Albans.

Official policy towards the conversion of mill buildings

The government's advice on the conversion of historic buildings to alternative uses is set out, most recently, in the National Planning Policy Framework: 'Where a development proposal will lead to less than substantial harm to the significance of a designated heritage asset, this harm should be weighed against the public benefits of the proposal, including securing its optimum viable use.'[1]

The advice to local authorities is to balance the benefits of conversion against any potential harm to the local heritage. Hertfordshire's local planning authorities have generally been favourably disposed towards the conversion of mill buildings to residential or office use as a route to preserving them. Their main concern is whether such proposals breach the strict green belt policy that operates over most of rural Hertfordshire. Several of the cases set out below were considered to be acceptable exceptions to green belt policy in that they enabled the preservation of an historic building to take place.

Local planning authorities have been faced with a variety of issues surrounding the conversion of mill buildings. These include accepting new uses for redundant buildings (Sele, Ware, Wheathampstead and Moor Mill), improving on unsatisfactory situations (Park Mill and Stanstead Abbotts), accepting expedients to retain historic buildings (Hertingfordbury and the fulling mill at Codicote), taking measures to

Figure 10.2 Sele Mill, Hertford, now converted to apartments.

salvage ruins (Reed and Breachwood Green windmills) and restorations after fires (Piccotts End and Bourne End).

North Herts District Council is typical of Hertfordshire local planning authorities in having a policy[2] that accepts that the maintenance of a genuinely redundant listed building may provide special circumstances to justify a relaxation of green belt policy. This policy is subject to the new use proposed not giving rise to any adverse environmental impact on the surrounding countryside. Where machinery has already gone the policy seeks to conserve what remains by accepting a residential use, even when to do so would normally be contrary to countryside and green belt policies.

Likewise, St Albans City Council pays 'particular attention to the continued use of historic buildings and consideration will be given to permitting appropriate new uses for them where this will ensure the preservation of their character and fabric'. Its relevant policy reads: 'Where there is a conflict between planning policies and a proposed change of use, the District Council may relax the policies in exceptional circumstances if this will best preserve the special character of the building and give it a new lease of life.'[3]

Local planning authorities also aim to retain complete mills where possible. This was the case presented by East Herts District Council at the public inquiry concerning the refusal of permission for the demolition of the smock mill at Little Hadham. Local planning authorities will normally seek the advice of the Mills Section of the Society for the Protection of Ancient Buildings (SPAB), which, while always favouring the retention of mills, will nevertheless critically examine each proposal on its merits. This policy was set out in a letter of 1970 concerning the conversion of Reed windmill, which has since been developed into a broad philosophy on the historical, technical and practical aspects of the protection and repair of mills: 'the first aim of the Section is to keep mills in being. Conversion to houses is undertaken and some are converted in a reasonably sympathetic manner with the existing structure: It is not an easy assignment but it can be done.'[4]

The Hertfordshire Building Preservation Trust was set up in 1963 with the aim of preserving buildings of special and historic interest in the county at a time when local planning authorities had very little power over the demolition of listed buildings. It is a private company initiated by the county council and is supported by the constituent local authorities. The voting members are drawn from district councils and the county council. There is a partially separate trading company with an advisory team, Built Environment Advisory Management Services, which provides technical advice to owners of listed buildings and carries out historical, environmental and site assessments.

The practicalities of conservation and restoration

The restoration of mills is technically skilled, expensive and ongoing, as shown by this brief summary of the phases of the restoration of Cromer windmill (Figure 10.3).

Figure 10.3 Cromer Mill in its heyday, c.1920. *Photo by T.W. Latchmore. Kindly supplied by R. Webb.*

RESTORATION AND PRESERVATION

First phase During 1968/9 a new ladder and fantail were constructed and a second set of sail frames was put on. This cost some £4,000, which was raised via an appeal to the members of the Trust and donations from local people.

Second phase In 1979/80 substantial steel reinforcing plates running the full length of the mill were added to the side girts†, which are often the weak point of a post mill. Several steel tie rods were added to take some of the diagonal strains. At the same time the sail frames were taken off because the timber was found to be substandard. In all, the cost was some £7,000.

Third phase In 1989–90 the late Vincent Pargeter, the acclaimed millwright, was commissioned to design an appropriate set of sails, which was installed in 1990. At the same time the brake wheel was rebuilt. It had been broken during a gale in 1923 and had not turned since then. The striking gear was replaced and a partial set of new shutters was installed. The internal restoration was also completed, with the addition of the bin floor and the millstone furniture. Dorothea Restorations Ltd undertook major structural repairs, including the renewal of the weatherboarding, the rebuilding of the brake wheel and the refitting of the sails.

In 2003 the fantail was rebuilt. All this cost £63,000, which was provided by grants from English Heritage and East Herts District Council, with a loan from the Architectural Heritage Fund. The work was again carried out by Dorothea Restorations. Since then the mill has been open to the public.

Fourth phase In 2010 the three white sides of the buck were reboarded to replace poor-quality timber. This cost £70,000 and was funded by grants from English Heritage and the Heritage Lottery Fund, with a contribution from the Trust itself.

Fifth phase In 2013 the steps, ladder and fantail, which were nearing the end of their life, were replaced. The new fantail is a faithful copy of the one present when the mill ceased working in 1923. The new ladder includes a sack slide. Finally, the tram wheels have been realigned so that they are splayed to follow the circular track.

In 1984 Letchworth Garden City Corporation campaigned for the complete removal of Cromer windmill, which it proposed to re-erect on another site. The view of SPAB was that this was a special case and an exception to their normal policy: 'Usually the Society does not approve of buildings being removed from their original site but, given the special circumstances of Cromer windmill, and the fact that there is a history of post mills being moved, in this particular case it will not object to the application.' However, the expense of this proposal, at £75,000, was more than could be afforded at the time and the move did not take place.

Case studies

There have been a number of cases over the years that have collectively provided a synthesis of official views and a robust policy stance on which local authorities have relied. This has meant that a small but significant number of the county's mills have been preserved for posterity.

Bourne End (see pp. 88–9)

There was an extant permission for conversion of the building, which was provisionally listed, to five flats. In 1967 there was a two-day public inquiry into two schemes, one for the demolition of the mill and the other involving the use of the mill as a ten-bedroom motel. At that time it had been used for the storage of waste paper. However, in 1970 fire seriously damaged the mill. Permission was then granted for a scheme for a 50-bedroom motel that incorporated existing buildings and retained the waterwheel.

Little Hadham and Roydon (see pp. 119 and 133–4)

These two cases saw planning inspectors resisting the calls for the demolition of mills on the basis that they were still capable of restoration and a successful new life. In both cases the secretary of state supported the local authority's policy.

In December 1978 listed building consent was sought for the demolition of the Grade II listed smock mill at Little Hadham on the grounds that its undisputed dilapidated and dangerous condition placed it beyond realistic restoration. Permission was refused by East Herts District Council for the reason that it was the only remaining smock mill in Hertfordshire and was considered to be of importance both architecturally and historically, reflecting a particular period in the evolution of windmill design and construction. The council considered that it was still capable of restoration and served a notice on the owner of the mill to the effect that if the necessary work was not carried out within the period specified the repairs would be put in hand by the authority.[5]

An appeal against the council's decision was duly lodged, the public inquiry providing the opportunity to set out the uniqueness of the mill, to assess the scale of work necessary for restoration and to establish the cost of doing so. The evidence of Millwrights International said that restoration would be more straightforward than at Lacey Green, the smock mill in Buckinghamshire on which the company had also worked. The witness provided a vivid reminder of the problems inherent in dealing with listed buildings: 'The crucial question appears to be whether or not this mill justifies preservation at some cost, possibly involving public expenditure and possibly requiring compulsory purchase.'⁶

The appeal was dismissed in July 1981 on the grounds that the possibility of restoration had not been fully pursued. The Chiltern Open Air Museum had expressed an interest in acquiring the mill and the appellant was willing to donate it. However, within a month the mill was destroyed by fire.

The same argument was used in the case of Roydon watermill (Figure 10.4), where an application had been submitted for its demolition. The local planning authority objected to the proposal because of the mill's rarity and the benefits of preserving it for future generations. On appeal the inspector expressed the view that the mill should, if at all possible, be preserved either in its present form or as a restored original mill structure. He was not convinced that such a restored building was incapable of being put to a valid use, possibly recreational or social, perhaps including some residential units. The mill has since been restored as part of the Roydon Mill Leisure Park (Plate 23).

Windmills at Breachwood Green and Reed (see pp. 141 and 145)

In both cases these former tower mills were in a ruinous state to the point of collapse. The local planning authorities took the view that conversion to residential use was

Figure 10.4 Roydon watermill towards the end of the nineteenth century. Reproduced by kind permission of W. Wright.

Figure 10.5 Breachwood Green windmill today.

RESTORATION AND PRESERVATION

the only way of preserving and restoring them, even at the expense of making an exception to the rigidly enforced green belt policy.

Permission was granted in 1993 for the conversion and change of use to a dwelling of the Breachwood Green tower mill. The planning officer stated that the disused windmill was in a poor state of repair and that the scheme to restore it to residential use was acceptable even in a green belt location. This conversion is unusual in that it did not involve any additional annexe or extension. The cap has been replaced as faithfully as possible. Mountings for sails are in place so that, in theory at least, sails could one day be attached (Figure 10.5).

Likewise, Reed windmill was considered to be in very poor condition and in a dangerous state, and the planning officer recommended that the top section should be removed completely and that serious consideration should perhaps be given to complete demolition.[7] However, this did not happen and the tower is now part of a house (Figure 10.6).

Figure 10.6 Reed windmill conversion, c.1978. Kindly supplied from the Tom Doig collection.

Goldfield windmill (see p. 145)

In this case the tower was in reasonable condition but lacked a long-term use. Unlike the other two cases, it was not situated in the green belt and hence a conversion, considered the best way of ensuring the preservation of the listed building, was more easily accepted.[8] A common problem with converting windmill towers is that, because of the battering of the courses of brickwork, it is notoriously difficult to ensure that the interior surface remains dry. Lime mortar is porous and pointing with cement mortar is undesirable for historic structures. Traditionally they were painted in tar, but modern opinion considers it regrettable to obscure the historic brickwork. Some form of external cladding may be the only way of overcoming this fundamental problem.

Hertingfordbury Mill (see p. 108)

The mill is listed Grade II and lies within the green belt. In 1943 it was converted to a corn-drying plant. Planning permission was granted to convert the 'redundant mill' to four dwellings, along with further dwellings in outbuildings, in November 1996.[9] The proposal was considered to be an acceptable exception to green belt policy as it ensured the preservation of this historic building[10] (Plates 19, 20 and 21).

Figure 10.7 The fulling mill at Codicote today.

RESTORATION AND PRESERVATION

Codicote fulling mill (see p. 179)

In 1989 permission was granted to convert an existing disused mill, previously used for industrial purposes but which had been redundant for over two years, and an adjacent barn situated to the north of the mill, for residential purposes. The council accepted that the proposal was an acceptable exception to green belt policy. Then, in 1990, applications for alterations to convert the existing mill building and detached barn to offices were submitted. North Herts District Council saw no material objection on the basis that the machinery was long gone. Neither the planning officer nor the conservation officer objected to the principle of the development, although the latter sought detailed improvements to the design.[11] The council was satisfied that the proposed use for offices would secure a suitable alternative use for the listed building while retaining the character of the mill and its reason for being listed (Figure 10.7).

Ware Park Mill (see p. 112)

A comprehensive proposal was submitted in 2008 for the 'reinstatement' of the ruins of Ware Park Mill to a five-storey block of eleven flats which also involved the conversion of a barn and garage and the provision of a restaurant, moorings and a car park. The local planning authority considered that the proposal, for what was essentially a new residential development, amounted to an inappropriate development in the green belt; in this case, there were no special circumstances to over-rule the green belt policy. Furthermore, the proposal would have been likely to damage what remained of the listed building rather than to enhance it. Permission was refused and the proposal was dismissed on appeal in 2009.[12]

Park Mill (see p. 93)

In some cases a local authority might decide that a change of use could result in a distinct improvement. This was the case when St Albans City Council granted permission in 1984 for the change of use of Park Mill, which was in a generally poor condition, from a breakers yard to offices, including a significant extension to the east. In planning terms this was a considerable benefit to the neighbourhood; over the previous 60 years undesirable uses of the mill had included a glue factory and then a scrap yard, all in a building rendered unsightly by the bricking up of its windows and its deteriorating condition (Figure 10.8). The conversion also allowed the preservation of the waterwheels, which were the only surviving pieces of the original mill machinery. The conversion was done to a high standard and no doubt the Park Street community has benefited from it (Figure 10.9).[13]

Wheathampstead Mill (see p. 97)

In this case the use of the building as a provender mill, with the consequent amount

Figure 10.8 Park Mill, before conversion. Reproduced by kind permission of Susan Watts.

Figure 10.9 Park Mill, after conversion to offices.

of traffic generated, was proving increasingly problematic. The change of use of the mill building to retail, business and residential use was considered by St Albans City Council to be more appropriate to the location (Plate 22).

Moor Mill (see p. 65)

This mill had a complicated planning history involving a blight order and a planning inquiry, in which the inspector allowed an appeal against the refusal of an application to change its use.

After it ceased working in 1939 it was used as part of a farm until 1980, when it was sold to the Department of Transport under a 'blight order' because of its proximity to the line of the proposed M25 motorway. The Department proceeded to lease the mill and surrounding buildings to a number of businesses, including a car repair garage. St Albans City Council refused permission for the temporary use for car repairs and a public inquiry took place in March 1984.[14]

At the same time a local businessman applied for permission to convert the mill into a restaurant and cocktail bar, with the prospect of restoring the building to its 'original' condition. This involved the clearance of untidy sheds and the restoration of an adjacent barn. 'Enabling development', to offset the costs of the restoration, included the erection of a motel. The motel would be in two new buildings similar in scale to the existing black-boarded and red-tiled barn. This proposal was seen as an acceptable exception to green belt policy. In 1985 the mill wheels turned for the first time since 1939.[15] Altogether, the outcome was far more satisfactory than might have been expected.

However, in 1986 the use of vibrating rollers during motorway construction brought the proposal to a premature end with the collapse of the barn and the development of cracks and damage to the mill house, requiring the building to be shored up. This led to the granting of an injunction against the motorway contractor.[16]

Subsequently a company specialising in old historic inns purchased the mill in 1989 and sought to renew the planning permission, which had nearly expired. A year later the company submitted a proposal for a larger scheme, with an additional motel block of 44 rooms and a car park. In addition to the conversion of the mill building itself, the Mill House was to become a manager's flat and residents' lounge. Permission was refused by St Albans City Council. A councillor was quoted as saying, 'There has got to be a balance between keeping the mill and an intensification of its use. We do not want to see more than the minimum allowed to maintain the mill.'[17] The council also served a repair notice on the applicant.[18]

In March 1991 a public inquiry was held into the council's refusal and the appeal was upheld. The inspector concluded:

> The principal issue in this appeal is the effect of the proposed alterations, extensions and new building upon the character and setting of the existing Grade Two listed building.
>
> The scheme would result in the removal of an unsightly collection of buildings which detract seriously from the appearance of the local scene.
>
> Although a greater area of the site would be covered by buildings, the removal of what exists would be a benefit.
>
> On balance, the setting of the listed buildings would be enhanced by the development.

The inspector argued that the retention, repair and reuse of the listed buildings justified an exception to normal green belt policy.[19]

In September that year work on the restoration of the mill finally started (Plates 3 and 4). Among other works, five craftsmen spent six weeks repairing both waterwheels. The restaurant was opened on 18 May 1992.[20]

On the Essex side of the river Stort are two encouraging examples of preserved watermills enjoying new uses. Parndon Mill is now a centre for the visual arts with art gallery, studios and craft workshops. And Roydon Mill, once the subject of a planning application for demolition, is now the centrepiece of the Roydon Village Marina (Plate 23).

Conclusion

One hundred and fifty years ago milling, in all its forms, was a major part of Hertfordshire's economy. Since that time it has been overtaken by many more modern and technically advanced forms of industry. Milling has declined in both relative and absolute terms.

Much of the heritage has inevitably been lost, but imaginative initiatives to find new uses for redundant mill buildings on the part of mill owners and developers, coupled with equally imaginative responses from planning authorities, have ensured that several interesting historic buildings have been saved. However, these successes cannot compensate for the extensive losses of mill buildings that have occurred.

I have suggested elsewhere that, when faced with a proposal for the conversion of a mill, local authorities should apply a sequential test, the first part of which should be to ascertain whether the use for which the building was designed can be continued and maintained. Only if that fails should an alternative optimum viable use, which may not necessarily be the most profitable one, be entertained.[21]

The ideal must be to conserve any mill in its state as a working mill. If this is not possible then there are a range of options which would allow the building to be conserved in its historic form. These might, for example, include an educational resource or a community centre for a variety of functions. Imagination is the key to success. This sequential test has been applied, consciously or unconsciously, to planning applications for the demolition or conversion of many of Hertfordshire's mills. The appeal decisions at Little Hadham and Roydon sought to retain mills in their original form. Conversions where the machinery had already been lost secured a future for the windmills at Breachwood Green, Reed and Goldfield and for the watermills at Hertingfordbury and Moor Mill. Making an exception to green belt policy was justified at Hertingfordbury and Breachwood Green, but not at Ware Park, where 'reinstatement' essentially meant a new development which would have done nothing to conserve an historic asset.

Much of Hertfordshire's milling heritage has already been lost. However, the county is still home to major flour-milling companies and two traditional vernacular watermills which produce stone-ground flour. There is also a lone example of a complete windmill. Tangible remains of two of Hertfordshire's milling industries, paper and silk, are also present.

This book has aimed to provide a comprehensive overview of a significant part of Hertfordshire's industrial heritage. It sets this overview within the dynamic of the nation's history from the time of the industrial revolution and the context of prevailing economic forces.

References

1. Department of Communities and Local Government, *National Planning Policy Framework,* Paragraph 134 (2012).
2. North Herts District Plan, Policy 7.
3. St Albans City Plan, Policy 88.
4. Society for the Protection of Ancient Buildings, *A philosophy of repair of windmills and watermills* (London, 2004).
5. East Hertfordshire District Council Report, Febuary 1979.
6. Proof of evidence, D.J. Nicholls.
7. D. Ogden, 'Report on Reed Windmill' (16 March 1970).
8. *Berkhamsted Gazette* (27 October 1967, 13 November 1970 and 11 June 1971).
9. East Hertfordshire District Council, Development Control Committee report (5 October 1996), Application 3/96/0092.
10. North Hertfordshire District Council applications nos 89/00075/1 89/00065/1 LB.
11. North Hertfordshire District Council report on planning applications nos 90/00757/1 90/00758/1LB Codicote.
12. Appeal Decision Ref APP/J1915/A/09/2104291.

13 *Herts Advertiser* (23 March 1984, 15 November 1984 and 14 December 1984).
14 *Herts Advertiser* (29 January 1982 and 16 March 1984); *Review* (21 March 1985).
15 *St Albans Observer* (4 July 1986 and 11 July 1986).
16 *Review* (7 November 1985).
17 *Herts Advertiser* (26 January 1990).
18 *Herts Advertiser* (20 April 1990, 14 September 1990); *Herald and Post* (19 April 1990).
19 *Herts Advertiser* (9 January 1991, 30 January 1991).
20 *Herts Advertiser* (3 April 1991); *St Albans Observer* (3 July 1991); *Herald and Post* (26 September 1991).
21 H. Howes, *The windmills and watermills of Bedfordshire – past, present and future* (Book Castle Publishing, Copt Hewick, N. Yorks, 2009).

Appendix 1

'The country mill in wartime', extract from *The Miller*, 1 April 1918

By 'Excelsior'

While looking through the back copies of THE MILLER I have just come across an article by Mr Charles Richardson, of Par, in a June issue of last year. The whole article is well worth looking up again for it has not grown out of date. To quote one sentence 'The miller who possesses the soundest and most extensive technical knowledge with practical experience and has a fully equipped and well flowed plant, had and has, the best chance to accomplish the results demanded in the shortest time with the least changes and expenses and ultimately has, and will produce a satisfactory sack of flour of the particular Regulation grade required'.

That statement points out that the only way to successful milling in War Time – but what should be also in peace time – sound and extensive technical knowledge backed up by practical working experience, leading the miller to the desired results in the shortest time with the least expense. In other words the best miller 'makes good' first. Today really first class millers are about as scarce as gold coins. Yet how could it be otherwise? Put the blame on the War if we like, but if we are wise then we shall think twice before doing so. The shortage of really first class men is not a War result. True, it has been accentuated by the War, but the cause does not all lie therein, nor will the closing of the War see the end of the troubles if millers revert to the suicidal policy of pre War days. So long as profitable milling, as an art, is subservient to wheat speculations and the commercial life made more attractive than mill life we cannot expect to find an adequate stream of young men entering the milling industry on the manufacturing side.

If the country miller, to be successful, must in most cases have personal technical knowledge at a fairly high standard. Less than that would not suffice, neither will the size of his business warrant the expense of buying such knowledge from anyone else capable of supplying the same. The country miller's fortune is clearly interlaced with the prosperity, or otherwise, of the farming industry in normal times, and is, therefore, very dependent on climatic conditions and other variable elements. The changing quality of our native grain crops, not only from one year to another, but also during the deliveries of any one season's yield continually, brings the practical miller face to face with many difficult problems. It must never be forgotten that the real solution of the agricultural problem depends somewhat on the ability of the country miller to produce from home grown wheats, a loaf satisfactory to the general public of these islands. The country miller therefore, at this stage has a large and vital part to play and he must not fail therein. He has already successfully extricated himself from many dark and dangerous corners into which circumstances beyond his control have pitched him. In the past when the milling trade has been too lean, he has developed a connection in stone-ground wheatmeal, or gone into the provender trade, or the corn trade, perhaps taken to farming or other kindred art, but whatever he has touched has usually been mastered. Many country millers have made quite pleasing profits on the wheat markets at times, but the attitude of the average miller to that does not match the view of the merchant miller. Ultimate success in business consists in giving such excellent value in goods that the purchasers come back with repeated orders. The first duty of the miller is to manufacture the best possible flour. The first precaution of the manufacturer is to maintain an adequate manufacturing profit based on a margin between the price of the day of the wheat and its products. A manufacturer's profit should consist of the value added to his raw material in his manufacturing process, over and above the cost of treatment. The miller, therefore, with wide practical experience reflected in a modern well-arranged mill, stands to ensure such a margin, and if that can be increased by commercial astuteness well and good. But the miller who sells his finished products of the day at, and often below, the value of his wheat, trusting almost entirely to his market manipulations to balance the job would probably make just as much money without his mill as with it.

Better conditions will not prevail in the milling industry until by agreement or compulsion, true milling knowledge is the real basis of success; when money cannot secure advantages for the one class that experience or brains on the part of the owner cannot ensure on the other hand. Experience is a valuable asset but its practical value depends on the ability to adjust it with advantage to one's own affairs.

Country millers have amassed considerable experience in dealing with many varieties of grain – wheat, oats, barley, rye, beans, maize and so forth; and various Government regulations have presented a unique chance of putting things to the test in many cases to the discomfort of those firms trusting in capital and commerce to see them through. I am not pitting myself against the large merchant millers 'en bloc' for we are all ready to recognise the superior technical knowledge of the leading individuals in certain of the largest concerns who only a few years ago had small

APPENDIX 1

country businesses but those are the cases where experience has already been put to the test and been found wanting.

It is my purpose here to set out how many country mills have with good success endeavoured to comply with the many and ever-changing milling regulations. Before control with the fixed extractions became the order of the day the progressive men had already begun to stir themselves. The rising value of raw materials and the widening gap between flour and offal prices together with the increasing demand for the lower grade flours all tended to enhance the value of good milling and make an increased extraction of flour a desirable, nay, a needful thing. The first Flour and Bread Order decreed that after November 1916/8 no flour other than Straight Run flour should be milled and that the extraction of flour from wheat should be on the basis of 76 per cent. English wheat and 78 per cent Australian. The flour made under that order was a great success proving how essential it is to maintain a well-milled, well-balanced flour. It is safe to assume that such a flour will in the future be a most desirable basis for further competitive trading. Quickly following came an Order demanding an extra 5 per cent of flour either by further extraction from the wheat or by the addition of flour derived from other cereals. It was at this point that the country miller's experience of handling other cereal than wheat stood him in good stead, although it was not a short time before the alternative clauses were both insisted upon. First hand experience on G.R. flour up to this stage proved that –

1 It was possible by good milling to add substantially to pre-War flour lengths without unduly lowering the quality of a Straight Run flour.

2 That the need for ample roll grading and dressing surface, aided by plenty of well-arranged and skilfully manipulated purifiers, increased as the percentage of extraction increased.

3 That whilst in conditioning wheat an increase in the weight of products is desirable, the real aim should be to make possible a maximum extraction of flour of the best possible quality.

4 That granted the above conditions exist, the maximum economy in the consumption of wheat is reached when the extraction of flow is about 78 per cent., that is, after that stage is passed the lower bread yield and the reduced quantity of cattle feed more than balance the value of the increased percentage of flour as a food for man, because then its food value is beyond the zenith.

Appendix 2

London: Docks and Mark Lane

From the late eighteenth century onwards grain was being imported up the Thames estuary, starting a trend which was ultimately to destroy the economics of local milling in the home counties. The ensuing large-scale mills were able to reap economic advantages in terms of economies of scale which local inland mills could not hope to achieve. They were not dependent on the vagaries of wind and water and could be relied upon to produce flour in the quantities required by a rapidly growing metropolis.

The first steam-powered mill, the Albion Mill in Bermondsey, opened in 1786 and at once demonstrated the advantages of taking grain directly from the river. Other mills, including those on the Lea, received grain by barges, which involved an additional transhipment.

The Millwall Dock, which opened in 1868, was built specifically to handle imported grain, replacing the Surrey Docks in that role. Its first mill, opened in 1869, was the Wheatsheaf Mill, built by the McDougall brothers, the first of the giant milling concerns. This was followed in 1903 by the Central Granary, which boasted a technological and economically beneficial innovation, the pneumatic suction elevator. This was far more efficient than the mechanical bucket scoop systems that had been used to unload ships until then.

The pre-eminence of the Millwall Dock gave way to the Royal Victoria Dock, where the first of three industrial-scale mills opened in 1901. This was the CWS's mill. It was closely followed by Joseph Rank's Premier Mill in 1904 and in 1905 by the Millennium Mills of William Vernon and Sons, a company that was to become Spillers in 1920. These mills were part of a complex of silos for grain storage. Despite suffering severe damage in 1917 in an explosion at a nearby munitions factory in Silvertown and bomb damage in World War II, these mills provided flour for white bread for London and the home counties until the 1960s, when the focus of mass milling once again moved east to Tilbury, where, in 1957, Rank Hovis McDougall founded the Bulk Grain Terminal.

The Mark Lane Corn Exchange

The Corn Exchange in Mark Lane was founded in the 1740s and the first exchange building was erected *c.*1750 on the east side of Mark Lane. The building was enlarged in 1827 and roofed in 1850. A rival exchange was set up immediately to the north. The two organisations were merged in 1929. In 1882 the 'old' corn exchange was demolished and replaced by a far larger building with an Italianate façade. The corn exchange was destroyed by 'enemy action' in 1941 and a replacement building was opened in 1953. By the 1970s the number of traders had declined and the traders moved to the Baltic Exchange on St Mary Axe, which was itself destroyed by a terrorist's bomb in 1992.

The growth of trading in Mark Lane led to the decline of local corn exchanges throughout the home counties. Gradually the business that had been transacted in corn was lost to the London Exchange. The local corn exchanges were fine civic buildings, often in neo-classical styles, and date from the middle of the nineteenth century. They became redundant in the 1960s and 1970s. As they occupied valuable town centre sites, they were threatened with proposals for redevelopment and consequent demolition. Happily, those in Hertfordshire – in Hertford, St Albans, Hitchin and Bishops Stortford – have found new uses, mostly as offices and shops, and have retained much of their original character. (Figures A1 and A2)

Figure 1 A busy day in the Hitchin Corn Exchange. Reproduced by kind permission of Jas. Bowman and Sons Ltd.

Figure 2 Bishops Stortford Corn Exchange today.

Mark Lane also became a national centre for milling and was described in *The Miller* as 'the "Mecca" of England's grain trade'.[1] It became a centre, or commercial hub, for the milling industry by the beginning of the twentieth century – a veritable cluster of concentrated expertise.

Several important suppliers of milling equipment congregated in Mark Lane. The leading firms were:

APPENDIX 2

- At No. 20, **J.J. Armfield & Co.** of Ringwood, a pioneer in the manufacture of roller mills, which were 'Made in 30 sizes to suit all plants'. The penstock operational gear, visible at Hertingfordbury Mill, was made by them. The company was noted for its turbines.

- At No. 26, **William R. Dell and Son**, who were millstone builders, machinists and mill furnishers. The company clearly marketed its 'small mill', powered by a 10 hp beam engine, fitted with automatic cut-off governors and capable of making four sacks of flour per hour, at the struggling 'country millers'.

- At No. 28, **Whitmore and Binyon**, who were 'Millwrights, Engineers, Founder and Boiler Makers, Flour Mill Machinery and Fittings'.

- At No. 56, **Bryan Corcoran**, a firm founded in 1780 and run by three generations of the same family. The company described itself as ' Builder of Best Quality French Millstones'.

- At No. 64, **S Howes**, who were 'General Mill Furnishers and contractors to H.M. Government also Russian, French, Indian, Egyptian and Cape Governments'. They advertised grain washers, turbines and graders for barley and rye.

- At No. 69, **Clarke and Dunham**, supplying machinery for flour millers.

- At No. 82, **E.R. and F. Turner**, manufacturing agricultural machines and stationary steam engines and progressing into flour milling machinery, particularly high-quality roller mills in the 1880s. The company features strongly in Hertfordshire, having supplied five mills with their equipment: Walkern, Ickleford, Bourne End, Kings Langley and Tring.

Today no trace of the corn exchange or the milling industry remains in Mark Lane. The contrasting recorded recollections of those who worked there are therefore particularly valuable. First, Peter Bowman:

> Peter always found the Mark Lane market in the City of London instructive and alive with trade. It was attended by upwards of 500 traders, including millers, maltsters, flour factors, flour buyers, grain merchants, sack and bag suppliers, insurance brokers, machine manufacturers and the occasional accountant among many others.[2]

Then Bryan Corcoran as a child:

> …was quite familiar with the fact that the millstone chips would often fly upwards and break little starry holes in the house windows. There was also the constant noise of the chipping itself, hammering and rivetting of the hoops, and the thud of the wire weaving looms. Great blazing fires were also burning for heating the hoops. A furnace was heated by day for baking the plaster of Paris by night, and the latter was also ground on the premises. Big jobs were often done in the yard itself under temporary erections, and the seams of large woven kiln floors were frequently being flattened by men hammering away at them with wooden mallets, on a pavement made of granite slabs.[3]

References

1   'After many days', *The Miller* (1 April 1901).
2   Bowman, 'Bill, thrift and damsel'.
3   'After many days', *The Miller* (1 April 1901).

Appendix 3

The archaeology of Hyde Mill, Ickleford

The mill house was demolished in the very late 1920s or possibly 1930. The mill probably ceased producing animal feed in the 1930s, but the mill building itself was not completely demolished until the late 1940s. The mill wheel, together with those of Bowman's Mill and possibly Oughton Head Mill, were taken to support the war effort in 1942/3 (Figure A3).

During 2011 a local archaeological group, under the aegis of the Ickleford Parish Council, uncovered the base of the walls and floors of the mill house and that part of the mill building on the north side of the river Oughton. The excavation revealed a rough and antiquated house with floors of varying levels consisting of tiles resting on

Figure 3 The mill race and site of the waterwheel today. Kindly supplied by R. Freeman.

Figure 4 Parts of the waterwheel have been recovered from the mill race; part of the rim is shown with a bracket for supporting a bucket.

Figure 5 A reconstruction of the waterwheel based on the parts recovered from the mill race. Reproduced by kind permission of R. Freeman.

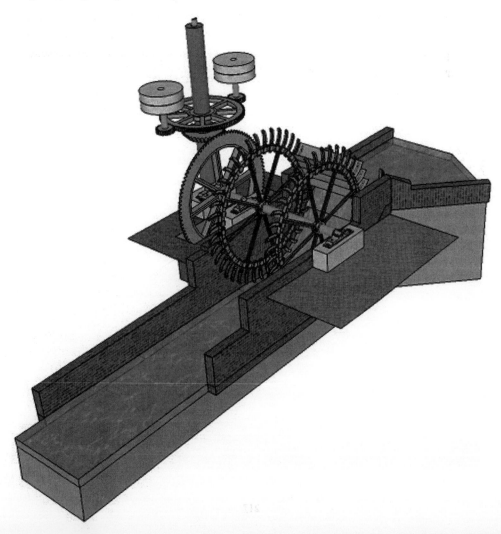

APPENDIX 3

bare earth. The building must have been demolished to within a few inches of floor level, with anything below this being covered over. The excavations have been recorded and the site re-covered with geotextile and earth from the excavations. During the excavations of the mill race several cast-iron pieces of the mill wheel were discovered (Figure A4). The following year the mill building on the south side was excavated and the outer walls and mounting blocks for the axle of the wheel were located. Further pieces of the wheel were discovered. So far it has not been possible to excavate the pit for the pit wheel.

The parts of the wheel included pieces of the rims and parts of the arms, including a section with a bolt hole that showed how the two halves of the wheel would have been joined. From these it has been possible to generate a synthetic model of the wheel (Figure A5). This suggests a breastshot wheel, probably dating from 1820, 12' in diameter and 6' in width, with the water being introduced at axle level. The position of the headstock is clearly visible. The wheel is likely to have had two rims and eight spokes cast integrally in two halves and bolted together with joints running down the centre of two of the arms. The brackets are of cast iron and are joined to the rims with cast-iron wedges supporting 40 floats (or paddles). The shape of the brackets, with a flat curve and large radius, suggests open-ended floats, which would be consistent with a breastshot wheel of the period.

Appendix 4

'Mr B. Coles new mill at Luton, Bedfordshire', extract from The Miller, 1 May 1893

(Gardner's System)

This mill, known as the Hyde Mills, near Luton, Bedfordshire, has recently been fitted up completely by Mr William Gardner, milling engineer of Gloucester, with one of his small roller plants, in which that gentleman employs three breaks and five reductions to reduce the wheat to flour and offal. In this plant Mr Gardner has, we understand, embodied machines of his latest type, and the illustration which is a longitudinal section of the mill, will give our readers some idea as to the method adopted by Mr Gardner in fitting up a mill of this capacity on his small roller system.

The building, which was originally the warehouse for stone flour, &c., is the part into which the plant is put, and it consists only of two floors, and much thought was required on the part of Mr Gardner and staff to place a plant in so small a compass.

On entering the mill it will at once be observed that an excavation was necessary to allow for the main drive and elevator bottoms, and a great feature of this mill is that though standing on the ground floor the miller can at once see the whole of the shafting with main drive, and also the roller mills with their adjustments, &c., which have been fixed on a very strong and rigid platform above this excavation, thus making a very neat and attractive roller floor.

The elevators run to the top of mill and have glass panes in their trunks on the two floors so that the flow of material can be seen at any time by the operator on the floor which he is attending.

The four double roller mills are fitted with rolls 6 in. diameter, and are of very neat design, and contain the necessary adjustments with long gun metal bearings, automatic feeds, and special lubrication arrangements. In this mill the rolls are firmly secured to the strong platform mentioned above, and so placed as to allow ample room to inspect the working of each machine. It should here be mentioned that in these roller mills special facilities are made for taking the rolls out quickly so as not

APPENDIX 4

to interfere with the frames of the machine. Above the roller mills is the shafting for driving the centrifugals and other machines on the floor above and arrangements have been made so that all the main drives, belts, and bearings are easily accessible from the ground floor.

On the first or top floor are placed the purifier, rotary scalper, centrifugals, break meal centrifugal and bran duster. The elevator tops are also observable here. The purifier is one of Gardner's dustless double sieve purifiers fitted with Bates' patent air tunnels over each sieve. The centrifugals are of Gardner's iron frame pattern, and take up very little room, and doors are provided for the inspection of the work as required. A double rotary scalper is used, and this is fitted with balance wheel and adjustable toe, so that the throw may be altered as desired. We notice that the exhaust is attached to all necessary points throughout the system.

The whole mill is very compact, well-finished, and presents a very neat appearance, turning out an excellent sack of flour, leaving the offals exceedingly well, the output being about two sacks an hour. The power is obtained from a horizontal engine, also a waterwheel, these also driving the stones for Mr Coles grist trade.

NB: The mill itself is in Hertfordshire and the mill house is in Bedfordshire.

Appendix 5

'Mr Toovey's New Roller Flour Mill At King's Langley, Herts', extract from *The Miller*, 4 September 1893

(Turner's System)

We had the pleasure during the past month of paying a visit to the King's Langley Flour Mills, which have been recently fitted with a roller plant by the well-known milling engineers Messrs. E.R. & F. Turner of 82 Mark lane, London E.C. and Ipswich, for Mr T.W. Toovey, whose great grandfather came into possession and worked these mills in the year 1780. The pretty village of King's Langley, or as it is sometimes called Langley King's, is situated about 17 miles W.S.W. of Hertford, and is noted for its ancient church, in which is the tomb of the fifth son of King Edward the Third. The flour mills are most advantageously placed for receiving the raw material by means of the Grand Junction Canal, and distributing flour to the northern suburbs of London by means of the water carriage thus provided. The mills were taken over by Mr Thomas Toovey in 1780, a few years before the Grand Junction Canal was built, so that its water rights remain unimpaired, and part of the power required today to drive the machinery in the roller mill and the old millstone mill is furnished by the water taken at the head of the mill from the canal. Mr Thomas Toovey, the founder of this flour milling business, married into the family owning the King's Langley Mill and surrounding property, and so came into possession of the mill in 1780 when he rebuilt the millhouse for the reception of his bride. In this house was born the son, Mr Thomas Toovey, who succeeded his father in the milling business, and in this house also Mr William Archibald Toovey, the father of the present occupier, saw the light, and welcomed us when we visited the mill in the company of Mr A.R. Tattersall, of Messrs Turners, on behalf of his son, who had been called away on some important business. Mr William Archibald Toovey, who was well known on Mark Lane market to millers of the last generation, after being in business for 51 years, handed over the mill and business to his son, the present occupier, Mr T.W. Toovey, on January 1 1886. Recently the mill, as before stated, has been equipped with a roller millplant having a capacity of five sacks per hour.

APPENDIX 5

Roller mill proper

The roller mill plant is situated in a brick building of three storeys and so arranged as to receive the power direct from the steam engine and also from a 'Hercules' turbine.

Ground floor

On the ground floor we noticed 12 elevator bottoms of the elevators used for carrying the material from one machine to be dealt with on the succeeding machine. Here also is the foreman's office.

First floor

The first floor is given up to the six double 'Turner' roller mills for breaking down the wheat on the system of four breaks, and reducing the semolina, middlings and dunst to flour on four double machines, and the different spouts for packing the flour and offals on this floor. The first, second, third and fourth breaks are accomplished on two double roller mills fitted each with four smooth chilled iron rolls 40 in by 10 in, two breaks being effected on one machine. The semolina, middlings, dunst and tailings are reduced on four double roller mills, fitted with four smooth chilled iron rolls 25 in by 9 in. One of the peculiarities of this mill is noticed on this floor, where, on account of the old water mill on the ground floor, it was found impossible to drive the roller mills excepting from above, so that there are on this floor two lines of shafting from which the roller mills are driven. The breaks rolls are driven from the first line of shafting on this floor by means of a six inch belt. One end of the main line shafting on this floor is connected by gearing, with clutch, to the vertical shaft of the 'Hercules' turbine, while at the opposite end of the shafting is driven direct from the engine by belting. We also noticed on this floor an offal sieve, a cockle cylinder and two elevator bottoms.

Second floor

The second floor contains five sieve purifiers of Messrs Turner' latest design, two centrifugal flour dressing machines, a dickey sieve, a unique dust collector and three pneumatic sorters, which beat the material received from the first, second and third break scalpers, thus relieving the succeeding breaks from material that it is not necessary for it to treat.

Third floor

The third or top, floor is given up to three inter-elevator scalpers placed in one line and driven by means of one shaft along a silk reel five sheets long for breaking the chop material, a centrifugal used as a bran duster, a dickey sieve, four centrifugal flour dressing machines, and an inter-elevator flour dresser. There are also on this floor the heads of the elevators, which are all driven by separate straps.

Motive power

The motive power necessary to drive the roller plant is obtained from a Marshall high pressure and condenser engine of 20 nominal horse power, with a fly-wheel of 8 ft, a stroke of 18 in, and a 10 in, cylinder, and a 'Hercules' turbine water wheel 36 in in diameter. There is also the old breast-shot water wheel which is 17 ft in diameter and 6 ft wide, which drives two pairs of millstones in the mill for gristing purposes.

It should be added that besides the machinery mentioned in the roller mill, we noticed two 'Eureka' smutters, one horizontal and one vertical, and a 'Victor' brush machine, for treating the wheat as it arrived at the mill.

There is such a demand for the flour produced by this mill, on account of the excellent manner in which it is run, that the roller plant is kept in full operation night and day.

Appendix 6

'Mr J.G. Knowles and Sons', extract from *The Miller*, 3 April 1911

That there is plenty of profitable business for energetic country millers with a knowledge of their trade and locality was borne in upon us last month when we paid a visit to the handsome substantial mills recently erected by Messrs J.G. Knowles and Son close to the railway station and on the side of the canal at Berkhampsted.

The founder of the business was the late Mr J.G. Knowles of Broadway Farm between Berkhampsted and Boxmoor. He did a very considerable trade in the district and in 1893 took a long lease of Bourne End Mill which is only a short distance from Broadway Farm. He ran the mill on the stone system till about the end of 1900 when he decided to install the rollers and placed his contract with Messrs E.R. and F. Turner of Ipswich, his son, Mr Alfred G. Knowles, taking over the practical management of the mill. Mr J.G. Knowles died a few years ago and his son has since carried on the business both of mills and farm. Bourne End Mill, like a good many country mills, lies at some little distance from a station, and Mr Alfred Knowles, who has largely increased the merchant side of the business, requiring more accommodation, recently secured a first class site in the town of Berkhamsted itself on the side of the Grand Junction Canal and with a road from the railway station where he has erected the substantial and modern block of buildings known as Castle Mills, that we are able to illustrate to-day. Having had such satisfactory results from the plant erected by Messrs E.R. and F. Turner at Bourne End Mills he naturally employed our Ipswich friends to design his new premises, and placed the order with them for the necessary machinery and the erection thereof.

The silo, the highest part of the building, has a dozen grain bins of large capacity, splendidly arranged to be automatically filled by elevators and conveyors so that grain can be automatically drawn out of any one or more bins in any desired proportion and carried to the grinding, washing or cleaning machines as required. The silo is fire-proof and separated from the mill proper by armoured, double fire-proof doors. Intake elevators receive the grain from waggons on the road side of the building, and from canal boats on the other side. These elevators are cleverly arranged so that grain can be sent directly to the silos, and lie there till it is required.

The basement of the mill contains a National gas engine and suction gas plant, and, having a concrete ceiling, a fire in the basement could not spread to the room above. The floor of the basement is just above the level of the canal and waggons can get to this lower room by means of a slope from the road.

This first floor is occupied by massive oat crushers and maize kibblers, grain cleaning machines, sacking off spouts &c., while the floor above contains a number of grinding bins, barley cylinders, cyclone dust catcher, &c. The top floor has the various intake elevator heads and sack hoist, which latter, by a neat arrangement of chains, can be used to hoist sacks either from boats or waggons, or if need be, to raise or lower sacks of stuff from one floor to another inside the mill.

A number of bins are fitted with automatic mixers so that chicken mixture and horse corn can be made without any manual labour. Messrs. Knowles do a large seed trade, and Messrs. Turner have installed various seed-cleaning machines, all being arranged in the most convenient manner. We were struck with a number of ingenious 'spout scalpers' for taking dust &c., out of grain, as also with the number of spouts going from most of the elevator heads, enabling, by means of valves, the stock to be sent to various machines and stock hoppers or into the silo elevators. The whole arrangement has been designed and installed by Messrs. E.R. and F. Turner for convenience of handling stock with a minimum of labour, and a more complete outfit than this it would be difficult to imagine.

As we remarked above, Bourne Mill is between two railway stations, and Castle Mill is partly – for the moment, at any rate – to act as a silo for the flour mill for wheat coming by rail or water. The firm's waggons are continually hauling flour to Berkhampsted town and station and thus able to load back with wheat at little or no cost.

The top of the mill and silo are flat roofed with solid parapet walls, carried up breast high all round, and a splendid view of all the country around can be had from thence. The offices are a lower block between the road and the silo end of the mill, and over the offices are three or four pleasant living rooms for one of the employees who will also be caretaker of the premises. There is considerable vacant land the other end of the building, which will allow of extending the mill at some future date, and we should not be surprised to hear of a roller plant being added.

Castle Mills are certainly an ornament to the town, and we must congratulate Messrs. Turner on the design and equipment of the buildings with which we learnt from Mr Knowles himself he is highly pleased.

Appendix 7

'Successful country mills', extract from *The Miller*, 4 August 1902

Our illustration represents Mr. W.N. Mead's mills at Tring, Herts. These mills, as will be seen, occupy a very commanding position, and are typical of both ancient and modern systems, forming a very interesting *ensemble*. The tower windmill was, we believe, built in the 18th century and fitted with three pairs of stones, and was successfully worked by Mr Thomas Mead (Mr W.N. Mead's father) for many years. That gentleman, however, found the old mill to be of insufficient capacity, and with the British miller's characteristic enterprise, decided on building the fine modern building with which we are for the present principally concerned. This structure was erected in 1875, and fitted up with what was, at that time, a model stone plant. The mill is charmingly situated in the centre of a good wheat growing district, and from the 'conning tower' rising from the roof a grand view of the surrounding country for many miles can be had. One specially interesting feature in the landscape is the view of the great reservoirs belonging to the Grand Junction Canal Company, and which are just now swarming with wild fowl, the shooting and fishing rights being held by Lord Nathaniel Rothschild. About 1891 the mills passed into the hands of Mr W.N. Mead. That gentleman at once decided upon the installation of a roller mill plant, and, after an exhaustive comparison of various systems, he placed his order with Messrs. E.R. and F. Turner, Ld, the well-known milling engineers of London and Ipswich, who erected a 2½ sack plant, which has, up to the last few months, been most successfully worked. Finding his business still increasing, and at the same time wishing to keep himself and his mill quite abreast of the times, Mr Mead decided in March last to again entrust the necessary alterations, and extensions to the hands of Messrs. E.R. and F. Turner, Ld, and the result is a mill now capable of turning out four sacks an hour, which for completeness in every detail would certainly be hard to beat, and we rejoice to see such an example of go-a-headness in a country miller, as well as to find from actual observation that it is possible to have a thoroughly good and complete plant on a comparatively small scale. The plant is actuated by a compound condensing beam engine, which, while only making 48 revolutions a minute and with a pressure of only 60 lbs of steam, seems to literally play with the whole mill. The dynamo house is hard by, and we here mention that Messrs Christy

Bros., of Chelmsford, have installed a very neat and effective electrical service. The breaking of the wheat is done on two double sets of 'Turner' rolls each 30 ins by 9 ins, and, at the time of our visit the work was being very correctly apportioned, having in view as large a quantity of semolina as possible, a small quantity of break flour, and a clean broad bran. The reductions are obtained through five double sets of smooth rolls, each 15 ins by 8 ins. All are thoroughly exhausted and work quite cool, and when we remark that in addition the ingeneously-arranged scraper both keeps the rolls absolutely clear and acts as a detacher as well, it will be inferred that we saw no flaking of the stock anywhere. There are four dustless purifiers, and right well do they justify the name in the work performed. They are of ample size, and the provision which is made to meet all manner of wheat and stock conditions compels our admiration. Ten centrifugals do the dressing, and an offal-dividing machine practically completes the plant proper. The flour, as might be expected from what we have already said, is very pure; the yield is satisfactory, the feed is well divided and the qualities arranged in first-class fashion. There was not a dirty feed in the mill, and all the machines were working smoothly, quietly and with apparent ease. There are many departures from the stereo-typed flow sheet. We have never before seen a like arrangement for break stock and product, but we thoroughly endorse the diagram. We took the trouble to go entirely through the whole system step by step, and the division of the middlings and the sub-division immediately following. The grouping of the feeds and the absence of unsuitable combinations gave us much pleasure. The chief aim is, of course, 'Patents' and the arrangement of the flow sheets to produce it is admirable, and can only be appreciated when seen in actual operation. The governing feature of a mill's diagram is to so arrange the connections that the machinery yields as large a proportion of absolutely pure stock as can be obtained for the head of the mill, a cutting off and a grouping of that which is not quite pure, and a re-purification of, and a further grouping of tailings which, later on, are rolled once and again divided and subdivided, so that nothing whatever is lost sight of or left to chance. The outcome is a very large percentage of the highest quality product, and an almost entire absence of anything in the neighbourhood of low grade. In the mill under notice we were witness that every purifier is treated with the utmost exactness and skill, and a complete system of safeguards is inaugurated in every part. We were much pleased to find a complete absence of dust on the purifier floor; it can be seen at a glance that without a doubt these machines well deserve their name of 'Dustless'. We have many times had opportunity of judging the principle upon which Messrs Turner build their purifiers, and to state the bare fact. Apart, however, from the machines themselves we wish to state for the benefit of all our readers that there is more real science called for in the purifier department than in any other place in the mill. From here spring all the perfections of well brocken stock, from here we expect to see the results of the mill's best efforts, and each and every attention bestowed will amply repay the miller in better Patent, and more of it, in enhanced grades all through and clean offal. All this we saw at work in Mr Mead's mill, and it was also being done within the ordinary compass of roll inches and dressing surface. The machines are arranged in a simple and get-at-able way, and room is ample everywhere.

The mill is situated on the Grand Junction Canal, and facilities are afforded for unloading from boat or barge. On the land side the intake plant is also handy and capable of dealing with wheat arriving by waggon. Both sides can be also utilised for loading the mill's output. At the time of our visit Mr Mead was fully employed in executing his many orders. This, it may be said, is normal, for he believes with us that the greatest good comes of being well equipped and in making a first-class article, the two together constituting the dominant factor of the milling trade of to-day. We commend the study of these matters to our friends in country districts, in the hope that will waken more ambition. There is plenty of room for improvement in our mills, and it ought not to be a matter of much difficulty or expense to be put and kept in the front line. We know that the country miller is 'waking up,' as we several times had the satisfaction of testifying to during late months, and we repeat that this gives us pleasure. The milling trade of England must grow, and that extensively, and we are always ready and willing to be the means of showing others what their fellows are doing. To Mr W.N. Mead belongs great credit for his enterprise and business ability, and to Messrs. E.R. and F. Turner, Ld., we tender our congratulations on the result of yet another instance of successful engineering. We wish in connection with the mill and with our visit, to mention the name of Mr H.R. Pertwee, Messrs. Turner's representative, who has had charge of the installation, and who was kind enough to show us over the premises and explain many of the problems connected with the latest system of flour milling.

Appendix 8

'A model country mill', extract from *The Miller*, 7 May 1906

At the pretty little village of Walkern, some four miles from Stevenage, Herts, are situated the roller flour mills of Mr A. Pearman. The mills have a long and unique history, for we learn that so long ago as 1838 the present proprietor's father went there with his uncle and he eventually took the mills over in 1881 and practically rebuilt them. Some time after his decease, in 1883 the Mr Pearman of today had the first roller plant installed by Messrs. E.R. and F. Turner, the well-known Ipswich firm of flour milling engineers. Originally the capacity was something under two casks an hour, but recently Messrs Turner increased it to about three sacks, and we learn that the owner is highly pleased with the results.

The mill has for motive power (other than its water wheel) a tandem compound condensing engine of Messrs Turner's high class make, and which was installed some half dozen years ago and we understand that Mr Pearman has found it a very effective and economical auxiliary.

We have pleasure in giving a reprint of both the miller and his mill, and we may just whisper the fact that, that in Mr Pearman's young son – now a year old – we may probably have another successful member of the craft in the coming years, and whose portrait may adorn a page of some future issue of THE MILLER.

As is well known THE MILLER is ever on the look-out for the trade's good, and always endeavours to foster the interests of the smaller members. Mr Pearman is progressive and up-to-date in his methods, he views things in the right spirit and we may once more repeat that only up-to-date millers can hope to do their trade at a profit.

The miller of Walkern has our hearty good wishes.

Glossary

backwatering, excess water in the tail race which immerses the lower part of a waterwheel and acts as a brake on its motion.

balance weights, iron or lead plates fitted to runner stones to counteract any imbalance and to ensure that the runner stone is completely level. Often carries the name of the maker of the stones.

beam engine, a traditional fixed steam engine where a pivoted overhead beam is used to transfer power from a piston to a connecting rod.

bedstone, the lower and fixed millstone.

bin, or granary, floor, the top floor of a mill, where the grain is stored in bins before it is fed to the stone floor below.

brake wheel, the primary gear wheel in a windmill mounted on the windshaft, having a braking mechanism for controlling the speed of the sails.

buck, a term used in eastern counties of England for the rotating body of a post mill.

butty, the unpowered trailer of a pair of narrow boats.

common or **plain,** the simpler form of sail to which cloths are attached to a wooden lattice frame.

crown wheel, a horizontal bevel gear wheel mounted above the great spur wheel, from which secondary drives may be taken to drive auxiliary machinery.

damozel, forked iron bar which feeds grain into the eye of the millstones.

fantail, a mechanism for automatically facing the sails of a windmill into the wind. It consists of a circular bladed fan set at right angles to the sails at the rear of the mill.

Fourdrinier, the pioneer of the continuous paper-making machine.

girt, or side girt, timbers running the length of a post mill supporting the buck.

governor, a centrifugal regulator to control the speed of the millstones.

great spur wheel, the large gear wheel on the main shaft transmitting drive to the stones via the stone nuts.

grist, corn to be milled. Generally refers to animal feed.

groundwater, water abstracted from subterranean strata using vertical boreholes.

hopper, a wooden box in the shape of a funnel from which grain is fed to the millstones.

horse, wooden framework which supports the hopper above the stones.

hurst frame, the framework, either timber or iron, holding the machinery of a watermill in place and supporting the millstones above.

laths, longitudinal bars of a plain sail which support the sail cloths.
launder, head race in the form of a wooden trough carrying water to a waterwheel.
lay-shaft, a horizontal driving shaft equipped with one or more spur wheels for driving millstones or other machinery.
leat, artificial channel carrying water to a waterwheel.
luccam, projecting structure of a watermill at roof level, enclosing a sack hoist.
offals, the husks of grain left over after the kernel has been milled, which is usually fed to livestock.
ogee-roofed, double curved shaped cap of a twoer windmill.
patent, or shuttered, sails, self-regulating sails with shutters designed to achieve a constant speed irrespective of the force of the wind.
pit wheel, the primary gear wheel mounted parallel to the waterwheel within the mill building.
Poncelet, Poncelet was a general in Napoleon's *Grande Armee* who applied scientific and mathematical principles to the design of waterwheels in order to feed the army. His designs greatly improved the efficiency of waterwheels from 30 per cent to 70 per cent.
post mill, the earliest form of windmill, in which the body carrying the machinery is turned into the wind about an upright timber post.
purifier, machine in the form of a rotating sieve for separating light flour particles from bran before the latter is fed to millstones or rollers.
roller mill, machines, similar to mangles, using parallel sets of rollers to separate grain from bran and to reduce the grain to flour.
roundhouse, a circular or octagonal brick or masonry structure enclosing the trestle of a post mill.
runner stone, the upper, revolving, millstone, as opposed to the lower, fixed, bedstone.
sack hoist, a chain or rope mechanism for hoisting sacks to the bin floor either within a mill via trapdoors in the intervening floors or outside into a luccam.
sails, the revolving arms of a windmill which are turned by wind to drive the machinery.
screw auger, an Archimedes screw revolving in a trough for the horizontal movement of grain.
shoe, a shallow trough feeding grain from the hopper into the eye of the millstones.
shutters, the hinged, adjustable vanes of patent sails.
sifter, sieve or straining device for separating fine from coarse particles of flour using brushes in a rotating wire mesh drum.
smock mill, a windmill similar to a tower mill but constructed in timber rather than stone or brick.
stitching, fluting, the process of 'dressing' millstones by cutting fine grooves with a thrift. These grooves need to be sharpened regularly.

GLOSSARY

stone floor, the middle floor of a mill where the mill stones are located.
stone furniture, a complete set of equipment for feeding grain into the millstones.
stone nut, a small pinion driving the runner stone from the great spur wheel.
stone spindle, the shaft on which the runner stone rotates.
tail pole, a spar projecting from the rear of a post mill for turning the mill to face the wind.
tentering screws, the mechanism for controlling the gap between the millstones.
tower mill, a windmill consisting of a brick tower with a revolving cap which carries the sails.
tuns, wooden casing which encloses the millstones.
turbine, a device more efficient than a waterwheel for extracting power from water using an enclosed impeller.
under-driven, refers to runner stones driven by a spindle from below through the eye of the bedstone.
wallower, a horizontal bevelled gear wheel transmitting power from the pit wheel to the main shaft.
winding, winded, turning a windmill to face the wind. 'Tail winded' refers to a situation in which the wind is blowing from behind a post mill, when it has not been possible to turn the mill to face the wind. This can cause great damage.
windshaft, the main shaft of a windmill which carries the sails and brake wheel.

Gazetteer

Name	Descriptor	Grid Ref	Historic Environment Record (HER)	River	Page
Abbots Langley, Hunton Bridge Mill	Demolished, waterwheel remains	TL 083 004	5795	Gade	87–88
Albury, Patmore Heath tower mill	Demolished 1921	TL 445 259	4753		149
Anstey post mill, Lincoln Hill	Demolished *c*.1920	TL 398 322	6182		130
Anstey smock mill, Snow End	Demolished *c*.1921	TL 403 322	5980		139
Apsley, Frogmore Paper Mills	Paper Trail Museum, a.k.a. Covent Mill	TL 058 055	5759	Gade	77, 159
Apsley, Nash Mills	Site of paper mill, now redeveloped for housing	TL 070 044	5762	Gade	160
Apsley paper mill	Site of paper mill, now redeveloped for retail	TL 062 050	5760	Gade	159
Arkley Mill	Existing preserved tower mill, a.k.a. Barnard Gate Mill	TQ 218 953			141
Ashwell Mill	Reconstructed watermill	TL 268 399	5772	Rhee	119
Aston smock mill	Demolished *c*.1875	TL 275231			141
Ayot St Lawrence Mill	Site of	TL 212 173		Mimram	104
Barkway post mill	Demolished *c*.1903, a.k.a. Rokey Mill	TL 382 361	1536		129
Barkway smock mill	Demolished *c*.1920, a.k.a. Newsells Mill	TL 383 364	1536		139

Name	Descriptor	Grid Ref	Historic Environment Record (HER)	River	Page
Barwick gunpowder works	Not used for manufacturing gunpowder since 1946	TL 386 194	5712		79
Berkhamsted, Bourne End Mill	Converted to motel	TL 021 063	5776	Bulbourne	88–9, 161, 196
Berkhamsted, Castle Mill	Converted to apartments	SP 993 081	5773		89, 223–4
Berkhamsted, Lower Mill	Mill building converted to restaurant	TL 001 074	7098	Bulbourne	89
Berkhamsted, Upper Mill	Demolished, remains in school grounds	SP 994 080	7087	Bulbourne	89
Bishops Stortford, Parsonage Mill	Demolished watermill	TL 494 224	6791	Stort	115
Bishops Stortford, South Mill	Demolished watermill, a.k.a. Garratt's Mill	TL 493 204	5775	Stort	115
Bishops Stortford, Town Mill	Working flour mill of Allinson's, a.k.a. Edwards' or Beech Flour Mill	TL 491 211	5774	Stort	47–8
Bishops Stortford, Twyford Mill	Converted to residential	TL494 193	5811	Stort	115
Boxmoor, Foster's sawmill	Site redeveloped for housing	TL 045 062		Bulbourne	185
Braughing steam mill	Demolished	TL 389 243	5778		109
Brent Pelham smock mill	Existing smock mill without machinery	TL 433 313	6252		137
Broxbourne Mill	Destroyed by fire. Waterwheel and turbine survive	TL 372 068	5779	Lea	104
Broxbourne, Pulhamite works	Surviving horse-drawn edge-runner stones	TL 372 071	5709		185
Buntingford Mill	Watermill converted to dwelling, a.k.a. Aspenden Mill	TL 363 289	5780	Rib	111

GAZETTEER

Name	Descriptor	Grid Ref	Historic Environment Record (HER)	River	Page
Buntingford post mill	Demolished	TL 368 287	13385		127
Bushey, Hamper Mill	Buildings preserved	TQ 097 939	5767	Colne	163
Bushey Heath smock mill	Demolished c.1910	TQ 152 943	1538		137
Bushey Mills	Site of watermill	TQ 121 981		Colne	82–3, 163
Cheshunt, Goff's Oak steam mill, Cuffley Hill	Shown as Flour Mill – Steam in 1873. No indication of when milling ceased	TL 322 030	16143		147
Cheshunt, Goff's Oak tower mill	Demolished 1953/4	TL 317 035	1907		147
Cheshunt Mill	Site of watermill	TL 367 033	11840	Lea	79
Chipperfield Common, smock mill	Demolished c.1890	TL 038 014	7306		134
Codicote fulling mill	Used for offices	TL 226 169	5781	Mimram	179, 201
Codicote Heath, smock mill	Unconfirmed	TL 206 184	7305		141
Codicote Mill	Converted to residential	TL 207 181	10985	Mimram	105
Colney Heath tower mill	Converted to residential	TL 205 055			147
Cromer post mill	Preserved	TL 304 286	5822		71–6, 193–6
Croxley Green tower mill	Converted to residential	TQ 068 953	5825		147
Croxley Paper Mills	Demolished	TQ 083 953	5763	Gade	160
Digswell Mill	Converted to residential	TL 247 149	686	Mimram	106

Name	Descriptor	Grid Ref	Historic Environment Record (HER)	River	Page
Enfield, Ponders End Mill	Working flour mill of G.R. Wright & Sons Ltd	TQ 361 956		Lea	53–5
Essendon Mill	Converted	TL 275 098	5782	Lea	98
Gorhambury, Pre Mill	Building remains but turbines removed	TL 129 084	9609	Ver	185
Graveley smock mill	Destroyed by fire *c*.1884	TL 238 298			137
Great Hormead post mill	Collapsed *c*.1940	TL 399 303	6216		130
Great Hormead smock mill	Collapsed *c*.1940	TL 399 302			139
Great Offley tower mill	Survives in part	TL 133 269	6328		145
Hallingbury Mill (Essex)	Surviving watermill	TL 496 169		Stort	117
Harlow Mill (Essex)	Converted to restaurant	TL 471 128		Stort	117
Harpenden, Batford Mill	Converted to offices	TL 148 150	5819	Lea	95
Harpenden, Hyde Mill	Mill complex survives	TL 132 170	5821	Lea	68–71, 218–19
Harpenden, Pickford Mill	Site redeveloped for industry	TL 143 153	7021	Lea	95, 164
Hatfield, Bush Hall Mill	Site of paper mill	TL 238 101		Lea	164
Hatfield, Cecil sawmill	Converted to other uses, a.k.a. Withy Mill	TL 250 097	5784	Lea	185
Hatfield, Mill Green Mill	Working mill and museum	TL 240 097	5785	Lea	60–3
Hatfield, Sherriff's Mill	Site redeveloped for residential	TL 233 092	5707		97
Hemel Hempstead, Noake Mill	Converted to residential	TL 043 097	5783	Gade	85

GAZETTEER

Name	Descriptor	Grid Ref	Historic Environment Record (HER)	River	Page
Hemel Hempstead, Piccotts End Mill	Converted to apartments	TL 050 092	5786	Gade	85
Hemel Hempstead, Two Waters paper mill	Destroyed by explosion 1919	TL 055 058	7112	Bulbourne	160
Hertford, Dicker Mill (later site)	Site redeveloped for industry	TL 330 132	7246	Lea	98, 185
Hertford, Dicker Mill (original site)	Site redeveloped for industry	TL 327 128	9479	Lea	98
Hertford, Horns Mill	Leather works. Site redeveloped for housing	TL 321 117	5787	Lea	181
Hertford, the Old Waterworks	Building preserved	TL 326 129	5654	Lea	98
Hertford, Sele Mill	Converted to apartments, a.k.a. Garratt's Mill	TL 320 127	5789	Beane	108–9, 165
Hertford, Town Mill	Site redeveloped as a leisure complex	TL 325 126	5790	Lea	98
Hertingfordbury Mill	Converted to dwellings	TL 307 121	5791	Mimram	108, 200
Hitchin, Grove Mill	Briefly a silk mill. Converted to commercial use, a.k.a. Burnt Mill or Shotling Mill	TL191 304	5768	Purwell	171
Hitchin, Lucas Windmill, Gaping Hills	Demolished	TL 173 292	5990		128
Hitchin, Purwell Mill	Converted to apartments	TL 204 294	5793	Purwell	119
Hitchin, Station Mills	Demolished, site redeveloped, a.k.a. Jas Bowman's Mill	TL 192 298			52–3
Hunsdon Mill	Demolished, mill house survives	TL 421 114	6362	Stort	117

Name	Descriptor	Grid Ref	Historic Environment Record (HER)	River	Page
Ickleford, Bowman's Mill	Working flour mill of Jas. Bowman Ltd	TL 182 313	5796	Oughton	52–3
Ickleford, Hyde Mill	Site has been archaeologically excavated	TL 185 314	11415	Oughton	119, 215–17
Ickleford, Oughton Head Mill or West Mill	Demolished	TL 171 308	5794	Oughton	119
Kimpton Mill	Converted to residential	TL 198 185	5797	Mimram	105
Kings Langley Mill	Site redeveloped, a.k.a. Toovey's Mill	TL 075 030	5798	Gade	85–7, 220–2
Kings Langley, Home Park Paper Mills	Site of former paper mill, now redeveloped	TL 078 021	5761	Gade	160
King's Walden, Breachwood Green tower mill	Converted to residential, a.k.a. Darley Hall Mill	TL 146 232	5838		145, 197
Knebworth, Rye End Mill	Site of	TL 196 190		Mimram	104
Lemsford Mill	Converted to offices	TL 219 124	5799	Lea	57, 97
Little Hadham smock mill	Destroyed by fire 1921	TL 438 228	5823		133–4, 196–7
Much Hadham tower mill	Demolished	TL 422 183			151
Parndon Mill (Essex)	Converted into arts centre	TL 433 111		Stort	204
Puckeridge, Gatesbury Mill	Demolished 1906	TL 393 239	5777	Rib	111
Redbourn, Little Mill	Demolished for road widening, a.k.a. Doolittle Mill	TL 113 112	7002	Ver	162–3
Redbourn, Woollam's Silk Mill	Converted to local museum	TL 106 120			176

GAZETTEER

Name	Descriptor	Grid Ref	Historic Environment Record (HER)	River	Page
Redbournbury Mill	Working flour mill	TL 119 108	5801	Ver	66–7
Reed, Mile End tower mill	Converted to residential	TL 359 385	5824		141, 197–9
Rickmansworth, Batchworth Mill	Water company offices	TQ 062 939	7148	Colne	162, 177
Rickmansworth, Loudwater Mill	Paper mill demolished 1890	TQ 053 961	5906	Chess	162
Rickmansworth, Mill End Mill	Demolished	TQ 046 939	7140	Colne	162
Rickmansworth, Scotsbridge Mill	Converted to restaurant	TQ 064 951	5764	Chess	161
Rickmansworth silk mill, 171 High Street	Site redeveloped	TQ 057 944	9264		177
Rickmansworth, Solesbridge Mill	Site of Roman watermill associated with villa complex	TQ 044 971	779	Chess	161
Roydon Mill (Essex)	Surviving watermill	TL 402 103		Stort	119, 196–7
Royston, Station Mill	Working soya flour mill of Cereform	TL 356 412	5802		49–50
Sarratt Mill	Demolished paper mill, mill house survives	TQ 036 980	13425	Chess	161
Sawbridgeworth, High Wych post mill	Dismantled and removed to Little Dunmow	TL 466 143	5874		133
Sawbridgeworth Town Mill,	Destroyed by fire, a.k.a. Burton's Mill	TL 486 151	5807	Stort	117
Shafford Mill	Converted to residential	TL 126 093	5806	Ver	90
Sheering Mill (Essex)	Demolished	TL 486 144		Stort	117
St Albans, Abbey Mills	Silk mill converted to residential	TL 142 069	5830	Ver	176

Name	Descriptor	Grid Ref	Historic Environment Record (HER)	River	Page
St Albans cotton mill	Demolished, site redeveloped as swimming pool	TL 150 066	7272	Ver	181
St Albans, Dixon's flour mill	Steam flour mill burnt down 1924. Site now occupied by housing	TL 145 071	7081		91
St Albans, Kingsbury Mill	Mill preserved largely intact, houses a restaurant	TL 138 075	5804	Ver	63–5
St Albans, Miskins' sawmill	Converted to offices	TL 144 072	7076		185
St Albans, Moor Mill, Colney Street	Converted to restaurant	TL 150 025	5889	Ver	65, 203–4
St Albans, New Barnes Mill	Converted to offices, a.k.a. Cowley Mill	TL 155 054	5805	Ver	93
St Albans, Park Mill, Park Street	Converted to offices, a.k.a. Corville Mill	TL 149 039	5832	Ver	93, 201
St Albans, Sopwell Mill	Mill preserved largely intact	TL 152 061	5765	Ver	91–2, 163
Standon New Mill	Converted to apartments, a.k.a. Chapman's Mill	TL 395 055	5808	Rib	111
Standon Old Mill	Little remains following fire in 1961	TL 396 226	5809	Rib	111
Standon smock mill	Demolished c.1930	TL 396 221	5810		139
Standon, the Old Paper Mill	Little remains apart from mill house	TL 393 222	5766	Rib	164
Stanstead Abbotts, Glenmire smock mill	Demolished c.1921	TL 386 118			133
Stanstead Abbotts Mill	Converted to offices	TL 386 119	5810	Lea	103
Stevenage, Corey's Mill	Demolished. Site now within Lister Hospital	TL 229 266			128

GAZETTEER

Name	Descriptor	Grid Ref	Historic Environment Record (HER)	River	Page
Tewin Bury Farm Mill	Demolished apart from waterwheel	TL 265 141		Mimram	108
Tewin Mill	Demolished 1970	TL 272 136	6340	Mimram	108
Tring, Gamnel End tower mill	Demolished 1911	SP 924 130	5827		141
Tring, Goldfield tower mill	Converted to residential	SP 915 117	5826		145
Tring, Grace's Mill	Site redeveloped for housing	SP 924 113	5454		88
Tring, New Mill, Gamnel End	Heygate's working flour mill, previously known as both Mead's Mill and Gamnel Mill	SP 926 130	9685		50–1, 225–7
Tring Silk Mills	Converted to small industrial units	SP 926 122			172–5
Wadesmill	Converted to residential	TL 359 174	6103	Rib	111
Walkern Mill	Converted to apartments, previously known as Pearman's Mill	TL 286 254	5813	Beane	108, 228
Waltham Abbey Mill (Essex)	Site of watermill	TL 380 005		Lea	79
Waltham Abbey, Royal Gunpowder Mills	Museum	TL 375 010		Lea	77–9
Ware Flour Mills, Amwell End	Converted to apartments 1987, previously known as French's Mill	TL 360 141	5814	Lea	102–3
Ware Park Mill	Largely demolished	TL 336 139	6360	Rib/Lea	112, 201
Ware Town Mill	Industrial premises of Glaxo Smith Kline	TL 353 144	5815	Lea	100
Ware, Westmill	Converted to residential	TL 338 163	5816	Rib	94

241

Name	Descriptor	Grid Ref	Historic Environment Record (HER)	River	Page
Wareside, Mardock Mill	Converted to residential	TL 393 148	6361	Ash	113
Waterford Mill	Site of	TL 314 158	6358	Beane	8
Watford flour mill	Destroyed by fire 1924	TQ 116 961		Colne	83
Watford, Grove Mill	Converted to apartments	TQ 087 986	5817	Gade	88
Watford, Rookery Mill	Site redeveloped	TQ 108 951	5872	Colne	177
Watton-at-Stone Mill	Demolished 1968	TL 300 195	5818	Beane	108
Welwyn Mill	Demolished 1921, millhouse survives	TL 232 161	7040	Mimram	106
Weston, Lannock tower mill	Converted to residential *c.*1950	TL253 306	5829		147
Wheathampstead Mill	Converted to retail units	TL 177 142	5820	Lea	97, 201
Whitwell Mill	Mostly demolished, waterwheel remains	TL 187 210	5803	Mimram	105
Whitwell, Pann Mill	Site of	TL 194 202		Mimram	104

Waterpumps					187
Cassiobury Park	Demolished	TQ 090 974			
Chaulden House	Demolished	TL 037 062			
Chorleywood House	Pumphouse preserved in original state	TQ 039 976			
Hatfield, Cecil sawmill (*see main entry above*)	Building survives	TL 250 097			
Hertingfordbury	Demolished	TL 299 098			

GAZETTEER

Name	Descriptor	Grid Ref
Langleybury	Mechanism visible but in a poor state	TQ 084 996
Marden Hill House	Mechanism visible in the open	TL 279 134
Panshanger	Mechanism visible in the open	TL 293 124
Panshanger	Mechanism visible in the open	TL 298 122
Panshanger	Mechanism visible in the open	TL 289 128
Shafford Mill (*see main entry above*)	Converted to residential	TL 126 093
Tewin Water	Not known	not known
Tring Silk Mills (*see main entry above*)	Building preserved as industrial units	SP 926 122
Watford, The Grove Hotel	Mechanism visible in the open	TQ 082 986

Select bibliography

Archer, P.C., *Historic Cheshunt* (Cheshunt, 1923).
Ashby, M., *The book of the river Lea* (Barracuda Books, Buckingham, 1991).
Austin, W., *Tring silk mill* (privately published, 2008).
Bennett, R., 'Hertford and its paper mills', *Hertfordshire Past*, 26 (Spring 1989).
Bonwick, L., *Cromer windmill history and guide* (Hertford, 1999).
Bourne, J.C., *Drawings of the London and Birmingham railway* (Ackerman and Co. Facsimile by David and Charles, Newton Abbot, 1970).
Bower, P., 'British paper mills: Standon Mill, Hertfordshire', *The Quarterly* (April 1996).
Branch Johnson, W., 'Trouble at Codicote Mill led to Star Chamber', *Hertfordshire Countryside* (June 1968).
Branch Johnson, W., *Industrial monuments in Hertfordshire* (Hertford, 1967).
Cauvain, S.P. and Young, L.S., *The Chorleywood bread process* (Cambridge, 2006).
Coleman, A., 'The compleatest mill on the stream. A concise history of Sarratt Mill on the river Chess', *Chess Valley Journal* (2009), pp. 22–6.
Cornwall, G., 'The paper mills of Rickmansworth', *Watford and District Industrial History Society Paper Journal*, 4 (1974), pp. 41–51.
Currey, J., *A mill on the Beane* (C. & J. Currey, Walkern, 2011).
Curtis, G., *A chronicle of small beer* (Chichester, 1970).
Dean, L., 'The history of King's Langley Mill', *Watford and District Industrial History Society Journal*, 1 (1971), pp. 3–9.
Dickinson, J., 'Supply of water from the chalk stratum in the neighbourhood of London', paper given to the Royal Society, Ref AP/33/10 (1850).
Evans, J., *The endless web: John Dickinson and Co Ltd, 1804–1954* (Jonathan Cape, London, 1955).
Evans, J., 'Hertfordshire and its water supply', *Hertfordshire Illustrated Review* (1893).
Fairbairn, W., 'On waterwheels with ventilated buckets', Institution of Civil Engineers paper 793 (9 January 1849).
Fairclough, K., 'James Fordham and the construction of Ware Park Mills', *Hertfordshire's Past*, 47 (1999).
Faulkner, A.H., *The Grand Junction Canal* (Rickmansworth, 1993).
Featherstone, A., *Silk mill to museum* (Redbourn, 2010).
Featherstone, A., *The mills of Redbourn* (privately published, 1993).

Finerty, E.T., 'The history of paper mills in Hertfordshire', *The Paper-maker and British Paper Trade Journal* (April 1957 pp. 308–26; May 1957 pp. 422–6; and June 1957 pp. 510–18).

Freeman, I., *The old order changeth*, The History Publishing Society, Book 5 (Wheathampstead and Harpenden, 1991).

Freese, S., *In search of English windmills* (Cecil Palmer, London, 1931).

Graham, M., 'Fulling in Hertfordshire', *Hertfordshire Countryside*, 54/479 (1999).

Hands, J. and R., *Bourne End and Boxmoor, old and new* (Boxmoor, 2013).

The Herts and Essex Observer Year Book, Directory and Almanac 1935.

Howes, H., *The windmills and watermills of Bedfordshire – past, present and future* (Book Castle Publishing, Copt Hewick, N. Yorks, 2009).

Hunn, J. and Zeepvat, B., 'The Old Mill, Berkhamsted: archaeological investigations', *Hertfordshire Archaeology and History*, 16 (2009), pp. 97–109.

Hutchin, D. and Mott, R., *We ploughed the fields and scattered* (privately published, 2005).

Ickleford Parish Council, *The mills of Ickleford* (Ickleford, 2014).

Jones, G., *The millers: a story of technological endeavour and industrial success 1870–2001* (Lancaster, 2001).

King, N., *Kingsbury water-mill museum* (Derby, 1993).

Lewis Evans, J., *The firm of John Dickinson and Co Ltd* (London, 1896).

Lewis, J., *London's Lea valley* (Chichester, 1999).

Liddle, H.D., *Notes on Old Chipperfield* (privately published, 1948).

Longman, G., *Mystery of Watford's short-lived silk industry* (Watford, 1985).

Lucas, J., *Phebe's Hitchin book* (Hitchin, 2009).

Lyddon, C., 'London's last miller', *World Grain* (September 2004), pp. 54–9.

Major, K., *Animal powered engines* (Batsford, London, 1978).

Moore, C., *Hertfordshire windmills and windmillers* (Sawbridgeworth, 1999).

Mullett, J.P., 'Goldfield Mill', *Hertfordshire Countryside* (May 1981).

Nunn, J.B., *The book of Watford* (Watford, 2003).

Pollard, M., *History of Waterford and Stapleford* (Hertford, 2001).

Ray, G., *The book of Chorleywood and Chenies* (Barracuda Books, Buckingham, 1983).

St Albans Teachers Centre, *Know St Albans: three St Albans watermills* (St Albans, 1976).

Savage, S., *A short history of Dundale* (Tring, 2009).

Sherwood, J., 'The changing face of Mill Street', *Berkhamsted Review* (July 2008), pp. 14–15.

Simon, H., 'Modern flour milling in England', Institution of Civil Engineers paper 1874 (16 May 1882).

Smith, R. and Carr, B., *A guide to the industrial archaeology of Hertfordshire and the Lea valley* (Association for Industrial Archaeology, Leicester, 2004).

Society for the Protection of Ancient Buildings, *A philosophy of repair of windmills and watermills* (London, 2004).

Stanners, C. and R., 'Chesham Bois: the mill's tale', *Journal of the Chess Valley Archaeological Society* (2006), pp. 19–23.

Stanyon, M., *Railways – the John Dickinson connection* (Apsley Paper Trail, Apsley, 2011).

Thomas, J., 'A kindly employer', *Hertfordshire People* (2013).

Thomas, R., *The waterways of the Royal Gunpowder Mills* (Waltham Abbey, 2009).

Tucker, L., *The listed buildings and other principal structures at the Royal Gunpowder Mills, Waltham Abbey* (Waltham Abbey, 2013).

Wallace, E., *Children of the labouring poor* (Hatfield, 2010).

Ward, M., 'Working in silk mills', *Hertfordshire People* (2005).

Ward, P., 'Corn milling in Dacorum', *Hertfordshire Past*, 29 (1990), pp. 3–14.

Young, J., *Silk throwing in Watford* (Watford, 1986).

Index

Abbots Langley
    Hunton Bridge Mill 60, 81, 87–8
Adams, B.D. archaeologist 93
Albury
    Patmore Heath windmill 5, 126, 149
Allen and Hanbury Ltd 73, 100
Allied Bakeries 46
American Civil War 7
Anstey windmills 126, 130, 139
Apsley Mills 21, 39, 77, 76, 155, 159, 161
    Frogmore Paper Mills 39, 77, 155, 156, 159
    Nash Mills 39, 159, 160
Archer, P., author 123
Arkley windmill 126, 141
Armfield, J.J., milling engineers 14, 15, 70, 108, 213
Ash, river 113
Ashwell Mill 119
Associated British Foods 46–7
Aston windmill 141
Ayot Mill 104
Barkway windmills 123, 129, 139
Barwick gunpowder works 79
Batchworth Mill 153, 155, 162, 169, 177
Batford Mill 32, 95
Beane, river 8, 32, 93, 165
Beeching Report 21, 111, 181
Berkhamsted
    Castle Mill 3, 19, 45, 81, 88, 89, 223–4
    Lower Mill 89
    Upper Mill 81, 89
    see also Bourne End Mill
Berkhamsted School 89
Bishops Stortford 3, 19, 48, 113
    Allinson 3, 26, 46, 47–8
    see also Castleford Mills and Edwards
    Corn Exchange 211
    Parsonage Mill 115
    South Mill 115
    Town Mill (Beech Flour Mill) 3, 14, 46, 48 *see also* Edwards
    see also Twyford Lock and Mill
Blackwell Hall Mill 161
Board of Governors and Directors of the Poor 170
Board of Ordnance 78, 79
Bois Mill 161
Bourne, J.C. 157
Bourne End Mill 3, 5, 11, 14, 45, 81, 88–9, 161, 193, 196, 223
Bowman, J. and Son 1, 3, 21, 25, 26, 46, 215
    Astwick Mill 19, 52
    Bowman, P. 53, 213
    transport 19, 21, 22
    see also Hitchin, Station Mills and Ickleford, Bowman's Mill
Boxmoor
    Foster's sawmill 185

Branch Johnson, W., archivist and author 5, 164
Braughing steam mill 109
Breachwood Green windmill *see* King's Walden
Brent Pelham windmill 127, 137
British Flour Research Committee 93
British Industries Baking Research Association 55
British Soya Products 49, 111
Brooke Bond 176
Brown, A.A., millers 3, 25, 33, 100, 102, 111
Broxbourne Mill 104
Broxbourne Terra Cotta and Artificial Stone Works *see* Pulhamite
Bugbrooke Mill 51
Bulbourne, river 32, 81, 160
Buntingford
   Mill 111
   windmill 127
Burton, Thomas, Harry and Owen, millers 3, 19, 22, 24, 25, 26, 37, 40, 115, 119
Bush Hall Mill *see* Hatfield
Bushey
   Hamper Mill 163
   Mills 82, 163
Bushey Heath windmill 126, 137
Cassiobury 187, 189
Castleford Mills, Yorks 57
Cereform Ltd 3, 25, 26, 46, 49, 50
Chapman Bros, millers 1, 3, 21, 111
Chaulden House 187
Cheshunt
   Mill 79
   see also Goff's Oak windmill
Chess, river 43, 81, 153, 161
Childwickbury Estate 90, 187–8

Chilterns
   chalk streams 31–2, 35, 104
   hydrology 33–5, 43, 123, 172
   Open Air Museum 134, 197
Chipperfield windmill 134
Chorleywood Bread Process 55, 57
Chorleywood House 187
Clarke and Dunham 92, 213
Cobden-Chevalier Commercial Treaty 7, 170
Codicote
   Mill 68, 105, 140–1
   fulling mill 179, 191, 201
Codicote Heath windmill 141
Cole, B., miller, 3, 68, 105 *see also* Hyde Mill, Harpenden
Colne, river 30–2, 34, 81, 161, 162, 169
Colne Valley Water Company 35
Colney Heath windmill 5, 127, 147
Cooperative Wholesale Society 26, 93
Corcoran, B. 213–14
Corey's windmill *see* Stevenage
Corn Laws, Repeal of 6, 7
Cow Roast 36, 40
Crimean War 7
Cromer windmill 3, 59, 123, 127, 130
   technical description 71–6, 191, 193–6
Croxley Green windmill 126, 147
Croxley Paper Mills 154, 156, 159, 160, 163
Dacorum Borough Council 88, 159
Dalgety 57
Dean, L. 7, 10, 24, 36, 85
Dell, W.R. and Sons, millwrights 67, 213
Department of Transport 203
Dickinson, J. and Co. Ltd, paper manufacturer 21, 25, 77, 155–9, 161

INDEX

disputes over water rights 33–6, 39–40
individual paper mills (Apsley, Croxley, Frogmore, Home Park and Nash) 159–60, 177
Digswell Mill, 106, 191
Dorothea Restorations Ltd 195
East Herts District Council 134, 193, 195, 196
Ebury Way 157
Edwards, S. and Son 3, 25, 47, 48 *see also* Bishops Stortford
Enfield
    Ponders End Mill 46
English Civil War 77
English Heritage 195
Environment Agency 43, 103
Essendon Mill 32, 60, 93, 98, 191
European Water Framework Directive 35
Evans, Sir J. 34–6, 40, 43, 159
Fairbairn, Sir W. 59, 63, 79
Fine Lady Bakery 51
Flour Milling and Baking Research Association
Foster's sawmill *see* Boxmoor
Fourdrinier 77, 155, 160, 161, 163
Freese, S., author 71, 74, 75, 123, 133
French, J.W. and Co. 3, 5, 14, 100, 103, 112
French and Jupp 103
Frenlite flour 103
Frogmore Paper Mills *see* Apsley Mills
Gade, river 32, 39, 81
Gade valley industries 34, 36, 39, 43, 81, 153, 154, 159
Garfield Weston 26, 46, 57, 117
Garratt, S. 3, 11, 13, 21, 14, 105, 109
Gaping Hills 127, 128
Gatesbury Mill *see* Puckeridge

GlaxoSmithKline 93, 100
Goff's Oak windmill 5, 14, 123, 126, 147
Golden Spray flour 85
Goldfield windmill *see* Tring
Gorhambury
    Estate 63
    Pre Mill 185
Grand Junction (Union) Canal
    rights and conflicts 30, 33, 39, 81, 220
    transport 19, 21, 46, 50, 85, 88, 141, 155
    water supplies 36, 172, 225
Graveley windmill 137
Great Eastern Railway 111, 151
Great Hormead windmills 126, 130, 139
Great Northern Railway 19, 46, 53, 87, 97, 106
Great Offley windmill 5, 126, 145
Green and Carter Ltd 168, 187
Green belt 193, 199
Hallingbury Mill 115, 117, 169
Hamper Mill *see* Bushey 163
Harlow Mill 114, 117
Harpenden
    Hyde Mill 3, 5, 14, 19, 32, 43, 45, 59, 68–71, 93, 191, 218–9
    modernising 14
    rail connection 19, 68, 70
    see also Batford Mill and Pickford Mill
Harrison Carter, J. 11
Hatfield 30, 32
    Bush Hall Mill 32, 60, 153, 164
    Cecil sawmill 32, 60, 185
    Historical Society 61
    Rural District Council 61
    Sherriff's Mill 1, 14, 19, 21, 97
    see also Mill Green Mill

251

Hatfield House 27, 60, 187
Hemel Hempstead 30, 33, 153
    Noake Mill 82, 85, 191
    Two Waters paper mill 160
    see also Piccotts End Mill
Heritage Lottery Fund 195
Hertford 19, 30, 33
    Dicker Mill 95, 98, 185
    Horns Mill 21, 32, 181
    Old Waterworks 98
    Paper Mill Ditch 98, 165
    Sele Mill 3, 21, 26, 46, 108–9, 153, 165, 189, 191
    Town Mill 98
Hertfordshire Building Preservation Trust 73, 193
Hertfordshire County Council 34
Hertingfordbury Mill 104, 108, 191, 199, 200, 205
Heygates Ltd, New Mill 3, 26, 46, 50–1 see also Mead and Tring
High Wych windmill 133
Hitchin 3, 127
    Corn Exchange 211
    Grove Mill 169, 171
    Lucas windmill 128
    Station Mills 52, 53
    see also Purwell Mill
Hiz, river 31, 119
Home Park Paper Mills see Kings Langley
Hughes Power Co. 63
Huguenots 169
Hunsdon Mill 117
Hunton Bridge Mill see Abbots Langley
Hyde Mill, Harpenden see Harpenden
Hyde Mill, Ickleford see Ickleford
HydroWatt, Karlsruhe 57

Ickleford
    Bowman's Mill 11, 52, 53
    Hyde Mill 119, 215–7
    Oughton Head Mill 119
Illustrated London News 153, 161
Institution of Civil Engineers 10
Institution of Mechanical Engineers 10, 11
Ivel, river 31, 52, 111
Jordan's Holme Mill, Biggleswade 70
Kimpton Mill 68, 105, 191
Kings Langley
    Home Park Paper Mills 155, 160
    Mill 5, 10, 11, 14, 24, 81, 85–6, 220-2
    see also Toovey
King's Walden
    Breachwood Green windmill 5, 126, 127, 145, 193 197, 199, 205
Knebworth Mill 104
Knowles 3, 11, 88, 89 see also Berkhamsted and Bourne End Mill
Lacey Green windmill 196
Langleybury 187
Lannock windmill see Weston
Lea (or Lee)
    Conservancy Board 38, 40, 115
    navigation 19, 21, 33, 37, 108
    river 3, 14, 25, 30, 31, 32, 46, 53, 57, 78, 93, 95, 100
    Trustees 37, 38
Lee Valley Regional Park Authority 104
Lemsford Mill 3, 32, 57, 93, 97
Letchworth Garden City Corporation 195
Limehouse Cut 40
Little Hadham windmill 126, 133, 193, 196, 205
London
    docks 19, 50
        Millwall 26, 210
        Royal 8, 210
        Surrey 8, 22, 25

INDEX

influence on Hertfordshire 7, 22, 26, 50, 52, 153, 154, 156
Mark Lane 8, 11, 67, 92, 210-3, 220
markets 7, 17, 22, 36, 46, 47, 50, 165, 169, 171
orphanages 169
Thames 32, 33, 47, 210
water supplies 30, 33, 34, 36
London North Western Railway 21, 89, 155, 157
Loudwater Mill 153, 162
Lucas, P., author 171
Lucas, S., artist 127-8
Lucas windmill *see* Hitchin
Luton 22, 32, 43
Macclesfield 169, 172
Major, K., molinologist 66
Marden Hill House 187
Mardock Mill *see* Wareside
Massie, S., artist 127, 128
Mauri, A.B. 46 *see also* Cereform
Maygrove, J. and Co. 25, 171, 176
Mead, T. and W., millers 3, 25, 51, 81
see also Tring
Mill End Mill 153, 162
Mill Green Mill 32, 45, 59, 60-3, 67, 93
Millers Mutual Association 26
Millwrights International 61, 145, 196
Mimram, river 32, 93, 104
Moor Mill 59, 65, 82, 90, 191, 203-4
Moore, C., author 126, 133, 141
Much Hadham windmill 5, 123, 151
Museum of English Rural Life 71
Napoleonic Wars 156, 169
Nash Mill House 159
Nash Mills *see* Apsley Mills
National Planning Policy Framework 191
New River and New River Company 33-5, 100, 103
Noake Mill *see* Hemel Hempstead
North Herts District Council 193, 201
Oughton Brook 119, 215
Oughton Head Mill *see* Ickleford
Pann Mill *see* Whitwell
Panshanger 187, 189
Paper Trail Museum 59, 77, 159
Pargeter, V. 195
Park Mill 82, 90, 93, 189, 191, 201
Parndon Mill 204
Patmore Heath windmill *see* Albury
Pearman, A., miller 11, 108, 228
Piccotts End Mill 82, 85
Pickford Mill 32, 95, 164
Ponders End Mill *see* Enfield
Pre Mill *see* Gorhambury
Puckeridge
    Gatesbury Mill 111
Pulhamite 3, 185
Purwell, river 119, 171
Purwell Mill 119
Ramblers Worldwide Holidays 3, 57, 97
    see also Lemsford Mill
Rank/Hovis McDougal 26, 46, 57, 210
Redbourn
    Little Mill 162
    Woollam's Silk Mill 170, 176
Redbournbury Mill 45, 90, 191
    technical description 59, 60, 66-71, 79, 92
    water supply 35
Reed windmill 127, 141, 193, 197, 199, 205
Regent's Canal 19, 50, 78
Rhee, river 31, 114 109, 112, 119
Rib, river 32, 93
Rickmansworth
    Scotsbridge Mill 153, 161
    silk mill 177

253

Solesbridge Mill 153, 161
  see also Batchworth Mill, Loudwater Mill, Mill End Mill
Rivers Pollution Commission and Act 42
Robinson, T. and Son, milling engineers 48, 55, 109
Roller mills 3, 5, 9–11, 14, 22, 27, 29 46
Rothschild, Baron L.W. and Lord N. 145, 174, 225
Royal Armaments Research and Development Establishment 77
Royal Gunpowder Mills 37, 59, 77–9
Royal Small Arms 77
Roydon Mill 119, 196, 197, 204, 205
Royston
  Station Mill 3, 14, 46, 49, 111
Ruston and Hornsby 47
St Albans
  Abbey Mills 82, 169, 171, 176, 191
  cotton mill 181
  Dixon's flour mill 14, 91,
  Kingsbury Mill 59, 60 63–5, 90
  Miskins sawmill 185
  New Barns Mill 93
  see also Moor Mill, Park Mill, Sopwell Mill
St Albans City Council 30, 193
Sarratt Mill 153, 161
Saundersons millwrights 151
Sawbridgeworth
  Town Mill 5, 14, 26, 41, 115, 117
    see also Burton
  transport 19, 22, 40
  see also High Wych windmill
Scowen, J., miller 71, 139
Shafford Mill 30, 82, 90, 187, 188
Sheering Mill 117
Silvertown 26
Simon, H.G., milling engineers 9–11, 47, 103, 108–9
Smith, A., author 141, 145
Smiths, Royston millers 1, 49,
Society for the Protection of Ancient Buildings (SPAB) 126, 193, 195
Sopwell Mill 66, 79, 82, 91–2, 153, 163, 191
Spillers 26, 46, 57, 103, 109
Standon
  New Mill 3, 19, 39, 49, 111
  Old Mill 111
  Old Paper Mill and sawmill 153, 164
  windmill 139
Stanstead Abbotts
  Glenmire windmill 123, 133
  Mill 14, 93, 103, 189, 191
Stevenage
  Corey's windmill 128
Stort
  river 25, 30, 33, 103, 113, 169, 204
  navigation 19, 37, 38, 40, 46, 47, 169, 204
Tangey water pump, 71, 185
Tate, J., paper-maker 104, 165
Tewin Bury Farm Mill 108
Tewin Mill 108
Tewin Water 187
Thompson, R., millwright 145
Tilbury 46, 50, 109, 210
Titmuss, G. and P., millers 95, 97
Toovey, T.W. 24, 25, 45, 82
  Kings Langley Mill see Kings Langley
  transport 19, 36
Tring
  Gamnel End windmill 81, 88, 126, 141
  Goldfield windmill 127, 145, 199, 205
  Grace's Mill 81, 88